Praise for *Vodka Shot, Pickle Chaser*

"David Kalis's wonderfully compelling memoir, *Vodka Shot, Pickle Chaser*, has all the attributes of storytelling at its best: masterful suspense and an engaging, voice-driven narrative that pulls us into the heart of an exotic adventure. It is an entertaining and intelligent portrayal of the defiant moodiness of Russian culture from the point of view of a young, endearing, and wholly American protagonist, who longs for connection to a world that is sometimes dangerous, often elusive, and almost always unfamiliar."

—Laurie Baker, *author*

"David Kalis has written an absorbing coming of age story with an unusual backdrop: Russia at the end of the Soviet Union. His many experiences, from comedic to terrifying and everything in between, make for great reading. Get this book!"

—Rabbi Keith Stern

"Reading Kalis's firsthand experiences through the former Soviet Union gave me the opportunity to witness history through his eyes. It gave me a much deeper perspective and understanding into a community where we now have a tremendous focus of our work. His story of tracing his roots and finding his connection to Judaism is compelling and straightforward, and most importantly will resonate with Jewish young adults."

—David Cygielman, *CEO, Moishe House*

VODKA SHOT, PICKLE CHASER

Temple Aliyah Community —
Enjoy the Journey!

David K[...]
10/26/14

VODKA SHOT, PICKLE CHASER

A TRUE STORY OF RISK, CORRUPTION,
AND SELF-DISCOVERY AMID THE
COLLAPSE OF THE SOVIET UNION

BY
DAVID A. KALIS

Kalis, David A.
Vodka Shot, Pickle Chaser: A true story of risk,
corruption and self-discovery amid the collapse of
the Soviet Union
ISBN 978-0-9912302-0-4
Library of Congress Control Number: 2013957737

Edited by The Threepenny Editor
Paperback book layout by Phillip Gessert
Cover design by Phillip Gessert

For inquiries, please contact:
David A. Kalis

www.davidakalis.com

CONTENTS

PROLOGUE

The following is a letter I received from my father, a few days after we discussed the anxiety I was feeling about my lack of post-collegiate plans. I often didn't fully appreciate his advice, but this time knew his instincts were just what I needed. Even so, instead of listening to his words of wisdom, I folded the letter and placed it atop the growing pile of important papers next to my computer monitor.

February 1991

Hi Dave!
DO NOT WORRY

1.   I think it is important that you have interviews with as many companies as possible—the interviews would be both informational and would have you improve your technique for interviewing—this is similar to being in the minor leagues before going to the major leagues and who knows, you may come across an interesting company.

2.   Utilize the resource center in order to determine jobs available, addresses of companies, addresses of international trade companies, addresses of consulting companies, addresses of international music companies, and international theater companies.

3.   In terms of the language program, we discussed what happens after the first four weeks—I am hopeful that you will be able to earn money so that you can stay on and obtain a job in the Soviet Union and progress with your Russian literacy as well as Spanish literacy.

4.   We have agreed that you should do the preparation for the GMATs; the LSATs will be put in the background for now although

I have not given up on it because I think that law would be good for you. Hopefully you will be able to take the GMATs before going on the trip so you can save time when you return.

5.   We have discussed what happens after the return from Europe and what would be gained by the language improvement—and we have agreed that this is an unknown quantity.

6.   You have agreed to get more information concerning business and law schools so that perhaps some applications can be made before you leave for the Soviet Union.

7.   Resumes—you have agreed that resumes should be sent to as many companies as possible including import/export companies.

8.   I strongly urge you to purchase the book listing companies that do business in the Soviet Union. I will *gladly* pay the $35 to you. *Please go ahead and get this book now.*

9.   You had indicated to me that there is an organization which encourages trade with the USSR—what is the name of that group and find out as much as you can about it.

10.   Russian program—you have indicated that you are interested in the program that has the job along with it. While you are in the Soviet Union you will look into the music business in Russia and in East Europe and perhaps try to contact some companies in New York City. I have the Manhattan yellow pages at home and you should be able to make use of that over the next couple weeks.

DO NOT WORRY

DA'VAY VWEPEEM!
LET'S DRINK!

THE ADVENTURE BEGINS

Sometimes you end up on the wrong side of a gun, and you're not really sure how you got there. While most college graduates think about what they are going to do for the next sixty years of their lives, I was standing on a Soviet tank in the center of Moscow trying to figure out how to survive my next sixty seconds. Somewhere between graduation and my first real job, I ended up impersonating a photojournalist while the 1991 Soviet *coup d'état* attempt unfolded around me. With just a camera in hand to defend myself against what seemed like most of the Soviet army, I knew I was putting my life at risk. But this was history!

I looked around, mumbling to myself. *That's it. Come on out. There you go. Show your face so I can take the picture! No...no...don't look that way—look towards me!* The smug-looking soldier peered out from the hatch of his tank and glanced at me. I pressed down and took the shot. Unbelievable! I was only three weeks into my journey and my mind was reeling. How could I have known that a side trip to Moscow, away from my tour group in Leningrad, would alter my view of the world? Could this actually be the beginning of the end of the Soviet Union?

Dozens of camouflage-green, idling tanks and countless somber-looking soldiers gathered near the Arbat, a tourist hotspot full of small shops and vendors. Russian citizens milled about, talking to the soldiers, most as surprised to see the tanks as I. From windows high above the street, neatly dressed businessmen in modern office buildings observed the commotion on the thoroughfare. I had put myself in a precarious spot. Running on adrenaline, I was taking risks I had never dreamed of, and relished every moment. I shifted my feet on the tank to improve my balance. As a former gymnast, muscular and short, I had a low center of gravity, but falling from here would be less than pleasant. Adjusting my oversized, brown plastic glasses to a more comfortable spot on my sloping nose, I peered through the camera lens and snapped photos. Soldiers cleaned their rifles, commanders barked orders, and everyone hustled to their next task. I was concerned that the situation might spiral out of control, but being in the center of the action, I couldn't make myself leave.

Out of the corner of my eye, I saw a soldier rush up out of a hatch about ten tanks in front of mine. He was tall with blonde hair, had broad shoulders, and was squinting around for something. I lowered my camera and our eyes met. I looked away, nervous and knowing that I had no explanation for why an awestruck, twenty-two-year-old American with a full head of bushy brown hair was standing on one of the Soviet army's tanks a few miles from Red Square.

A woman began screaming in Russian. Her shrill voice caught my attention. She was yelling wildly, waving her arms, hollering at me to get down. Soon, more middle-aged onlookers joined her, all trying to warn me. They looked legitimately concerned. Peripherally, I noticed more movement. Crap. The strapping soldier began running towards me, jumping from tank to tank. He seemed to have orders—and it appeared I was his target. Suddenly, the tank I stood on jolted to life. What was happening?

Exhaust fumes filled the air. Tank hatches dropped shut. The approaching soldier yelled something unintelligible, but the scowl on his face spoke volumes.

I grew disoriented in the plumes of smoke, and panicked.

HIDING BEHIND PICKLES

Growing up, I was somewhat of a peacemaker. I avoided fights in high school, but if one broke out around me I'd jump in to break it up. At a towering five-feet-zero-inches, I wasn't the starting quarterback for the varsity football team, but it was my nature to want people to get along. Trusted by most, I learned to listen intently—a critical skill if you don't want to be pigeonholed into any one group or clique. And so, because I was friendly to everyone, I often played the conciliatory role.

Being social helped me make many friends and develop a strong sense of self-confidence. My stable, upper-class Northeast suburb surrounded me with support and encouragement, and taught me to expect great things from myself. The height thing certainly made me the butt of many jokes, but it seemed to bother others more than me. Ignoring what some would see as a limitation, I pursued my interests in singing, athletics, politics, and yes—short girls.

High school wasn't just about pursuing the paths presented to me. Math wasn't my thing, and while I enjoyed other subjects like social studies, my courses seemed to merely scratch the surface. Unexpectedly, I'd become intrigued by the broader world. I watched *The Day After*, a made-for-TV movie, and it left a deep imprint on my psyche: Nuclear war and the bitter divide between the Soviet Union and United States was an unsettling thought on its own, but the movie also showed how interconnected our planet truly was. I lay awake, angst-ridden. I wanted to be able to take action and bring people together to foster understanding. I decided to take Russian in high school, naïvely thinking that if I became fluent, I'd be able to visit the country I had grown to fear, meet its people, and maybe find a way to change perceptions of how Russian people viewed Americans and vice versa.

In college, I pursued a degree in Soviet East European Studies. I enjoyed learning how the Soviet Union was formed, how each leader left his mark on the country, and how its politics developed over time. But as college graduation approached, where did that leave me? It never occurred to me that this niche degree had little value in the real world. In fact, throughout my college years, the real world remained far away, never encroaching on my life. I assumed I would graduate, but never contemplated it seriously. And then, all of a sudden, there it was, right in front of me.

Leading up to graduation, I began feeling the pressure of having a future plan before even completing the present one. With the day nearing, I felt as if the safety net of college was being hauled in. My choices—or lack thereof—paralyzed me. I became uncharacteristically insecure and envious of peers who had solid plans to go to Wall Street, medical school, or law school. My life felt like a game of chess, leaving me stumped for a next move. I knew I could land a typical nine-to-five job doing something really boring. Graduate school seemed like a cop-out. Another possibility was moving home and taking it from there, but I wanted to avoid any needless friction with my parents. Then, there was the money problem. Like everyone else, I had to make ends meet.

I wondered if I was the only person who felt this way at this stage of life. My friends who had concrete plans seemed pleased with their decisions. But was their satisfaction real, or just false confidence in a stressful time? Soon, we didn't have as much in common and I began to feel isolated. I couldn't share my fears with my parents, either, because they would simply ask the same questions I was asking myself. Overwhelmed by thoughts of a career that might span sixty years, I retreated. Social conversations became cumbersome, so I began to avoid occasions where I could be pinned down by questions about my future. I felt like Dustin Hoffman in The Graduate, whose future is summed up in one word—"plastics." It was a disturbing thought, but was this me?

Graduation day came and went, and a week later I found myself applying for that nine-to-five job I didn't want. The interview went fine but, as expected, lacked passion. I shook my interviewer's hand

and as I walked out of the office recalled the letter my dad had written a few months earlier. It was spot-on, with one exception: I was a worrier. I had tried to listen to his first and last lines: "DO NOT WORRY." It was no use. Despite its step-by-step approach and ease of understanding, I wore the burden of worry on my back like Atlas carried the world. His letter outlined a whole plan for me to pursue my Russian language interest abroad. It should have been easy! But, for one reason or another, I didn't follow his advice and was lost. I trudged down the stairs of the Brookline office building and out onto the street, preoccupied with worry, heading into a state of depression.

Out of the corner of my mind, I overheard a conversation in Russian nearby. Looking up, I found myself in front of a new Russian mini-grocery store. Without any real purpose or conviction, I walked down three steps into a basement store that immediately transported me to another place. I looked around at the Russian newspapers, the Russian food products, and then at the shoppers. Although dressed like Americans, they were all Russian and everyone was speaking in their mother tongue. The distinctive reek of fish emanated from the walls. The first aisle was full of foreign candies I had seen only at my Russian language professor's house. Another aisle featured dark rye bread and unfamiliar desserts. I paused at the condiments and eavesdropped.

The accents were stronger than I expected and the words flowed quickly. Frowning and feigning interest in a jar of marinated pickles, I realized that although I had taken two years of Russian in high school and four in college, I still couldn't understand the language. Sure, I got some words here and there, but to understand a complete sentence was out of my league.

Lingering between the pickles and the dark rye bread, I thought back to why I'd pursued Russian in the first place. My dream was to use my skills on a world stage to make a difference and to bring people together. Maybe the thought of going to the Soviet Union was actually a good one. Maybe my dad's letter was just the approach I needed. If I could go for an extended period to master the language, the sky might be the limit. I could influence international relations, policy, and the way America interacted with its so-called enemy.

And then it dawned on me. I had prepared to take action toward a goal, but stalled somewhere along the way, allowing fear and worry to determine my fate. My education and interests had led me down a road that I was hesitant to explore. Even my parents, who preferred a "safe" career for me, encouraged me to take the next step. What was I doing, interviewing for a job I already hated? I placed the pickles back on the shelf and walked out of the store, feeling the weight beginning to lift from my shoulders.

Finding an intensive language tour to the Soviet Union was easy. Returning a few weeks later to the Russian section of Brookline, I found the store where I had hidden behind the pickles. Next door was a travel agency specializing in trips to the Soviet Union. I sat down with a middle-aged, Russian agent who quickly found a thirty-day group tour that would get me to the motherland and only partially deplete my savings earned from a previous summer job as an ice-cream man. I would have to monitor my travel budget closely.

"Your passport looks good, but now you need a visa," said the frazzled agent in her monotone, guttural English. She pushed some papers to the side, and avoiding my eyes, looked for more items to move around on her desk.

"I don't know what that is," I replied, hoping she could offer some help.

"Well, you'll need to get one," she stated firmly. She still refused to look at me. "Without it, you won't be able to enter the country."

"Okay, but what is a visa and where do I get one?"

"Call the Consulate. They can help."

"In Washington?"

"Maybe Washington. Maybe New York," she said, matter-of-factly. *How could she not know?*

"You'll also need an invitation."

"An invitation to what?" I asked, a bit frustrated with the slow drip of information.

Looking in her desk drawer and shuffling through papers, it seemed she wasn't even listening to me. "Here, fill this out," she mumbled, and placed a form in front of me.

"What's this?"

"An invitation form."

I was lost. A form to be invited? How much red tape would this require? I looked at it and decided to be quiet. I filled it out and handed it to her.

"So, now what?"

"Nothing."

"Nothing?" I repeated.

"No, nothing. We'll process this and get you the invite and requisite visa. Thank you."

I walked out, pleased that I was on my way, but a bit bewildered. What just happened? I had never heard of a country requiring a visa, and assumed this was part of the Soviet Union's strict Cold War entrance policies.

With my travel plans complete, it was time to listen to my dad's letter. Preparation would be critical if I wanted to find real job opportunities abroad. There was no classifieds section for Americans looking for work in Cold War Moscow and no Internet, so I scoured libraries and searched Boston-based economic development commissions, looking for American companies doing business in the USSR. I visited nearby colleges that had Russian language programs and connected with professors who had contacts. And, as uncomfortable as it was, I cold-called my parents' friends who were in industries that had connections—even minor ones—to the Soviet Union. These conversations were tough, as they would ask the unanswerable question, "What do you want to do?" The truth was I would do anything, but that was a bad interview response. Instead, I made up empty responses: "To get in on the ground floor" and "Learn the business from a mentor." With practice, however, these became easier to recite, and more convincing.

By the time wheels were up, I had identified a few US companies with offices in Moscow and had uncovered some leads. I was ready to take my search to the USSR, hopeful that my college degree would be meaningful somewhere.

THE INTERVIEW

As we touched down in Leningrad, the tour group was palpably thrilled to be in a foreign country, but unlike them, I had a thirty-day goal: to find a reason not to go home.

The first few days were full of excitement—tasting my first bowl of borscht, visiting ornate palaces, gardens, and museums, trying to communicate in Russian, and navigating the Metro. Even with our hectic schedule of visits to tourist sites, the tour operators followed through on their commitment to intense Russian language learning. Each morning we had mandatory classes, and throughout the day were challenged to speak only in Russian.

Our gregarious tour guide, Ivan, was a towering middle-aged man with curly brown hair and a thick beard. He had a jovial yet casual approach to introducing us to historical places, and made it easy for me to go through the sightseeing motions. It's not that I wasn't interested in the sites, but I knew that if I could find a job, I'd be able to visit these spots at my leisure. Fortunately, my aggressive job search quickly paid off. Two weeks into the trip, I landed an interview in Moscow. Ivan was very supportive of my goals, and called some friends in Moscow so I would have a place to stay for a few nights.

I was on my way.

The overnight train was a new and exciting experience. Longer than I anticipated, the train seemed to span a few city blocks. Having never seen a *cupet*—a sleeping compartment—I was surprised by the layout. I opened the sliding wood-paneled door, and immediately at my feet was a narrow, thinly carpeted corridor leading to an old wooden table that sat beneath an undersized train window with small floral curtains. With two shiny, maroon, pleather beds in bunk formation on either side of the center walkway, it was tough to maneuver. I tried to decide which way to turn, but felt so cramped that standing and looking straight ahead seemed the only option. The entire *cupet* couldn't have been larger than ten-by-ten, so beyond the beds, the table, and a storage area near the ceiling, there wasn't much space for anything else.

I settled in, a bit nervous about who might walk in next. Maybe I'd get lucky and meet a cute Russian girl. I sat near the window and looked at the station outside. The conductor in his blue uniform and cap was taking tickets, people were saying their goodbyes, and a few elderly ladies struggled to get their bags on the train. Russian signage was everywhere, and while I could understand individual words, many phrases remained a mystery. Street vendors hollered to passersby, trying to interest them in European candies, magazines, and other snacks and knickknacks. I could hear shouting from the hallway, drunks in adjacent rooms, and boarding announcements from the outside loudspeaker at the station. I shut the *cupet* door, but that didn't help. With each passing moment, it seemed like a new sound vied for my attention. Then, without warning, the door opened and a head popped in.

"*Eto coopet dvadset pyat?*"

I looked at the man, dumbfounded, unable to understand the quick outburst of Russian.

"Huh?"

"*Neechevo. Cpokoyse.*" Nothing, don't worry about it.

He walked in, threw his bags on the lower bunk opposite mine, and sat down. Within minutes this happened two more times, and before I knew it, I was sitting in a small room with three Russian travelers, all looking at me with curiosity.

"*Nu, kto vwee? Amerikanetz?*" So, who are you? An American? asked one, slurring his words, glancing at my jeans and American-branded luggage. He smiled widely, displaying his shiny gold teeth.

"Leave him alone," interrupted a neatly dressed, younger one with glasses.

"Yes, you can see he doesn't speak Russian well. Give him a break," added the middle-aged man who seemed a bit perturbed by the entire exchange.

I was able to understand their brief statements, pulling the meaning of words together in my head, but I knew a complete conversation would be impossible. "I can understand you if you speak slowly, but it's difficult for me to speak in Russian," I responded tentatively. "Yes, I am American."

And with that, the discussion flowed. At least, from them it did. I listened a lot, and tried to respond and add to the dialogue where I could. Vlad, an unemployed farmer with the gold teeth, was on his way to the outskirts of Moscow to visit friends. Friendly and drunk by eight o'clock, he didn't care that I could hardly understand him, and talked nonstop until he passed out around ten. Sasha and Pyotr, the other two in the room, were less abrasive. They adapted to my limited Russian, speaking in a more deliberate way, trying to use simpler words. To make things easier, they even tested their broken English, which helped us make connections. From an outsider's perspective, the combination of their broken English, my basic Russian, and our hand movements must have been amusing. I learned that Sasha, a neatly groomed thirty-something, was an artist looking to sell his landscape paintings in Moscow. Pyotr, dressed in slacks and a short-sleeve button-down, was a family man with two kids, and was on his way to visit his brother.

"Why you here in Soviet Union?" Sasha asked.

"I'm looking for work in Moscow," I replied in English.

"Yes, but why? No jobs in America?"

"No, there are jobs. I just wanted to travel in Russia."

Furrowing his brow and looking stone-faced at me, Pyotr squinted his eyes. "Just want to travel? You know it's not easy living here? I never meet American who want work here. Seems strange. You are different." His tone was thoughtful, yet bothered. He looked out the dirty window and began tapping his fingernails against the Formica tea table. He turned back to me. "I would like if my kids could to travel to America—someday," he said, pondering his statement. The room fell silent.

He then waved his hand in frustration, crossed his arms over his chest, and looking away, muttered something angrily under his breath.

I looked at Sasha who avoided my glance.

With that, the two of them began a terse conversation, shouting back and forth vigorously. I couldn't follow their exchange but it ended abruptly, and for the rest of our overnight journey, our *cupet* was quiet. Something about my presence disturbed Pyotr. Whether it was the fact that I had the means to travel abroad, or that he was frustrated with his own lot in life, I wasn't sure. From rising unemployment and food shortages to the growing influence of the black market, I had learned in college that life in the Soviet Union was different from life in America. I quickly realized that my classroom and books taught me only so much.

As the train sped from Leningrad to Moscow, the evenness and reliability of its noise on the tracks soothed my nerves, but not enough to invite sleep. My mind was whirring, preparing for the upcoming interview and silently practicing Russian. I lay there a bit nervous and even intimidated by my situation. In a foreign country, on a train between two unfamiliar cities, I had never felt so alone. I could barely understand the three strangers with whom I shared sleeping quarters, not to mention everyone else on the train.

Exhausted, dazed, and in need of a shower, I arrived in Moscow around 8 a.m. The August air was already hot and steamy. Suitcase in hand, I walked through the masses of people on the platform into the main station, which was even more crowded. I pushed through the ticketing lines and zigzagged to avoid people running to catch trains. As I exited the station, I looked back and admired the massive building: With tall ground-floor windows rounded at their tops, the multi-level, Italian-inspired structure was surprisingly beautiful for a train station. Painted yellow with white trim that accentuated the intricate detail, the facade was now dirty and faded, and at its center stood a huge clock tower.[1] Looking around, I hoped to catch a glimpse of the Kremlin, but instead was barraged by a horde of taxi drivers and individuals hawking their wares.

"You want matrioshka doll? Very nice."

"This is new t-shirt. Look, you see picture of St. Basil's. You like? I have others, too!"

I wasn't in the mood to shop nor negotiate and found a low-key driver standing by his taxi. I slumped in, closed my eyes and hoped for a nap. Twenty minutes later, I awoke outside a five-story apartment complex.

Hidden behind mature, leafy trees and littered with sagging clotheslines on slab balconies, the prefabricated, Kruschev-style building lacked character, and was in dire need of care. Broken windows, chipped and decaying exterior walls, and dilapidated concrete stairs had me questioning whether it was safe to live here. In the courtyard a rusted, three-legged swing set stood alone among weeds and broken glass. I looked for the entrance and found a door propped open by a cinder block. Finding my host family's apartment, I said a brief hello, dropped off my luggage, and hailed another taxi to take me to the interview. It was a chaotic morning, but I soon found myself outside a monochromatic cement office building on the outskirts of Moscow. I took a deep breath, and paused outside the door. This was the time to push my exhaustion aside and perform.

Upon entering, I immediately noticed the office's blandness. Ordinary wood-panel walls. A tiny waiting area. Well-worn carpeting. No plants or wall hangings. But, who was I to be picky? I had little to offer except a willingness to live abroad and learn the trade. They had a growing enterprise in an exciting economic, political, and business environment. Their partnership with UPDK, a department at the Ministry of Foreign Affairs for the USSR, made the joint venture possible, and was quickly becoming a model for how international business could be conducted in the Soviet Union. Gorbachev's policy of Glasnost—openness—was taking shape, and I was hoping to be part of it.

An older, red-haired Russian woman with bright pink lipstick sat behind a shiny, laminate reception desk. I gave her my name and sat down in one of two uncomfortable chairs. Running through talking points in my head, I quietly whispered why I wanted the job, what I could offer, and why this company was for me. I mumbled to myself, certain that if anyone saw me they would quickly diagnose any of a few mental disorders. I was like a cannon waiting to be lit—ask a question and out would shoot my prepared answer.

I waited for about twenty minutes until a burly man approached through a doorway behind the receptionist. He had thinning brown hair combed straight back off his forehead. His casual dress slacks and loose-fitting shirt tried to hide his large stomach. Over six feet tall, he towered over me, and his thick neck and muscular physique indicated he'd probably played rugby or football in college. Approaching with a smile, he extended his bear claw of a hand to shake mine. I crossed my fingers, hoping he would speak English.

"David? Hello, my name is Kevin O'Shea." He pumped my hand one more time and released it. "I believe you spoke with Irina earlier on the phone? What brings you to Moscow, and how did you hear about us?"

His strong Boston accent immediately put me at ease. My parents and grandparents all had grown up and still lived in Boston, and had thick accents that I was glad I had not inherited. But still, being halfway around the world, it was comforting to hear someone speak in the familiar tongue.

"I was a Soviet East European studies major at Tufts University and came over a few weeks ago with a tour group. I'm hoping to find an opportunity that will keep me here a bit longer." I made sure to immediately float the idea of staying in the Soviet Union. This was an important point, as my travel visa lasted only as long as the thirty-day tour. Companies like Kevin's had the ability to grant or extend visas for business purposes. Without one, I'd be obligated to leave the country.

"Okay, sounds good," he replied quickly, almost dismissively. "Come on back so we can talk in my office and I'll show you what we have going on here." He motioned for me to follow him past the reception desk.

In the bright corridor leading to his office I was surprised to see a few large, glass window displays built into the walls, each featuring different American-branded products. It was as if Kevin's company had set their office up as a gallery. Each arrangement was meticulous in design, and featured consumer products like beer and soap as a way of advertising wares to Soviet import companies.

Given the lawlessness and turmoil that characterized the current Soviet business environment, it was no wonder these brands wanted help navigating the marketplace. Gorbachev's Glasnost and Perestroika—economic speed—were impressive policies that were opening up opportunities for Western businesses. But progress was slow. Nearly seventy-five years of communist rule had dulled the nation's entrepreneurial spirit, and beaten almost any glimmer of free market enterprise from its consciousness. Foreign firms needed the help of an importer who could navigate the changing landscape and who had contacts throughout the country.

Despite the well-thought-out product displays, the corridor to his office was filthy. Kernels of dirt, food, and other pellets in a variety of colors seemed to jump as our feet made contact with the thin carpet. The dark finger-like smudges on the walls were hard to ignore. I entered his office and sat down. Pictures of Kevin and his Soviet partners lined the walls. Kevin sat down, looked at me, but didn't speak.

I'd never been comfortable with awkward silences.

"Kevin, I'm excited to be potentially helping a business get in on the ground level of opportunities in the USSR," I blurted out. "Correct me if I'm wrong, but with Gorbachev in power and Glasnost gaining momentum, it appears there could be some great opportunities for American businesses here." I intentionally gave him a lay-up of an observation and an opportunity to speak.

He certainly took it. It was as if he'd been waiting for me to walk in so he could just let it all out. And once he started, he couldn't stop. He spoke about the challenges of doing business in the Soviet Union. Lamenting, he went on and on about the constant and pervasive bribery, the lack of a standard set of laws, the language barrier, and the challenges of trying to get goods out of customs. He described situations where Soviet businesses ordered products one day, but due to factors beyond their control, backed out of deals the next. There were no real consequences for reneging on contracts, and I could hear the frustration in his voice. He was aware that his warehouse security personnel skimmed, but he stuck with them, fearing that the unknown might be worse. And then his monologue turned personal. He missed his family, and although he got back to the States periodically, it wasn't frequent enough.

"I'm sorry. I've taken over the conversation," Kevin acknowledged, interrupting himself. "Tell me, what exactly are you looking to do?"

My body tensed up as I heard the dreaded question.

I tried to answer, but in reality, I didn't know. This job interview thing was new to me, and I still had only a vague idea of what the company did or how my college degree could fit in. I fumbled with my words, trying to hit on some area that triggered his interest. But as I watched his face, his expressions, and his body language, there seemed to be nothing that piqued his curiosity. I harkened back to the interview skills workshop I'd taken in college, and even though its content seemed unrelated, I tried to articulate how my passion, experience, and skills were relevant to his company. I talked about how I'd become interested in the Soviet Union and that I wanted to better understand the import–export business. At this, he seemed to wake up.

His eyes opened wide. He talked again: this time about how long he had been traveling to the USSR, what he liked and didn't, and his impressions of the political situation and Gorbachev's tenuous role. It was interesting, but he rambled, and even made himself laugh.

He leaned back in his black swivel chair, and I relaxed a bit. He had a Celtics banner and a Red Sox pennant hanging on one wall, and pictures of himself and his family on another. His desk was nothing fancy; it didn't need to be. I presumed they were saving money on the office to invest in the business. Papers were strewn about the desk in what looked like a mess, but maybe it was his organizational technique. Behind him, through the large window, I noticed we were looking out onto Leninsky Prospekt, a major thoroughfare running in and out of the center of Moscow.

I sensed the end of Kevin's monologue, and realized he was probably about to revisit the question of my specific area of interest. I decided to preempt him.

"Wow, I didn't realize you had such extensive experience in the Soviet Union," I exclaimed, feigning an interest in his story. "Because I don't know much about the import–export business, I was hoping you could tell me where you think I could best fit in. I'm willing to start at any level. The most important thing for me is having the opportunity to stay in the USSR and see where things go from there." My preparation had gone out the window.

He paused and started in again. I really tried to bear down and listen. But, as he spoke, my eyes wandered. My gaze returned to the window behind him, overlooking Leninsky Prospekt. It was an unusually wide road with multiple lanes traveling both north and south. Locked in on both sides by looming, multi-story, block-long, rectangular Stalinist apartment buildings, storefronts, and mature trees, it was similar to an American multi-lane highway running through a primarily residential area. As I peered outside, I noticed something didn't seem right. Where was the traffic? For a cloudy but pleasant summer day, things were very quiet. I noticed that while many cars were heading south, away from the city, few were heading the other way. Maybe it was the time of day, or maybe the road wasn't used much—I wasn't sure.

That's when I saw a few large greenish vehicles crawling toward the building. What were those? They weren't cars but they were using the roadway. I tried to make them out without missing too much of Kevin's story. I leaned forward, struggling to focus on Kevin as the vehicles neared. Wait a minute. Could those be Soviet tanks? They got closer and I could clearly see their long cannons, turrets, and distinct track-based wheels. I expected them to veer off the road, or stop and turn around. But they steadily continued their approach. The closer they got the more real they became. And there weren't just tanks. Behind two rows of tanks were camouflage transport trucks and armored vehicles rolling in what appeared to be an organized formation.

I tried to rationalize what I was seeing. Military vehicles on American highways weren't unusual. I was probably observing an exercise of some sort. But, somehow, in my gut, this seemed different. There were dozens upon dozens of vehicles, and the road was void of cars.

As the transport units passed, the sullen faces of troops seated on benches, looking aimlessly out on to the street were visible. Most disturbing, however, was that each held a large automatic rifle. This was no exercise.

"Kevin," I said, almost whispering.

Engrossed in his monologue, he didn't hear me.

"Kevin," I said louder, cutting him off mid-sentence. As respectfully as I could, I pointed to the street and said, "Sorry to interrupt you, but is that a normal sight in Moscow?" He turned around in his chair and slid to the edge of his seat. His slouch disappeared. Standing up, he rubbed his cheeks and placed a hand under his chin, thoughtfully. He then shuffled over to the side of the desk, as if to move further away from the window. I could tell he was more startled than I, and he yelled for his secretary.

"Irina, what's going on out there?" he demanded.

She hurried in. "What do you mean?" Then looking for herself, she saw the vehicles. "Oh my goodness, look at that," she said, rather calmly. "Let me call some friends."

I looked at a flustered Kevin. Sweat was beading up on his forehead, and his neck grew pinker. We watched in silence as the parade of camouflage vehicles rolled past the window. None of the soldiers was smiling, and despite their youth, they looked intimidating.

A few minutes later Irina reappeared, but had little news. Her friends were also confused. But they did have some information. Another group of tanks was reportedly moving towards the center of town from the north of the city. Kevin and I looked at each other.

"Needless to say, Dave, this situation is not normal. In fact, I like you and I bet we could find a place for you here, but given what we have going on out there..." He trailed off, motioning to the street, uncertain where to point. "Let's suspend this interview and talk later. I don't know what to tell you except be careful out there. Or, if you'd like, feel free to stay here until we have more information."

"Nice to meet you, Mr. O'Shea," I replied. "I think I'll go back to the apartment to learn what I can from there."

As soon as I said it, I knew it was a lie.

Running through the hallways and then out to the street, I was surprised by what I didn't see. Given the excitement, where was the crowd? The locals were uninterested, or at least pretended to be. An elderly woman with long hair and a mesh satchel over her shoulder limped past me, looked at my suit, and sneered. College had not prepared me for how Russians might react to an unexpected, well-dressed American in their midst. Nearby, a young couple was exiting a milk store; they glanced nonchalantly at the tanks. A few kids played in a grassy area between apartments. They paused and looked up, but thought nothing of the tanks, and even less of me.

Having never seen a tank up close, I walked to the edge of the sidewalk and watched. A few Russian civilians stopped to look, but they seemed disgusted, as if thinking, "No military is going to help this country." Gorbachev's economic and political changes had come at a cost. Not only did his reduction in armed forces spending anger the military, but his economic decisions hurt ordinary people. Long food lines, hyperinflation, and the growing mafia wreaked havoc on his overall support. While the promise of a more democratic state sounded appealing to Westerners, who equated democracy with the right to vote, the protection of freedoms, and economic prosperity, this notion fell on deaf ears in Russia. Yes, they cared that he was opening up society, but they were more concerned about their wallets and families. Watching the tanks, I wondered if this was the coup that many of my professors had predicted.

The noise of the metal treads grinding against asphalt combined with diesel exhaust and my lack of sleep, made me nauseated. I retreated onto a side street and stopped for a minute to think. It was close to two o'clock and the interview was over. Did I want to go back to the apartment or follow the tanks into the city? With so much apparently happening, how could I simply go inside and wait for news? I was never one to shy away from risk—but what if this really was a *coup d'état*? Might I get caught in a potential firefight between armed forces? Was I crazy?

I hailed a cab and gave the driver the address of the apartment. I had very little idea where in the city it was, and knew even less about my hosts. But they were friends of friends, were warm and welcoming, and since their son Igor was my age, I knew it would be fine for a few days. The cab driver was quiet, and his radio gave us no new information. We pulled up to the apartment complex and I asked him to wait for me. I ran inside, changed clothes, found my camera, and grabbed a bite to eat. Nobody was home to question what I was doing. In less than twenty minutes, I was on my way to the Kremlin, Red Square, and the center of Moscow with my camera in hand, and my imagination working overtime.

WALKING ON TANKS

"To the Kremlin," I told my driver, using my best Russian.

I must have done well, as he responded by swearing at me, gesticulating, and blurting out an entire paragraph in Russian that I couldn't understand.

"Can you take me to the center of town?" I asked in English.

"You are crazy American," he hollered back at me in English. "Do you not know what I just hear on radio? Do you understand what is going on? There is coup happening and military taking over downtown! Already Novy Arbat (a popular retail district in the heart of Moscow) is overrun with tanks!"

"Oh—I didn't know," I murmured. "How close can you get me?"

The taxi's ripped seats hinted that he might try to accommodate in some way.

"I don't know, but we can see. You pay in dollars, yes? You have big camera—are you journalist?" He looked back at me and removed an old baseball cap from his head, revealing a full head of hair and a mischievous smile.

I seized upon this bit of genius. "Yes, and I want to report on what is happening downtown. If this is a coup, I need to send pictures and information to the US."

"Okay, then. For that, I get you where you need to go. It is important for world to see."

As we drove, I peppered him with questions. "Who is leading the coup? Where is Gorbachev? Is he okay? Has there been any bloodshed? What are the news reports saying?"

He informed me that Gorbachev was on vacation at his *dacha*—vacation home—in the Crimea and that nobody had heard from him for days. It was unclear whether he was a prisoner of the plotters or able to react freely to the situation. I later learned that he was under house arrest and had no contact with the outside world for three days. My driver then went on to explain that eight military officials, led by a general named Pugachev, had launched the coup. This made sense, as the military vehemently disagreed with Gorbachev's approach to satellite states. The proposed Union Treaty decentralized the structure of the Soviet Union, giving neighboring countries more control over their internal affairs to the point where they were forming their own governments and becoming independent nations. The Gang of Eight, as the coup leaders were being called, preferred a strong, unified Soviet Union. Given that the Union Treaty had already been signed by some states and was planned to be signed the next day by the largest three, the Russian Federation, Kazakhstan, and Uzbekistan, it appeared the military believed it had little choice but to initiate a takeover.[2]

On the heels of the tanks, we sped down a deserted Leninsky Prospekt towards the Kremlin. Clouds darkened overhead and people bustled to and fro on the sidewalks. They looked to be stocking up on groceries in the event of a siege. Lines for food were not uncommon, but today they were longer. Babushka after babushka—Russian grandmothers—filed in and out of stores, dressed in floral, loose-fitting gowns with faded, triangular, multi-color kerchiefs covering their hair. Bulging, worn satchels filled with food and supplies pulled at their arms, causing their bodies to droop as they hurried to their destinations. Closer to the center of town, the apartment buildings became more ominous. They were built to meet Stalin's demands—tall, imposing, and intricately grandiose with wide archways leading to shared courtyards—and the overcast sky exacerbated their menace. We passed the towering statue of Yuri Gagarin, the first Soviet Cosmonaut, and I thought how interesting it might be to actually witness a non-American historic event.

The driver turned off the main road and approached Red Square via back roads surrounding the Kremlin. He let me know that the plotters had control of the media, and though there had been neither bloodshed nor shootings reported downtown, the news on the radio was unreliable. Continually rerouted by police, we rolled slowly past distressed hordes of older, gray-haired people banding together in protest.

"Those people look angry," I noted to my driver. "Are they supporters of the coup?" Many were draped in red Soviet flags and had military medals on their chests.

"These people you see—they live well with communism. I think you call them die-hard communists, yes? They feel strongly for days of Stalin and are proud of Soviet progress. They live their entire life under communism. They don't like change and want keep Soviet Union. *Ponemayesh?*"

"*Da, ya ponemayu.*" Yes, I understand.

"But, what about those protesters? Are they backing Gorbachev?" I asked, pointing to a second group who were similar in age, but weren't draped in Soviet-looking garb.

"These are people who do like change. You see, they know in here that our country needs change." He touched his jacket near his heart. "But they don't know who to trust. It is complicated."

"So they want to end communism, right?"

"Well, they don't know exactly what they are wanting, except change. But to know what change, that is difficult part."

"Hmm...Interesting."

"And you ask about Gorbachev? He is okay but not great. But, he is showing us that communism is full of lies. We now know that communism has simply meant dictator. We see glimpses of how other countries are. Business is coming here slowly. Foreigners are visiting more. We like his changes, but will they last is question. These political types all want power. Power and money." He paused to extinguish his cigarette in the almost full car ashtray.

"Ahhh. I understand." I leaned back in my seat. "I've heard about other leaders like Sobchak in Leningrad, so I get what you are saying."

"Oh, you know of Mayor Sobchak? He is reformer like Gorbachev. Many new politicians we see now. I am hoping things work out for him."

Closer to the center of the city, we continued past throngs of people who held umbrellas, stood in the newly formed mist, and listened to protest leaders shout through bullhorns. Organizers bellowed to anyone who would listen, fighting to be heard over each other. The sheer number of gatherings attested to a general sense of frustration, but also to a sincere interest in their country's future. The passion on all sides was evident, but the rage and determination in the eyes of the hard-line communists was beyond comparison. It was then that I started to understand their heartfelt sense of responsibility for, and ownership of, their country.

"This is where I take you—I am not going further and want to get home," he said, waving his arms, referencing the scene outside, but at nothing in particular. I looked around. I was at the Tverskaya Metro Station across the street from the most prominent symbol of capitalism in the USSR: the only McDonald's in the country.

"Excellent, thank you—and best of luck." I opened my map and pointed to a few places. "If I go straight down this road will I get to Red Square? And is the Arbat located over that way?"

"Yes, yes...And please show pictures to America!"

"Will do!" I yelled as I handed him a combination of rubles and dollars. I knew he'd be able to use the rubles immediately in stores, and although there were very few places he could use the dollars, Russians appreciated receiving them, as they were a nice hedge against inflation. I could see him smiling as I closed the door.

At first I didn't think twice about saying my photos would be seen in America, but as I walked toward Red Square, more and more Russians who saw me with a large camera bag hollered in English, "Tell the world so we can stop them," or, "Make sure Bush knows!" I began to feel truly responsible for sharing these photos. It's not as if I was an amazing photographer; I was just snapping shots of the tanks, the various demonstrations, and the soldiers. But to the majority of Russians who had never traveled abroad, who lived under the yoke and intimidation of the KGB, and who were un-accustomed to demonstrations of any kind, these pictures meant something. Whether or not the coup was successful, in their minds it was critical that the world know that the Russian people were fighting for democracy—that the coup plotters did not have broad support.

My instinct was that any larger demonstrations would be happening at the political center of the USSR, Red Square and the Kremlin. Following Tverskaya Street toward the Kremlin, I encountered a few well-contained protests. An elderly man yelled into his bullhorn, trying to be heard over the gathering of people in front of him. He was dressed in an old Soviet military outfit with red and gold medals hanging from his lapel. Another group formed on the opposite side of the main post office, across from the Intourist Hotel. Groups of onlookers watched, milling about as if they weren't sure if they should keep walking or stop and listen. Most continued walking, no doubt afraid that the mere act of stopping and observing might lead to involvement. At the bottom of the hill and near the entrance to Red Square, a bus blocked the roadway. Teens and college age protesters stood on it, yelling and holding homemade signs. As I got closer I realized that the bus had intentionally stopped in the middle of an intersection to stop the progression of a column of tanks that appeared to be heading directly for Red Square.

Anti-coup protestors were swarming the area, walking among the stationary tanks, challenging the soldiers to explain what they were doing in their city. Meanwhile, soldiers were casually working on their vehicles, smoking cigarettes, listening and watching quietly, or just standing around, disinterested. It was clear they were awaiting orders and didn't want to harm anyone. Each had a rifle either slung over his shoulder or in hand, and maintained a calm passivity toward the protestors. They kept their distance, and I wondered if they had orders not to engage. The passion and vitriol coming from the populace was palpable and could easily lure soldiers in, so it was safer for them to remain detached. Either way, their composed, patient approach was a positive sign.

Despite the feeling of danger, I couldn't resist taking a peek at the center of communism. I walked to the other side of the bus and followed the road towards the Kremlin. An imperfect cobblestone path, reminding me of Boston's historic streets, led up a slight incline and widened to become Red Square. It was truly a sight to behold. Breathless, I looked around at the various icons, absorbing the magnificence of it all. The square must have measured at least two football fields long and one field wide. With the expansive Kremlin walls on one side and GUM, a massive department store, on the other, Red Square was an embodiment of the intimidation that was the Soviet Union. Both structures were gargantuan. While the Kremlin façade was streamlined with tall, red brick walls, turrets and Soviet stars on top, GUM was an Italian-inspired masterpiece, including large arched windows, a partially glass-covered roof, and fine architectural details up and down the massive, multi-story structure.

The square also highlighted the beauty and inspiration of the multi-colored, domed St. Basil's Cathedral at one end, the red brick Lenin Museum on the other, and Lenin's tomb, located in front of the Kremlin walls, towards the center of the square. I paused and admired St. Basil's, recalling from college that it was built by an artist whose eyes were then removed by Ivan the Terrible so he could never replicate the beauty. Focusing my gaze on Lenin's red granite mausoleum, I noticed the ever-present guards standing at attention, dressed impeccably in dark military suits and caps, cradling their rifles.

To my surprise, the square was quiet, empty of tourists and protestors alike. I watched as black, boxy cars, Volgas used by political dignitaries, shuttled in and out through the Kremlin's turreted arches. Behind its walls was a series of office buildings, golden domed cathedrals, and meeting halls. There was plenty of political activity today, most of it happening out of sight. With so few people on the square it took a while for me to find someone to ask where people were congregating. I was told the soldiers had gone to the White House, the Russian parliament building, and Arbat Street, so checking my map, I backtracked up Tverskaya to see what I could find.

The Arbat has always been a unique place in Moscow. Representing a combination of periods, the area included two streets: the New Arbat with its paved roads, high-rise apartment buildings and offices, and the Old Arbat, where the cobblestone streets and smaller, irregular buildings had become a popular walking route for tourists intent on admiring local Russian artwork and trinkets. Everything from matrioshka dolls and paintings to T-shirts and key-chains were on sale. As I turned onto the New Arbat, I walked into a wall of camouflage green tanks.

Soldiers were hurrying around, barking orders, preparing for something. Others seemed to be just sitting on their tanks, observing the crowds that had gathered around them. From my vantage point on the ground, I couldn't tell how many soldiers or tanks were assembled, so I climbed a light post to get a better view. Finding a spot to place my feet, I stood amazed at the line of tanks in front of me. From here, I could see a few soldiers peeking out of the round hatches, while further down the line of vehicles, others seemed to be checking their machinery. Some stood around chatting, and overall, the scene was subdued.

The entire situation was a bit surreal. The military appeared to be trying to take control of the city, but they weren't actually doing anything, and seemed confused. Neither the military nor the civilian onlookers knew how to react or what to expect. Would they actually attack their own people? Would they try to take control of buildings? How long would they be in the center of Moscow? Did they even know why they were in Moscow? People tried to talk with the soldiers, hoping to understand what was happening, but were ignored.

My position on the light post provided a good view, but I still couldn't get a full picture. There were plenty of rooftops nearby, but they were inaccessible. I wasn't about to climb on any of the parked cars for fear of denting them, and I couldn't climb any higher on my post. I was about to give up when I realized there was nobody restricting people from climbing on the tanks. People had lined up five or six deep, and seemed only interested in observing or speaking with soldiers.

Feeling empowered by my camera and my successful impersonation of a Western journalist, I jumped off the pole and made my way through the crowd to the nearest tank. Although the wheelbase was large, metal rungs, reminiscent of the rings in gymnastics, were mounted to the side of the vehicle. The coast was as clear as it could be—no soldiers nearby. I reached up, grabbed a rung, and scampered to the top of the tank. Without looking for approval, I began snapping as many pictures as I could.

Now I saw much more. To my immediate right and left were more tanks, set in formation. From the pole, I could only see one line of tanks at a time, but from where I stood now, I saw about forty vehicles lined up in a tri-columned brigade. Some had their hatches closed and looked like bugs, while soldiers on farther tanks were at work on top. Considering the damage a single tank might inflict, the gathered military might was frightening. I snapped photos of soldiers walking on tanks and jumping in and out of hatches. I tried to juxtapose the military buildup with the high-rise apartment and office buildings surrounding the Arbat.

Through my viewfinder, my whole outlook on the world was changing. I was no longer studying history, but living it. The country had become my classroom, and the people I met, my teachers. Emboldened by adrenaline, I continued to snap pictures, unafraid of where this could lead.

Suddenly, people near the tanks started yelling at me.

"*Ostorosheno! Shto delaesh?*" Be careful! What are you doing? one woman yelled. I caught her eye and was suddenly brought back to reality. The situation was literally shifting around me. A young man next to her started shouting, too.

"Look out! A soldier is coming toward you. Jump down, I'll help you!"

I quickly scanned the area and saw a grimacing, muscular soldier hopping from tank to tank, coming my way. Where were those rungs? Was he really coming for me? He started hollering something at me in Russian. I definitely was his target. This wasn't the college police—it was the Soviet military, which locked fraudulent journalists into Soviet prisons! It was time to get down. Flustered and not thinking straight, I frantically looked around for a way off. Reading my movements, he paused, watching me from a few tanks away. His glare was piercing, warning me to get down and stay away.

Within seconds, I better understood his urgency. Suddenly, engines rumbled to life, and with a jerk forward and an overwhelming smell of diesel, the tanks starting rolling. The battalion's exhaust formed a cloud of dirty smoke that engulfed the area. For an instant I was paralyzed. I couldn't breathe and couldn't see. I was disoriented but had to make my way off the tank—fast.

Shoving the camera in its bag, I crouched on my hands and knees so I wouldn't lose my balance. I felt the slope of the metal and began crawling down. In one area the smoke cleared a bit, and I could see the street packed with people yelling at the tanks. Fists in the air, looking down the line and at each other, they were concerned that the movement meant an imminent attack on something, somewhere. Making my way slowly down the tank towards daylight, the tank jolted again. I lost my balance. Out of nowhere, and out of sheer luck, one of my searching hands landed on a well-placed rung. My other hand quickly followed suit as my legs dangled. Heart beating out of my chest and palms sweating, I held on for dear life. Hugging the tank, I edged along the slow-moving vehicle. As I got closer to the street, I jumped down, rolling to minimize the impact. I stumbled to my hands and knees in a cloud of exhaust, coughing and wheezing. Beyond the crowd was a grassy slope. I crawled to it and lay on my back, gasping for air. The tanks moved on, the sound of metal on asphalt diminished, and the exhaust dissipated.

What was I thinking?

☭

By now it was close to 5:30 p.m. I started to make my way back to Red Square. It was getting dark, but my curiosity was piqued. Any lingering exhaustion from my poor night's sleep on the train was gone, veiled by adrenaline. As I turned the corner back onto Tverskaya Street, near Pushkin Square, I saw a gathering of young protesters sitting on a low roof, using tanks and armored vehicles as stepstools. A few soldiers were walking the area, but seemed to have abandoned their posts or surrendered to the crowd.

A multitude of pre-Soviet red, white, and blue Russian flags flew atop the vehicles and roof. The number of flags and the soldiers' indifference proclaimed that despite the military muscle all around, the coup was bound to fail. I stopped to watch, thinking about joining in. The tanks were parked, and if I could climb to the roof, I might be able to take more photos.

With the camera around my neck, I approached a tank. Russians were very possessive of their country and their government. Would the protestors mind a foreigner joining them? How would the soldiers react? Taking one last glance around to assess my safety, I slotted my foot into a toehold and muscled my way up the side of the vehicle. *Just get up there, get a picture, and get down.*

People on the vehicle were sitting calmly, not moving. I had over-thought things—they couldn't care less about my being here. Onlookers watched me climb, but were no more interested in me than in copies of a recent *OOKAZ*—Decree—that the coup leaders had published to inform the populace of what was taking place. Apparently, it included little detail and clarified nothing. I, too, had tried to read the single-page document, but only made out a few words here and there. From where I was, I grabbed hold of the roof ledge and pulled myself up. I was safely on top and inconspicuously crouched down.

I rested, surveying the street, the people, and the distant walls of the Kremlin. A calm drizzle that had been falling on and off throughout the day began anew, creating a soft mist that dampened the city. Daylight was fading and the slight breeze helped cool me down from the day's thrilling exertion.

The streets were alive with activity. There was no evident violence, but I watched the passion of debate, conversation, and protest. The ease of viewing history from the walls of a classroom faded. People from each side argued the nuances of why their path was the best way forward. In some cases, conversations became shouting matches, while in others, cordial handshakes indicated agreements to disagree or the accomplishment of finding common ground. As reformers and communists debated, the impressive and overarching sentiment I witnessed was one of shared frustration: frustration with their government, frustration with their economy, and frustration with an obscure future. They could agree on their shared national pride, as well as their respect for fellow countrymen—and it was this that kept the coup peaceful.

Not wanting to overstay my welcome, I crawled to the edge of the roof and lay on my stomach, searching for a trustworthy face on the ground. There! A young woman approached with two girlfriends. I called her over and in my broken Russian asked her to take a picture of me with the flags in the background. I knew by the expression on her face that she had a hard time understanding me, but once she saw the camera, she knew what to do. Trusting her, I dropped my camera into her waiting hands, stood back and posed with the Russian flag. But as I stood there smiling, questions swirled in my head. Was this the end of Gorbachev? Would the coup plotters succeed? Would the apparent calm turn violent? I took one last look, climbed down and thanked the nice woman, hoping the picture would come out.

☭

Fatigue finally caught up to me, and I wanted to get home safely. As I walked down the street, I stuck to the edge of the sidewalk, kept to myself, and refrained from staring at people. Any misunderstanding or perceived suspicion, especially with a foreigner, could set off an already volatile and emotionally charged situation. The nationalists already had an inherent mistrust of the West.

A group of people in their twenties stumbled towards me, obviously drunk. They didn't appear belligerent. We brushed past each other, and as the last two women walked by, they grabbed my coat.

"You are not from Moscow?" they asked in English, taking their cue from my designer glasses.

"No," I answered reluctantly in Russian. I pulled away from their grasp. Others from their group approached.

Looking at me, their faces softened but became serious. "Please tell the world what is going on here. We know the word will not get out, so please let them know about the coup. We need help."

Skeptical at first, I was now drawn in. I assured them I would let people know what was going on. I told them I would get the pictures out.

"You are from America? You are lucky," said one of the young men. "You are free! You know, we like Bush very much and think he and Gorbachev should work together and can help each other. We need to make more business here, more opportunity. You understand? We want a different life than our parents and grandparents." He spoke so passionately that froth dotted the sides of his mouth. He was drunk, but sincere. The younger generation had heard stories of the repression that characterized previous regimes, and was hopeful that Gorbachev's progressive leadership would last.

On my way to the Metro I passed more troops and armored vehicles. I was intrigued when a truckload of soldiers stopped at a stoplight and began speaking with citizens.

"*Shto vwee delayate zdeys?*" What are you doing here? asked one man to the young soldiers.

"You won't open fire on us, right?" asked another, hopefully.

"*Da, net.*" No, no, they replied with shy smiles.

"Will you be here long?"

"We don't know. We are following our orders but hope to go home soon."

I walked up to them and asked if I could take a picture. They immediately invited me into the truck. Reluctant to jump in, I peered inside, taking stock of what I saw. There must have been fourteen men stuffed into a space comfortable for ten, and with their camouflage guns, military gear, and enormous boots, there was no room for me. Pushed up against the soft, dark green, fabric walls, the men shuffled around to make space. An encouraging crowd formed as I stepped up and basically fell in, landing on a few laps. The soldiers huddled around and a picture was taken. We exchanged pleasantries and as I jumped out, they told me to be sure to get off the streets, as it was their job was to patrol them that night.

I looked at their faces—I was only twenty-two, and they looked younger. Each one had an automatic rifle that I wondered if they would actually use. It was scary to see them wielding so much power at such a young age. Young men often joined the military, but to see them on the front lines of a significant military endeavor in the capitol of a superpower—it was eye-opening.

Next, I stopped at the Intourist Hotel located down the street from the Kremlin, on Tverskaya. One of the largest hotels in Moscow, it was where foreign reporters and Soviet and foreign dignitaries stayed when visiting. I flashed my passport at the door, a requirement for access, and walked into a wall of humanity. The lobby was a beehive of reporters, tourists, and official-looking people. My eyes immediately were drawn to the TV at the bar, which was displaying an image of tanks barricading the White House, surrounding it to ensure nobody went in or out. Were these the same tanks I'd walked on? From the blaring TV to the people talking over each other in various languages to others yelling into international phones, the cacophony was deafening. I made my way through the crowd and got in line at one of the international phones.

With everything going on, I felt it was important to call my parents to let them know I was okay. Using an international phone was a luxury in Moscow. Calling the US from an apartment involved making reservations with an international operator, being lucky enough to have a viable connection, and hoping someone on the other end was home to pick up. From the hotel, it would be a direct line.

What I didn't realize at the time was that there were very few tanks in Leningrad, where I was supposed to be, and only a few small demonstrations there. So when I finally got through, the first thing my parents said was how thankful they were that I was in Leningrad and not in Moscow.

"What are you seeing in the news about Moscow?" I asked urgently, yearning to understand how widespread and dangerous the situation was.

"They keep showing the White House surrounded by barricades, tanks and armed troops in the streets, and now they are showing a few fatalities near the Arbat Street," they said. "It looks pretty touch-and-go there."

"It's not as bad as it looks on the news," I said, trying to downplay the danger while remaining vague about which city I was calling from.

"You mean in Leningrad? Yes. That we know. But Moscow doesn't look safe."

I sighed and began talking in the same way my dad had used in his letter to me. "Mom and Dad, first let me say, do not worry." I paused and silence descended on our conversation. "I'm in the center of Moscow, across from the Kremlin, at a Soviet hotel where many foreigners stay." I paused and waited for their eruption of disapproval.

"What!? What are you doing there? Are you okay? Why are you not in Leningrad? How did you get there?" They were talking over each other, on two telephones.

"I'm fine, really I'm fine. You know the news makes things seem worse than they really are. They are probably only showing you the flashpoint areas. It's actually quite calm here."

"But you just said you are near the Kremlin," my dad persisted. "That's where protests are. That's where tanks are. Aren't you near the center of everything?" He had a good point.

"I was just at the Arbat, in fact, and did run into a few soldiers and tanks, but everything was peaceful. I'm okay and am leaving the area now to go to back to the apartment. I had an interview today with one of the companies we identified a few months ago and am staying with friends here in Moscow, so I'll be okay."

They weren't exactly pleased. "Just get to the apartment and be safe. You never know what can happen in these types of situations," my mom said. "And, who are these friends? We had no idea you were going to Moscow!"

"Don't worry—they are friends of one of the tour group leaders in Leningrad," I said, not realizing I was actually making them feel more uncomfortable.

My dad, who was a bit more interested in politics, asked if I had seen Boris Yeltsin on a tank, defending the White House and giving a defiant speech. I didn't know he was even involved, much less active in front of the White House. Having resigned from the communist party in 1990, Yeltsin had recently returned to politics as the first freely elected President of Russia. Portraying himself as a reformer who was not afraid to make tough decisions if they were right for the people, Yeltsin, similar to Gorbachev, was a new breed of leader. The fact that he was involved in the current situation seemed to be a good thing.

"Enough, Paul," my mom interrupted. "Get home, Dave, and call us later."

"I know, I'll get going now. I just wanted to check in to let you know I'm okay," I said.

And then, without thinking, I kept talking. "There's one more thing I wanted to tell you." *Should I bring this up or leave it alone?* Prior to calling them I'd had a fleeting thought that maybe, even if things didn't work out with the interview, I would do everything I could to stay in Russia a bit longer. I hadn't thought the idea through, so it surprised me to hear the words pop out of my mouth.

"I may not return home with the tour group. I'm trying to work some things out in Leningrad so I'll be able to extend my stay abroad. I may try to live with a family and possibly teach English. Depending on what happens with this coup, there could be a lot of opportunity here so I want to stay a bit longer. I know I'll have to get my visa extended and work some details out, but I think I can do this." I held my breath waiting for their response.

The phone was silent for a few seconds.

"David"—my dad used my full name when he was serious—"didn't we agree that you would stay only if you were able to find a job? How did the interview go?"

"It went well, but was cut short due to the circumstances. It's hard to know if it will work out, but either way, I think this is the right thing for me."

"I'm not so sure. But, I understand that you need to do what you feel is right. Just be careful. You aren't in Boston and there's a lot going on politically right now."

"I know," I said thoughtfully.

"And David, you realize that given the uncertainty there, this specific job may not pan out. Are you ready for that?"

"Is this the right time to be doing this?" my mom jumped in, probing to see if I had doubts. "I mean it seems dangerous over there. I'm...I..."

"I admit I don't have all the answers right now and this sounds unplanned. I think it sounds more risky than it really is. But I've met some great people and think I can set up some sort of life here and see where things go. I know this is far from a concrete plan and it's not graduate school by any means, but it feels like the right thing for me now."

"If this is what you want to do," my mom said, "then we're not going to stop you. But just be careful and keep us informed. We worry a lot so call as often as you can so we know you are safe."

We spoke a little more and I could sense that they trusted me on this adventure. They were giving me the benefit of the doubt, and it felt good.

When we hung up I made my way through the dimly lit streets of Moscow to the Metro and returned to the apartment. I took long drags of the fresh air. The rain had stopped and I thought about how fortunate I was for all I'd witnessed. My being here seemed so random. A few months back I had no direction and decided to visit the Soviet Union on a whim. Now, I felt energized. I couldn't help but think of the possibilities that a government in transition might bring to entrepreneurs and foreign businesses. It could be the beginning of a road I'd never imagined.

ZA ZNAKOMSTVO!
TO GETTING ACQUAINTED!

BONDING WITH BABUSHKA

Over the next few days, I learned that the Gang of Eight had been arrested, Gorbachev had returned to Moscow, and that Yeltsin had emerged as the defender of the Russian White House. What this meant for the Soviet Union, beyond the fact that Gorbachev had become a weakened leader, was unclear. Instead of spending some time in Moscow as planned, I reluctantly returned to Leningrad. Given the unusual circumstances, I felt obligated to touch base with Ivan as soon as possible. Having thought further about the idea of remaining in Russia longer, I was now firm about this decision. Just as the coup altered the fate of the USSR, it had also altered mine. I was now intent on not only mastering the Russian language, but also on creating a life for myself in this foreign land. I had no idea what that entailed, but returning to the US was no longer on the table.

Arriving at the *Moscovsky Vokzal*, the Moscow train station in Leningrad I bought myself a chocolate cone. The ice cream in Russia was different from American ice cream—less creamy, a bit icier, and far less flavorful. Despite its flaws, it was just as satisfying.

I thought maybe I would see some protests, possibly a gathering of people listening to someone speaking through a bullhorn, or maybe a few tanks or transport units on the streets. But the train station was filled with the typical assortment of people: Armenians and Azerbaijanis selling fruits and vegetables off wheeled carts, Russians selling lacquer boxes, matrioshka dolls, and original landscape paintings, and big-boned babushkas rushing to and from trains with large sacks of potatoes, beets, or carrots over their shoulders. The layer of dirt and dust that blanketed the train station surfaces was just as it was when I left, and on the street, people were going about their business. The ice cream stands and other kiosks that lined the sidewalks were busy with travelers out in the pleasant summer weather.

Beyond satisfying my ice cream craving, I had work to do that afternoon. I found Ivan in his office near the Hermitage and let him know I was planning on changing my flight home to make it open-ended.

"Is that really a good decision?" he asked, leaning back in his swivel chair behind his tidy desk.

"Honestly, I'm not sure it is, but I want to stay. I have a lot more Russian to learn, and I'm just not ready to leave," I persisted.

Looking at me sternly, hands clasped behind his head, he continued, "You know you won't be part of a group once the others leave? You will be on your own."

I could tell I had some convincing to do so I sat down to meet him at his eye level. "I get it. I'm ready."

"You're sure? There's a lot happening in this country right now."

"I'm sure. And, yes, I know you won't be able to ensure my safety and that the political environment is questionable, but I want to stay," I offered, trying to answer his unspoken questions.

I think it was then he realized I wasn't typical tourist. He sighed deeply.

"Okay, okay. Sounds like you know what you want." He smiled and opened one of his drawers.

"Can you help me find a place to stay?"

"I can," he replied, pulling out his Rolodex.

Ivan provided some leads, recommending I start with a young woman named Zhanna who lived with her mother. Apparently, they had a large apartment and were looking for a way to supplement their income.

My Russian was still poor, and I would somehow have to explain to Zhanna who I was, what I was looking for, and that I was actually a decent person who could be trusted to live with her family. Understanding this, Ivan agreed to host a meeting, and to help translate.

But before I called her, I needed one more thing from him.

"If I call her and this works out, will I legally be able to stay in country or will I have to leave and return on another visa?" I asked.

He knew I was hoping he would extend my visa. The implications of not having it done in-country were expensive and included having to fly home, applying for a new visa, and purchasing a ticket back to Leningrad. I had heard that in-country extensions were possible, but I also heard you had to know people on the black market to make it happen.

He looked at me, massaged his beard thoughtfully, and seemed to be searching my face for something. If this was considered an illegal transaction, I'd have to allay his fears.

"You let me know how much it costs and I'll double it for your trouble," I added, feeling a momentary exhilaration of being a big spender—until I remembered that I wasn't. "Well, maybe not double it, but I'll pay you well. Can you have the expiration date pushed out a few months?"

"I can do this for you, but you'll need to trust me," he responded, wagging his finger at me. "I'll need your passport, current visa, and fifty dollars. I'll return the passport and the new visa to you in a few days."

"But, if I give you my passport, I'll have no international identification." I was confused and felt a bit uneasy by the request. I had heard rumors of the mafia stealing and selling US passports on the black market as a means of exiting the country. I looked at him and knew I had no reason not to trust him. I knew where he worked and lived, so if anything happened, I'd know where to find him.

"Don't worry," he smiled. "I know people have been trying to steal American passports to sell them, but I will not do this. You know me."

I weighed my options. I really wanted to stay in Russia. I counted out $75 and hoped for the best.

The next day, I went to Ivan's home and met Zhanna over some tea and crackers. A soft-spoken, gentle woman in her late twenties, Zhanna had the admirable quality of patience. She spoke limited English, so we trudged through a conversation about our backgrounds and the type of arrangement we were looking for, and made small talk to get to know each other. Her big greenish-blue eyes were expressive and warm, and she had a head of bouncy blonde hair that framed a heart-shaped face. She seemed very sweet and instinctively caring, so I was hopeful we could work out an arrangement.

She also had a five-year-old son who lived with her. His father had left the family. She had been on her own for about a year and wanted to assure me that her former husband was not returning. Her interest in having me move in was not only for the additional income, but also to help her improve her English language skills. It quickly became clear that we both wanted to make this work, so we agreed on an $80 monthly rent. We planned to reconvene the next day at the apartment so I could meet her mother and son, see my potential new home, and maybe even move in.

☭

My muted, yellow-colored new home stood six stories high, had oversized vertical windows, and was a full city block in length. Multiple archways led to what looked like a parking lot and a common grassy area for the tenants. The apartment building had four entrances, each with a different numbered address despite being part of a single building. Although in disrepair with cracks running up and down the patched concrete façade, it still looked bomb-proof. I kicked aside a piece of loose cement and rang the buzzer.

Zhanna came downstairs to meet me outside and led me in through one of the large wooden doors. It creaked and rocked on its hinges. As in other apartment complexes I'd visited, a broken elevator shaft was in the center of the hallway, and the cement stairwell reeked of dried urine. On the fourth floor we paused. I watched Zhanna extract a small key ring with a few three-inch-long keys from her pocketbook. I had never seen keys that size except in medieval movies. To my surprise, one fit the door, turned the lock, and we were in. Zhanna looked at me, smiled, and took a deep breath as if to say, here we go. I wasn't sure what to expect, and followed quietly.

As if on cue, her mom was standing in the hallway, holding a kitchen towel in one hand and a frying pan in the other. She shuffled toward me wearing a tightly knotted kerchief on her head, an old flowery, free-flowing dress, and slippers. Big-boned, taller than me, and solidly built, she had a serious, almost grim look on her face. I assumed Zhanna told her about the new living arrangement, but it seemed that she was either surprised or disappointed by my presence. Her dark eyes were set deep into her leathery skin, and they were unabashedly evaluating me.

She fulfilled my preconceived notion of what an elderly Russian peasant would look like. I couldn't help but attach my own historical perspective to her. Hardened by the state, protective of her family and country, and probably saddened by the loss of someone in World War II, this older woman was someone I didn't simply want to meet, but someone I wanted to get to know. I'd had plenty of opportunities to socialize with younger Russians, but few chances to mingle with the elder Soviet generation.

She stood in front of me and instead of offering a handshake or any other welcoming gesture, mumbled some Russian words to herself, and turned to go back to her business in the kitchen. As she walked away, she grumbled, "You are shorter than I expected. Call me Babushka."

I looked quizzically at Zhanna, confused by Babushka's gruff exterior. She met my glance and shrugged her shoulders as if to say, "That's her," and we brought the luggage into the hallway.

The apartment was larger than many Soviet-style apartments. The entrance hallway ran for about twenty feet and then curved to the right, creating a thoroughfare for the unit. Similar to other pre-WWII apartment buildings in Russia, this one was constructed primarily of concrete, and the walls were painted tastelessly—the bottom half of the wall was an odd faded green, and the upper half was off-white. No pictures hung from the walls, and I noticed three closed doors on the left of the hall, two bedrooms on the right, and an open bathroom door at the curve heading to the kitchen. What was behind these closed doors was a mystery to me, but no apartment I had visited in Leningrad had this much space, or this many doors. The apartment was certainly tidy, but concrete dust from the breakdown of the walls gathered in corners where the linoleum floors met the walls.

"Don't mind Babushka," Zhanna said nicely. "She is wary of foreigners but I think over time you will like her. I hope she didn't offend you."

"No, not at all. People notice my height here. It seems everything is built big and people..." I fumbled with my dictionary looking for the word *appreciate*, "*otseneevat* size here, but I'm short and make the best of it."

"That's good. I like how you think about it. I hope you will like it here."

"I think I will."

"So, David, now that you are moving in, there's one more thing I'd like to tell you about the apartment," Zhanna began, as we brought my luggage into one of the bedrooms. "When you go inside the bathroom you will notice many pots in the bathtub. This is because the state is doing work on the pipes, so we have no hot water. I don't know how long this will last, so depending on if you need hot water, you can use the stove to heat some up prior to washing or showering."

I stood, unresponsive. No hot water? This was not good news. We were heading into autumn and I loved taking hot showers.

"What kind of project is it?" I asked, hoping for more detail, and a hint of when it would end.

"We don't know. This happened last autumn as well, and lasted into late October, so we'll see," she said casually.

I cringed but was intent on making the best of it.

"Also, the other bedroom is for Babushka, my son, and me. We hope you will respect our privacy."

"Of course," I replied immediately. I felt embarrassed about having an entire room to myself and wondered how they felt about sleeping in one room, together.

"By the way, this envelope is for you." She reached for an envelope sitting on a small table in the entranceway. "It's from Ivan," she said smiling, handing me a sealed envelope.

I opened it quickly hoping it was what I was waiting for. It was. My passport and a new visa were inside. How he did it in one day, I'll never know, and I didn't care.

"You look relieved," Zhanna said quietly.

"Very, thank you," I responded, a bit surprised that he had dropped it off in a random envelope at my new apartment. Either he was foolish and a bit cavalier with my documents, or he trusted my new family.

☭

Over the next few weeks, Babushka and I got more acquainted, but the first few weeks were awkward and our interactions were limited to pleasantries.

"Good morning," I'd say to Babushka and Zhanna in Russian.

"Good morning," Zhanna would respond in English, with her cotton-candy smile.

"*Nu, dobroe utro,*" Babushka would reluctantly mutter—well, good morning.

Thanks to a combination of her Cold War upbringing, my limited Russian vocabulary and mediocre pronunciation, and her nonexistent English, an unavoidable mistrust hovered between us. She knew that I left every morning to attend Russian language tutoring sessions, which I had set up with a private tutor (thanks, again, to Ivan), but I could tell she was suspicious.

She had every right to wonder what I was doing in her land, why I was friendly with her daughter, and why I was so intent on learning the Russian language. There was nothing I could do about it. I tried to tiptoe around the apartment, washing up at odd hours, eating out of the house when possible, and going to bed early to avoid intruding on her space. But, as time went on, my routine normalized, my language skills improved, and she seemed to accept me a bit less reluctantly.

Soon, Zhanna's schedule changed, and she began leaving earlier than both Babushka and me. With our mediator gone, we were forced to interact. The mornings continued to be a challenge. Neither of us was a morning talker, and the bone-chilling showers put me in a foul mood. But things began to change in the afternoons and evenings. At times, after I'd return home from my tutoring sessions,

Babushka and I would be alone in the apartment. We couldn't help but run into each other, and with tea a Russian ritual during the afternoon hours, we naturally began sharing conversation around the small Formica table. At times, she seemed to be holding back, and we would say very little. As our comfort level grew, she developed a tendency to lecture me, asserting herself as she saw fit. I didn't mind. I thoroughly enjoyed her company and accepted her as an authority on Russia, its people, and its culture.

I learned that Babushka was a communist and her outlook had been molded by the likes of Stalin, Khrushchev, and Brezhnev. Her Russia was the Soviet Union, and her country was one where the KGB had the last word, the state provided for the people, and behavior was a by-product of fear rather than any sense of law or morality. And because Babushka benefited from these policies, she supported the communist regime with a prototypical hard line, conservative, Soviet-era stance. Unlike many other people her age who had fallen through the cracks of the state safety net, Babushka continued to have housing and a job she enjoyed. She believed in the state's role in her life, and knew no other way. In her mind, the idea of protesting, or showing distrust of her leaders was never an option. It was inappropriate and, in fact, for much of her life was not tolerated, and could be reported as insubordination. She didn't enjoy waiting in lines for food or losing hot water for months at a time, but she understood the state had many priorities, and sometimes people had to sacrifice for the betterment of the country.

There was also a soft side to Babushka. Underneath her thick skin, she was not so unlike her daughter. Even the grizzle and moles on her face could not hide the warmth and curiosity that characterized her soul. It took some time for her to trust me, and while I don't know specifically when I turned the corner, I do know that somewhere between the tea and the borscht, we ended up bonding.

I grew to appreciate that the unadorned concrete walls of her apartment had witnessed more than I could have imagined. The seven-room apartment had been her home since she was married in the early sixties, but was occupied by four families as a communal apartment. This was a Stalinist invention intended to help provide housing for all. Although difficult for her to admit, Babushka talked of how crowded the apartment used to be, how uncomfortable it could get emotionally, and how challenging it was to live in such cramped quarters with so little personal space. But, when she and her husband moved in, it met their expectations and was considered a good situation. Her choices at the time were to share the apartment with strangers or live with her parents. She chose the apartment.

"Did you get along with the people you shared the space with?" I had learned about communal apartments in college, but didn't truly understand the implications so was eager to learn from someone who lived in one.

She looked at me blankly. This was the familiar look of someone trying to understand my garbled Russian. I rephrased the question and used my dictionary to look up "get along with."

A small smirk emerged. Babushka never really used a wide smile, so this was a good thing. She got up and shuffled to put some tea on the stove. "In principle, yes, we did our best," she responded. By the way she used the words "in principle," I knew there was more to her response than what was said. Russians often used this phrase "in principle" to answer questions while allowing listeners to make their own interpretation of the actual meaning. I grew accustomed to this quickly, and usually asked clarifying questions.

"In principle?" I questioned, as she sat back down.

"Yes," she said, looking away. "Things were not always perfect and in fact, we were luckier than most. It's true we had a family in each room. But we were fortunate. One family was elderly with grown children who lived elsewhere, the married couple did not have kids, and the other family had two kids. So considering what we could have had, it was not a bad situation."

"And you shared the bathroom, kitchen, and living room?"

"Yes. We made it work."

I sat back in my chair sipping the tea, appreciating how powerful a thing perspective could be. Whereas she "made it work," living in an apartment with three other families, I never thought twice about how lucky I was to have grown up in a house where nobody shared a room except my parents, where we had multiple bathrooms, and where space and privacy were not a luxury, but the norm.

I noticed her looking at me and she asked abruptly, "What else do you want to know?"

I didn't want to admit how fortunate my childhood was, so I asked a few more questions. "What happened to the other families? Is this your apartment now? Do you own it?"

"Technically, it is owned by the government, but in principle, it is ours," she answered.

There it was again, the "in principle" line, so I assumed with no other families living here, she had squatter's rights, if that notion existed in Russia.

"The elderly family passed away, the couple found a better arrangement, and the family that had children recently moved out, so we are very fortunate to have the space that we do."

"I can see that. I've been to a few other apartments and few are of this size. It's great. But, what do you do with the extra rooms? Do you often have periodic boarders (a word I looked up in my dictionary during the conversation) staying with you?" I had never asked about the doors that seemed to remain permanently shut. I wanted to, but knew it wasn't my place. But every day I'd pass them in the main hall, and every day my curiosity would grow.

She smiled a knowing smile and waved her large, calloused hand at me. "Others? No, you are our first and we'll see how that goes," she said, smirking and chuckling. She then stood up and began heading down the hall out of the kitchen. She stopped, looked at me and waved her arm indicating I should follow. Not knowing what to expect, and not accustomed to having such an involved conversation with Babushka, I followed like a puppy.

Around the corner, she stopped at the first locked door down the hall. She leaned against the green cement wall and fiddled with some keys she had removed from her pocket. As she sorted out the right key, again I was mesmerized by their size—like dungeon keys. Only in castles and really old homes had I seen keyholes that accommodated such large keys. She found the right one, opened the door and stepped back to let me in. She then went to open the second door down the hall, and then the third.

What I saw shocked me. The same ugly paint job continued inside each of the three rooms, and each had large windows overlooking the street. The light fixtures and drapes were nice enough to indicate someone used to live in each room. But there was no furniture. No furniture in the first room, the second, or the third. Instead, upon opening each door, I saw nothing but a huge pile of unwashed potatoes in one room, dirt-covered carrots in another, and whole beets in the third. Except for a small area to stand in each room, these mounds of vegetables covered the entire floor and rose close to the ceiling of each twelve-by-twelve room.

"I don't understand."

She smiled.

I thought of the food lines around the city and wondered what was going on. Did she have some secret supplier or was she hoarding food, anticipating a famine?

"It's a lot of food, I know," Babushka said as she closed each door and began walking back to the kitchen. She sat down and I followed. "You see, when I leave every morning to go to work, I oversee the distribution of the vegetables in this region."

"*You* do?" I said, sounding more surprised than I wanted.

"Yes, I do," she answered proudly. "What, you don't think I can?"

I was embarrassed that I had underestimated her. "No, it's not that. But knowing the little I do about the current food shortages and the lines that I see daily, that must be a difficult job."

"Yes, it is, and at times it's not pleasant. I know the lines exist. I know which stores have food, and I understand the shortages better than I want to. This is why I like Gorbachev. To me, he is not a true communist. But, I accept him and think he is a smart man who understands some of our most serious problems. You see, I know we need a better system of transportation, storage, and distribution. These things are very important, and without them we cannot succeed."

I was impressed with Babushka. She was an intelligent woman who didn't allow her Soviet perspective to cloud what she ultimately knew was necessary for her country.

She continued. "You know I lived under Brezhnev when times were also difficult, but it was different then. At least we knew what we could count on—low crime, food on the table, and a strong Soviet state that enforced laws. Brezhnev did not care so much about domestic concerns, and he didn't need to. Gorbachev, on the other hand, knows what is important and what our state needs, but his efforts seem to be leading to hyperinflation and corruption. We now have these hooligans who simply take what they want!" A note of despair entered her voice. "Nobody—not me, or anyone else— knows what to expect with them. I would like to see Gorbachev be stronger, tougher, and stand up to the crime, but...I just don't know."

At this point, I was thoroughly intrigued.

"So, you admired past communist leaders like Brezhnev, but you also respect Gorbachev? Did you support the KGB's role as strong people?" I didn't know the Russian word for "enforcers."

"Yes, Brezhnev was a good leader, but I am old enough to know that not everything is black and white. The KGB? They did some good and some bad. What I do know is that we felt their presence. So people followed the law. But, who am I to say? All I know is that we need someone to fight this growing group of Russian mafia. They are becoming bolder, stealing from those who cannot protect themselves, requiring bribes from those who cannot pay, and even resorting to murder. It is dangerous and we need a stronger government to help maintain control."

"When you say mafia, who do you mean? Is there an organized group of hooligans?" I wanted to understand what exactly she and others were talking about when they mentioned the mafia.

"This is hard for me to know. Some say they are organized, others say they are not. To me, it doesn't matter. I just know they are not good for our country."

I took a sip of tea and thought about what she was saying. I knew that Russian society was changing, but because I had yet to experience the mafia or the effects of inflation, I remained an outsider, unable to truly relate. I had heard so much about Gorbachev supporting more of a free-market approach. I knew the situation was tough on ordinary Russians, but had never discussed it at length with someone experiencing it firsthand. I thought about the people who had no choice but to live with these societal shifts and who were scared by the dramatic changes taking place around them. Babushka was a strong woman who surprisingly believed in Gorbachev. If she was uncertain of his goals and questioned his policies and enforcement, how would other, less convinced Russians react?

And just as I thought we would dive into politics and the economy, her phone rang, and her attention was quickly diverted to other things. But this was a big step for Babushka and me, and in the coming months, we would grow even closer.

ANONYMITY

The failed coup of 1991 ended up being the straw that broke the Soviet Union. Within a few days, Gorbachev resigned as General Secretary of the Communist Party, but held on to his role as President of the Soviet Union. Soon thereafter, without a centralized communist leader and ideology to follow, states that made up the Soviet Union began clamoring for, and declaring, their independence from the Kremlin. It quickly became evident that the Soviet Union, known as the "other" superpower, was in disarray. Gorbachev tried to establish a new economic agreement to help hold it together, but with his diminishing authority, he was in no position to deny these states that which he had essentially already granted—freedom. Whether he saw it coming or not, his role had all but evaporated, and the formal dissolution of the Soviet Union had begun.

The country was now in a race to make a clean break from its communist past. With fewer restrictions and less scrutiny from the state, private enterprise grew and more people began embracing change, hoping to take a chance on their dreams. Others stayed on the sidelines, afraid to dip their toes in a business environment they didn't fully understand. Either on their own or with foreign partners, businesses began popping up throughout St. Petersburg (Leningrad reverted to its original name in September, 1991)[3] and Moscow. They quickly learned that the new brand of Russian capitalism had its benefits, but as Babushka mentioned, its drawbacks as well. Without a clear and tested legal system, the mafia grew unchecked. To small businesses, this meant paying for protection or facing potential consequences. Threats, firebombs, and unsustainable bribes were not uncommon. Many legitimately questioned whether mafia-infested capitalism was an improvement on KGB-sponsored communism.

With my newfound independence and desire to stay in St. Petersburg, I was forced to adapt, too. Unlike the country I was living in, I wasn't trying to run away from my past, but questioned my direction and purpose. Everything—my college degree in Soviet East European Studies, my travel timeframe, finding a job based on pre-coup research—had blown up. It was crazy to think that I had spent four years studying a country that no longer existed. Now, because many Western companies were exiting the market to avoid the perils of a civil war that never materialized, opportunities were scarce. In fact, Kevin O'Shea never returned any of my follow-up calls, and from what I heard, had closed up shop. Many of the companies that did remain preferred hiring low-cost Russians, whom they could pay in rubles, to Americans who demanded dollars, health insurance, and a safe work environment.

Since moving in with Babushka and Zhanna, my routine of studying Russian, meeting and socializing with new friends, and learning more about the city was tremendously satisfying. I took pleasure in having the time to walk the city, demystify the Metro, and try new bus routes. On a daily basis, I'd take the Metro from the center of the city to the outskirts, where my tutor lived. To reach her building, I'd then transfer to a bus that would wind through the bleak, gray, uniform expanse of uninspired government-built tenements. Privatization was literally a foreign concept, and people depended on the state to provide housing. At last I'd find my tutor's building, take the stairs to the fifth floor, and study with her for two to three hours a day, trying to approach the Russian language in a disciplined and effective way.

Afterward, I'd return to the center of St. Petersburg and get to know my adopted city by visiting outdoor markets, meeting people, and using the language. I remembered being told many times that St. Petersburg was the Venice of the North. As I grew to know the city, however, I tried to reconcile what I saw and what I had heard. Years before, I had traveled to Venice and admired the sculptures, enjoyed feeding the birds at the outdoor piazzas, and marveled at the frescoed church interiors. The city was full of vibrant storefronts, cafés, restaurants, and an evening scene rich with culture, fine wine, long strolls, and romantic boat rides on the canals. There was a relaxed feel to the city. Overall, Italy was impressive not only for its individual treasures, but also for its collective attitude of commitment to preserving its history and art.

Maybe I'd hoped to truly find a Venice of the North. More probably it was a direct result of the troubled economy, but the more I observed of St. Petersburg, the less I found the cities comparable. Despite its attractive canals, Italian-inspired architecture, sculptures, and museums, St. Petersburg was a pale imitation. At first, I wasn't sure what I was missing. Each day I'd walk a different route hoping to find the Venetian spirit in these Russian streets. I didn't. What stood out to me was the dark soot covering many of the public sculptures, the disrepair of the domes, and the dust that seemed to cover the entire city like a light blanket of snow. Many of the larger museums such as The Hermitage were national jewels, but their upkeep was second-rate at best. Peeling paint, dilapidated columns, and extended exhibit closures contributed to a feeling of malaise and failure. And because I wasn't intrigued by my surroundings, I focused on the people, which made for an even grimmer picture.

Frustrated by the economy, angered by the long lines, and fed up with the political environment, Russians rarely smiled in public. Going from store to store, line to line, looking for staples like bread, milk, and cabbage was maddening. I'd often see the wide sidewalks filled with people alone with their thoughts, sullen and frustrated. They'd walk out of stores empty-handed, cursing a situation they blamed on the government. While the mafia grew louder and stronger, reveling in their newfound wealth, the everyday person felt more frustrated and alienated.

As an alternative to typical stores, markets emerged outside of each Metro station. Vendors would set up card tables, share a temporary stall with a friend, or simply hold a few items up for sale hoping to walk away with a handful of rubles. From Western cosmetics, cigarettes, chocolates, and magazines to loaves of bread and jarred pickles, the variety was enticing. These pop-up markets were crowded with bargain hunters, and as their popularity grew, became just another outlet for the mafia to exploit. Although the money was small, I heard that each vendor was required to pay a certain percentage of their take to the local mafia. I'd sometimes browse, but rarely buy. I never knew how any of these products were acquired, if they were genuine, or if they had been tampered with.

One day as I exited the nearest Metro station to my house, I walked through one of these markets and got in line at a local bread store. I stood with my head down, quiet and deferential, trying to blend in. Sandwiched between two babushkas holding old satchels and dressed in loose-fitting, rugged dresses, I recalled the song, "One of These Things Is Not Like the Other." My newer jeans, fashion-forward eyeglasses, and brand-name sneakers all identified me as a foreigner. I listened as one babushka complained about the lines and how she spent all day looking for bread. Another vigorously chimed in to complain about the rising prices. Neither was speaking to anyone in particular, but others responded with similar stories and soon I was caught between a group of babushkas grousing to each other, growing more irate by the minute.

I stood quietly and looked in the store window. Supplies were dwindling, but I would get a loaf. What suddenly struck me, and shamefully hadn't earlier, was the fact that this was a bread store and only a bread store. I should have known by the generic sign out front, *Chleb,* that most stores were a generic version of the item it was selling. In fact, these stores often sold only one product, and to make things worse, only one variation on that product. The milk stores sold milk, the cabbage stores, cabbage, and the meat stores, meat. Multi-product food stores did exist, but in reality and all too often, they had only one or two products on their shelves at a time. I thought about how much time these old ladies must spend searching for food, week after week, going from one store to the next, standing in line for one product at a time. It was mind-boggling. Needless to say, I was lucky to be living with Zhanna and Babushka.

Although I had stood for thirty minutes, I knew I didn't need bread as much as these folks. I also had the option of visiting one of the few dollar stores—small, Western supermarket-style stores that accepted foreign currency—that were popping up throughout St. Petersburg. I slowly walked out of line and made my way across the street. I didn't look back, but could feel eyeballs peering at me, wondering why I was abandoning my treasured spot in the queue.

As time passed, the revelation that I was truly on my own in a foreign land at last sunk in. Parents, longtime friends, and relatives surrounded me in childhood, and it was rare that I would do anything absolutely on my own, or more accurately, feel alone. My instinct to travel to Russia was based on my thirst for knowledge and a connection to another culture. I never anticipated feeling such a powerful sense of independence, anonymity, and complete self-reliance.

This newfound emotional reality was not a negative thing, just different. Without the academic pressure to run to a class or the social pressure of doing something "productive," I alone decided what I would do with my days. On many occasions, I'd simply wander the city, observing people, admiring detailed architecture, and marveling at Russian history. My long walks became practice sessions in which I would talk to myself to reinforce new Russian phrases and vocabulary. I spent days in The Hermitage, wandering the opulent gold-leaf hallways, looking at masterpieces and wondering why they had earned so much acclaim. In many instances I didn't see their charm or beauty. At home I would have dwelled on a piece, trying to appreciate it as society instructed me I should. Here, I simply observed and continued walking. The freedom of only answering to myself was liberating, even if my conclusions, thoughts, and impressions were directionless and even a bit pedestrian.

This feeling of anonymity was unlike any I'd felt before. Even on my first day in college I knew a few people. The more I considered my situation, the more it looked like a chance to reinvent myself. Everything I'd once seen as impossible or forbidden was now permissible. This new freedom was half-glimpsed, mostly subconscious, but nevertheless rooting itself inside me.

Throughout this period of discovery, Zhanna and I would spend time taking walks, going to friends' houses for dinner parties, or hanging around the apartment, listening to music and talking. Most of the time, we had fun together. But, at other times, there seemed to be an awkward undercurrent in our relationship. Whether because she was single and on the hunt, or because I was paying to live with her, our dynamic was sometimes uncomfortable. And, oddly, she tried to fill the role of my mother abroad, something I didn't appreciate. She couldn't help herself, and incessantly nagged me over what constituted appropriate winter clothing, and reminded me how disappointed she would be if I didn't tell her where I was going or where I'd been. In response, I chose to do what Babushka had done when she had lived with three other families: In short, I did my best to ignore what bothered me, and we all managed to get along.

One evening, while sitting around the table sipping tea with Zhanna, her longtime friend Pavel stopped by. Dressed in a fine, pressed suit with everything just so, he said hello, sat down, and crossed his legs. With his long face, pointy features dulled by a full, reddish-brown beard, and bronze-rimmed spectacles, he seemed like an intellectual character from a nineteenth-century Russian novel. He looked at me, assessing. Based on his mannerisms and appearance, I anticipated a formal, conservative, and intellectual conversation. While he met my expectations on some counts, on others, I was surprised.

"So, you are the American?" he asked, nodding his head up and down, knowing full well the answer. He formally extended his hand with his arm straight in front of him, and we locked eyes.

"Yes, nice to meet you," I replied.

"I'm excited to get to know you and to ask questions about American music and culture—would that be okay?" he asked, looking intently at me, pronouncing each word distinctly. "I don't speak English, so please let me know if you don't understand me. Additionally, if you have questions for me, please feel free to ask."

"Of course." Even though predictable, his formality was almost unnatural. I went along, amused by his demeanor, not knowing what to expect. I looked at Zhanna, who shrugged, not knowing where this was going, either. "Okay. It's about the blacks in your country.

I don't understand them. You know, here, in Russia, we don't have a large black population. There are students from African countries, but I've not met any, and don't know them."

I was a bit taken aback at how direct his question was, but realized that without a significant black population, and a history so different from America's, he had probably not experienced nor understood the sensitivities of race relations. It was a sincere question.

"I've noticed there are very few blacks here," I offered. "But what don't you understand?"

"Well, how do I ask this?" He looked away. "Are they bad in your country? I mean, I know there are many who do amazing things like Michael Jackson and Michael Jordan, but I hear so much about gangsters, poverty, and crime and then I see something about this Rodney King man, and I don't understand. I mean, did they beat him so badly because he was black? From what I can see, they are just like you and me, so why are there so many problems?"

I thought for a moment and didn't respond. Zhanna was obviously interested as well, leaning on the table, sipping her tea, peering at me over her cup. How could I explain race relations in a way that someone who has no background in American history could understand? I was impressed with his question; others might never have asked and merely believed what they heard or saw, but not Pavel.

I tried to respond in the simplest way possible. "They are absolutely not bad, and in fact many of my good friends from college are African-American."

"Ahh, interesting." He pushed the middle part of his glasses between his brows and seemed to lean back in his chair and settle in.

"Yes, I noticed a black man on the cover of your CD," Zhanna chimed in referencing the collegiate *a cappella* CD I had brought from home. I had sung in the group, The Tufts University Beelzebubs.

I struggled to map out what I would say next. I knew this conversation would challenge my Russian language skills, and given its potential scope, I needed to frame it so they could understand my thoughts. "Relations between whites and blacks in America go back many years. What you need to know is that in America today there are different backgrounds, economic statuses, and religions, and that people don't always agree or share the same point of view. To me, the important thing is finding out who people are for yourself and then deciding how you, as an individual, feel about that person. I look at blacks, whites, Asians, and other nationalities all the same. It reminds me of why I'm here in Russia. To me, people are people no matter where they live or who they are."

After sifting through my dictionary and finding the verbs "to owe" and "to assume," I went on. "We owe it to each other never to assume behaviors or beliefs based on outward appearance alone. The issue of misunderstanding one another is often due to stereotyping an entire race as either good or bad. We can't do that. People need to avoid generalizations about groups because everyone is unique. We all have different backgrounds, beliefs, and things we hold dear, but at our core, we are still just people."

"I understand and agree, but unfortunately, I don't think most people look at things that way," he lamented. "So, this Rodney King fellow, why did this happen? It seems unfair."

"I agree that it was excessive and although I can't answer definitively if race was involved, I think it played a significant role, and so it shows you that even now, America has problems with race and is still working them out."

"I tend to think we will have similar issues in St. Petersburg. Maybe not race-related, but ethnicity related," Pavel surmised.

"What do you mean?"

"I've seen many more Armenians and Azerbaijanis at the train station lately and they are not well received here. Many believe they are associated with our increase in crime."

"Why are there more now?"

"With Gorbachev's new policies, it is easier to travel to the larger cities," Zhanna explained.

"That is exactly my concern, Zhanna," Pavel interjected. "I am worried about where his policies might take us and that unforeseen challenges will crop up."

We eyed each other for a moment, thoughtfully. The silence was awkward. "You will face many challenges, but the one you bring up isn't one I had considered. Very interesting," I said, thoughtfully.

Sitting back in his seat, Pavel looked at me intently. His head kept bobbing up and down in agreement.

"Well, my explanation of our situation in America is far from complete, but it seems you understand what I'm saying. I hope it helps," I said, still intrigued by his question.

As I quickly discovered, living abroad had its share of quirks and oddities, and plenty of learning moments. Most Russians I encountered, including Pavel, had never traveled outside of Moscow, not to mention out of the country, so these kinds of contemplative questions were frequent. With each question, I was given the opportunity to step back, think about my own perceptions of America, apply what I had learned in college and life, and provide a thoughtful answer. As time went on and similar deep questions persisted, I found myself really enjoying the act of explaining the American culture and comparing it to the Russian situation.

"Thank you for your insight, David." He grew even more formal, if that were possible. "You know, I'd like to ask another question, if I may."

Knowing he was a thinker and also quite bold, I braced myself for what would follow.

"I also wanted to ask about the Jews. Do you know any and what are they like? I've heard there are many in Boston."

I paused for a moment. I knew there was a long, ugly history of anti-Semitism in Russia and the Soviet Union[4]. Even today, I had heard that many Russians blamed their economic plight on the Jews. But, still, one of my wishes in traveling to Russia was to dispel misconceptions.

"There are, and yes, I've met many," I said guardedly and still a bit surprised by his straightforward approach. "How do you feel about the Jews?"

"I don't know any," he said. "It's similar to my question about the blacks, in that many people have opinions, but because I don't have experience with either group, I don't know what to think."

"Ah, okay." I was relieved. He seemed to have no agenda and genuinely wanted to learn. "I myself am Jewish, so I hope you'll get to know me and decide for yourself what you think."

He smiled broadly and blushed a bit. "I didn't know."

"Yes, my grandparents are from Eastern Europe, actually Ukraine, and are Jewish. They came over to America in the early 1900s."

"Interesting." He looked at me thoughtfully, caressing his beard.

"Am I what you expected?"

"I didn't know what to expect. But, it is nice to know you and will be great getting to know you further." He was still smiling.

"Enough, Pavel—leave him alone," Zhanna interrupted, taking on her tone of a nagging mother. "It's probably tiring for him to be speaking with you, given your tough questions. You'll have time."

"*Da, da, chorosho*—yes, yes, okay," he conceded. "Oh—Zhanna, guess what?" He was suddenly so excited that he didn't let her respond. "You know my friend Sergei who wanted to open a studio? Well, he did it!"

"I don't believe it. Really?"

"No joke. He's so excited about it." He went on to explain that despite the economy, or more appropriately, because of Glasnost, he was able to open a recording studio and was looking to recruit new artists. He had formed a company and was hoping to generate interest by offering inexpensive studio time to attract up-and-comers who would spread the word. The wheels in my brain jolted into action.

"You know, Pavel, I sang in an *a cappella* group in college, and was on a few albums. What kind of music is he looking for?"

"You mentioned that CD earlier. I didn't realize you had a talent here," Pavel said, looking at Zhanna and then at me.

"Oh, yes. He brought his guitar and sings for us sometimes. He does the Beatles and other songs. He's quite good," Zhanna boasted.

"Do you think he would help an American looking to get into the music business?" I asked. My interest in music was sincere, but I had doubts about how far I could go. Singing with The Beelzebubs was one of the most rewarding, exciting, and fun experiences in my life, but writing and singing music on my own was in an entirely different class of commitment. Yet I had always wondered what might happen if I really applied myself.

Pavel leaned forward and put his teacup down. "I'm meeting him tomorrow to look at the studio if you'd like to come."

I looked at Zhanna. *Why not?* Pavel gave me the address and closest Metro station, and we were set to meet his friend the next day.

☭

I showed up at the appointed time and walked into the studio. I didn't see Pavel, but a tall, thin man with long, straight, black hair and a prominent nose appeared.

"I speak with Pavel today and he not come, but he say an American singer and songwriter would be here. Is this you?" He asked softly.

The songwriter designation threw me for a loop. I contemplated whether I should correct him, as I had never really written a song. Then again, there was no reason to cut my knees out from under myself before seeing where this could go.

"Yes, that's me. Are you Sergei?"

He looked relieved. "Ah, you speak Russian. Much better. Come in!" In his mother tongue, his voice became more robust—almost bellowing. "Would you like some tea? We can make some and sit down to talk."

"No, I'm fine, thank you." I didn't know Sergei at all and didn't want to end up spending the entire afternoon at his studio. "So, this is the studio Pavel was telling me about?"

"Yes, come in and see. He told me that you had recorded before. Is this right?" He switched to a more polite form of address.

I peered through the glass into the recording studio. "Yes, I have, with a group in college. We were fortunate to be able to record in New York City, at the same studio where Billy Joel recorded a few of his albums."

"Does the equipment compare to what you've used?"

Sergei's studio had plenty of professional-looking microphones, various instruments including a drum set neatly positioned against a wall, wood floors with wood paneling, and sound-proofing materials to optimize the acoustics. The soundboard in the main room was large, and though I was no expert, it looked like a serious piece of equipment. "You seem to have great setup here!"

"Yes, thank you," he said as if that was what he expected to hear. "We put a lot into this. So, Pavel mentioned you might like to record and you know, because you have experience, there is an opportunity I'd like to ask you about."

This was my chance to clarify my level of experience. I didn't take it.

"You see, a well-known St. Petersburg filmmaker has asked me to find an artist to write music for his film. Is this something you think you could do?"

It took all the focus and energy I had to conceal my true feelings of doubt. There was no way I could say yes. Sure, I had recorded with a group, but I had never written music, performed my own songs, or arranged a score. And to do it in the context of a Russian movie that I probably wouldn't even understand—it was totally unrealistic.

I decided to do it anyway.

"When is he looking to have the music complete? Would he mind if it is in English? And I'd need to know what the movie is about so I can write lyrics that make sense for the plot," I responded, trying to maintain my confident façade.

"All good questions. First things first, however. He is well established and has done many films. I think it's best if we record a variety of your songs, submit to him, and see what he thinks. That way, we will know if he likes your style and then you can discuss other questions with him. When would you like to come in to record?" He flipped to a page in his scheduling book.

His response initially put me at ease, knowing I'd have a first pass at recording to see if the filmmaker even liked my music. The second part, however, scared me. He spoke to me as if I were a recording artist from the US with a rich catalogue of songs. The reality was that I had one unfinished song I had never played for anyone and had some scattered ideas for others. *How many would they be expecting?* I didn't ask. We settled on a date a few weeks out, and planned for two days of recording time.

Reminded of a challenge my gymnastics coach presented to me as a sophomore in high school, I was determined to make a go of this recording opportunity. Coach had not so subtly let me know that I had the potential to become one of the best gymnasts in the state. My body type—short yet muscular with little body fat—was telling. He believed in me, more than I did in myself, kept me focused, and pushed me until I almost quit. Over the next few years I worked hard, eventually placing second in the state for rings and in the top ten for parallel bars.

Similarly, music was a passion and a dream of mine, and although I only pursued it as a hobby, this was my chance to see what I could do. Absent the influence and expectations of family and friends, the downside was merely personal, and I could handle rejection. The upside? I wasn't sure, but imagined the possibilities.

Over the next few weeks, I focused all my efforts on preparing for the recording sessions. I dreamt about recording a hit, and visions of grandeur pushed me to do things I had never done before. I wrote lyrics, crafted melodies, and practiced my songs until I knew them back and forth. I added harmonies on the fly and mastered a few original guitar licks, repeating them time and again to build fluency. By the time we were ready to record, my fingers had calloused over and I had never played better guitar.

☭

When the time came to work in studio, I felt nervous, but ready. I had seven prepared songs, one in Russian. The lyrics were complete, and I was ready to play both the rhythm and solo guitar parts as well as sing the melodies and harmonies. In the back of my mind, I wondered if they would throw me out after one song—but secretly hoped they would rush the studio and embrace me.

Neither occurred.

Sergei attended both days of the recording session. The morning of the first day he obviously had high expectations. He was gregarious and repeatedly offered anything I wanted to make me feel more comfortable. I loved his attention and faith, but his true feelings would show in how he reacted to the music.

At first, he seemed to like it. I could see him humming along and he went out of his way to offer ideas, input, and advice that improved the songs. But, by day two, he was done with me. He stopped paying close attention to the process. When he did engage, his demeanor had shifted, as though he was more interested in completion than improvement. He was mentally absent, possibly deciding how he would break the news to his client.

Either way, I was ecstatic about the final product. I had no band accompaniment, so ended up doing multiple takes to record harmonies over myself, add guitar sections, and delete areas that didn't work. Even the song I wrote in Russian, which wasn't grammatically perfect at first, received some help from others in the studio, and developed into an understandable and catchy tune. When all of the songs were complete, I listened to the full recording with Sergei. While he said very little, his thoughts were obvious. He let me know he would submit the tape and they would call within a few weeks, but I knew I would never hear from him. He wasn't angry, just disappointed.

I, on the other hand, felt both relieved and triumphant. I had taken a shot at something I had always wanted to do. For me, that was enough. It would have been incredibly satisfying to have met Sergei's expectations, but I knew I gave it my all. When I left the studio for the last time, I walked out and looked down the street. People walked on and looked past me. I watched as two Russian men standing nearby shared a cigarette and a handshake, grinning their gold-toothed smiles. I found myself alone, anonymous, and rich with free time. I walked home along a canal embankment and paused to admire the reflection of an apartment building on the river.

OPENING MY EYES

By Russian standards, Babushka was a very good cook. She had a limited choice of ingredients, but did her best to present food in ways that made meals unique. I was grateful, but let's just say dinner was rarely a surprise. Staple items included brown bread, beets, carrots, some kind of meat, and potatoes. She was partial to frying food, but at times would bake or boil. On occasion, she'd confuse me by encasing meat in some kind of gelatin, a preparation technique I found revolting. I think she sometimes enjoyed watching me squirm; I'd pick around the gelatin, trying to get to the meat. Soup, on the other hand, red beet borscht or white Ukrainian borscht, was a staple and delicious.

Although she put care and effort in to preparing meals, Babushka's food rarely agreed with my system. Maybe it was the lack of variety, the lack of fresh fruit, or possibly the unidentified meat, but my sensitive stomach was queasy almost every day. Because of this, I took the precaution of finding and noting each and every public bathroom in St. Petersburg. And knowing these bathrooms as I did, I carried emergency toilet paper with me at all times.

Despite the consequences, I savored her meals, and while dessert was rare, our customary tea after dinner was unexpectedly pleasant. Prior to traveling to Russia, the idea of sitting around a table sipping tea, winding down, and reflecting on the day was completely foreign and unappealing. But, I grew to rely on this bond with my adopted family. At first, our conversations centered on our daily lives, but soon I noticed a shift. Ever so gently, Babushka and Zhanna would ask simple questions about how safe I felt outside of the apartment. As things progressed, it became clear that they were very protective of me. Did I speak with strangers? Was I able to communicate with people on the street? Had I run into any mafia trouble?

They would talk to me about the growing crime in Russia, but never lingered on the topic, probably for fear of alarming me. Even so, I was aware that foreigners were a prime target of thieves looking to accumulate dollars. Babushka was particularly serious about my taking safety precautions, and if I was going out at night, wanted to know where I was going, who I was going with, and when I would be back. She wanted a local at my side at all times to keep me from hanging out with people she classified as *hooligani*. Eventually, their questions became overbearing. In the same placating tone I used with my parents, I reminded them that I was eager to listen to advice, but would need to make my own decisions.

As Zhanna introduced me to more of her friends and I met others through Ivan, my circle expanded, and to Babushka's dismay, I'd frequently be out at night. We would often end up at the only jazz club we knew, *Malenkaya Pteetza*. The clientele were wealthy Russians seeking a safe, respectable place to spend time with friends and family. It didn't appear that these people were looking to harass foreigners. As long as we were careful in our choice of late-night taxis, and traveled in groups, we felt safe.

It was a great nightspot, and reminded me of mid-century American lounges I'd seen in movies. The entrance was discreet—marked with just a small, white neon saxophone above a creaky wooden door on the corner of two streets. Bouncers flanked the entrance, and after a pat-down, you passed through a black curtain that kept the cold winter wind at bay. Inside, the dimly lit, egg-shaped room featured high, ornate, ceilings with an elevated stage at the front and seating close enough to see the performers sweat. With the exception of a small dance floor near the stage, the room had plush wall-to-wall carpeting. The combination of dark velvet drapery with large, framed paintings imparted a classy, yet casual atmosphere. Two well-stocked bars hugged the walls and on the almost-hidden second level, a few booths were tucked away, overlooking the stage. It made for a cozy and inviting place to spend time with friends.

We quickly became regulars. Zhanna, Pavel, a few of their longtime friends, and I were known by the bouncers and familiar with the wait staff. One evening when Zhanna wasn't around, however, I had been drinking too much and decided to save money by taking the Metro home alone. After all, it was close to both the club and the apartment—it was probably safe. Stumbling into the station and onto the platform, I sat on a bench, hoping the train would come soon. There was an emptiness that filled the air and quietly, almost surreptitiously, others joined me on the platform. My eyelids grew heavy. I had grown accustomed to taking brief, late-night naps on the Metro, so wasn't concerned. The rumble of an oncoming train filled the station and on cue, the muffled loudspeaker bellowed instructions. When the train arrived, I got on, slumped into my seat, and took a quick look around the car. Someone glanced up at me, but not in an alarming way. I made a mental note and settled in.

I closed my eyes. The gentle swaying of the train on the tracks lulled me into an intoxicated trance. I had been in Russia just long enough to fully understand the recorded, female voice announcing station stops and warning people that the doors would be closing. Listening to the voice usually kept my mind whirring—I would think of the complexity of the language and remain somewhat alert. After a few stops, I opened my eyes to see who was still on the train. A disheveled older man with wild gray hair and a dirty salt-and-pepper beard was now seated opposite me, staring strangely at me. He reminded me of a picture I had seen of Karl Marx and for an instant I thought I was dreaming. The man who had looked my way previously was still there, but made no movement to get off at the next stop, where I planned to disembark.

A bit more lucid, I stepped casually off the train and made my way to the long escalator up to the street. The expansive Russian Metro system was built deep underground in the 1950s. Much of it was developed as a showpiece for early communism, featuring beautiful sculptures, intricate tile work, and spacious walkways to accommodate the growing population in St. Petersburg and Moscow. I was always shocked at how clean the stations were, and this one was no different. But here, there was no artwork. Instead large, golden chandeliers hung from the ceilings, marble benches adorned the sides, and one of the longest escalators in the system transported passengers who chose not to use the stairs. I typically used the escalator—not because it was easier, but so I could peer down the tunnel from above to see if someone was behind me.

At first, I noticed nothing unusual. It was late, so there were few people in the station and even fewer on the escalator. Approaching the top, I took one last look behind me and noticed the same man from the train getting on the escalator. Must be a coincidence. I didn't think he had exited the train, though, and his presence struck me as a little odd. He looked up the tunnel as if searching for something. I stepped up my pace and headed across the platform towards the exit.

I glanced back. He crested the escalator, hunched over, gasping for breath. He had just finished running up the stairs! I was concerned, but not overly so. I turned and walked briskly down a few streets and sped up. Needless to say, my buzz had worn off. Another glance backward revealed the man about twenty-five yards behind me. I crossed the street to see if I could get a good look at him, hoping to understand what I was up against. He was maybe six feet tall, wore a black leather jacket, and because he wouldn't look up at me, his features were obscure. He started closing in.

As we approached the street where Babushka and Zhanna lived, his footsteps became louder and I knew I had to do something. I turned the final corner onto my street and ran to the door and up two flights of stairs, bypassing the unreliable elevator. Gripping the banister tight, I jumped two steps at a time, got to the landing at the top of the second flight and listened. I heard the door creak open.

Still gripped around the banister, my knuckles ached and my body temperature rose. A series of slow footsteps followed, approaching the stairs. I wondered if I could get to the door of the apartment and open it quickly enough to avoid a confrontation. I wasn't convinced. The large keys were clumsy and there were three locks on the door. Knowing I had nothing to defend myself with except my fists and speed, I decided that if the pursuer got halfway up the first flight, I would awaken my neighbors by yelling for help. I wasn't a good fighter, and as a shorter guy, always believed that acknowledging my weaknesses was one of my best strengths. I listened intently and heard the footsteps creeping closer.

His shadow slid along the wall and slowly ascended the stairs. *Is now the time to yell or should I wait?* My hands began sweating. I couldn't wait any longer.

"Help! Somebody help!"

Despite my accent, people knew what I was yelling. The sound of opening doors echoed in the halls, followed by the sound of fleeing footsteps on the stairs, and the front door slamming shut.

☭

The next morning I sat down and told Babushka what had happened. Her face grew stern as we talked, her lips pursing at the corners. Concerned, but relieved nothing serious had occurred, she waved her finger at me and shuffled out of the room mumbling something potentially offensive, but for me, unintelligible.

Later that day, Zhanna sat me down and told me not to worry about Babushka. She advised that I keep stories like that to myself unless they contained something that was critical for Babushka to know. She was a worrier, and because she wasn't in the best of health and often internalized her troubles, telling her a frightening story did more harm than keeping it a secret. Zhanna also told me about a friend of hers who could sell me a bottle of mace as protection. Within a day, I had one in my pocket and carried it everywhere. I didn't know if I would have the guts to actually use it or even if it would work, but preparation was wise. Although Babushka's concern was justified, I wouldn't stop exploring St. Petersburg because of one bad experience.

AN OPPORTUNITY
PRESENTS ITSELF

Bottled Coke was foreign to Babushka and Zhanna. I, on the other hand, craved the carbonated beverage because it helped soothe my stomach. Unlike in the United States, where soft drinks were available anywhere, Coke in St. Petersburg came in glass bottles and was hard to find. Few stores carried it, and I began noting both the locations and delivery days to ensure I'd be there to pick some up.

One day, after an unsuccessful search for my source of comfort, I was ascending one of the longer Metro escalators when two young women approached me. As often happened, I wasn't simply listening to music on my Walkman, but was singing along a bit louder than I thought. As they climbed past me, they stopped and turned around. I quickly lowered my volume and started humming instead, hoping I had not offended them. I felt their gaze, and peripherally could see them edging their way closer to me until we were standing on adjacent steps.

"What are you listening to?" one asked in heavily accented English. Her dark, eye-shadow-accentuated eyes were eager and large.

Hearing the question over the chorus of "Italian Restaurant," I replied, "Billy Joel. Do you like him?"

"Sure," she answered, smiling. "What's your name and what are you doing in Russia?" She had straight black hair, a pronounced, pointy nose, and was thin as a rail.

I removed my headphones and explained that I'd arrived about three months ago on a tour but was now living with a family, studying Russian, and looking for work.

"I am Galina and this is my friend Sonia." She motioned to her blonde friend who hadn't said a word, but stood there chewing gum.

"I know this might sound forward or strange, but I run an English-as-a-second-language school here in St. Petersburg. We are always looking for new teachers, if you are interested." She was trying to be nonchalant, but with her assertive approach, gave off a vibe of desperation.

I thought about it for a second. "I have no experience teaching and I'm not sure I'd know how to explain grammar or sentence structure to students. It sounds interesting, but probably isn't for me."

"Don't worry about it. Your inexperience doesn't matter. I look for English speakers who can lead conversation groups. And while we have many British English speakers, we have few American English teachers, so you would fit in well."

She was relentless, I thought.

"Of course, there will be times when students might ask complex grammatical questions that you may not know how to answer. That's okay. These students really just want someone foreign to speak with so they can practice their English, hear your accent, listen to your intonation, and understand your perspectives."

We had reached the platform and stepped out of the stream of commuters. How hard could it be to lead a conversation group?

"Do you pay your teachers?" I asked.

"Sure we do, but in rubles. In dollar terms you will probably only be making about twenty-five cents an hour, but in Russian terms, it's quite good. You could come see the school right now, if you'd like. We're going there anyway."

"Sure, why not?" We were on our way. While the pay wasn't great, it *was* good by Russian standards, and would give me some much needed spending money.

Two blocks from St. Petersburg's central thoroughfare, Nevsky Prospekt, the school's location was ideal. It would give me another destination to visit when I didn't feel like spending time in the apartment. From the quick tour Galina gave me, I understood that it was less of an official school and more of a small business trying to meet a need. I wasn't surprised to see that the school building was nothing more than two large apartments connected by a hallway. There were plenty of rooms, some with doors and others without. Students and teachers were unsure of where they were supposed to be, and the environment was chaotic.

After observing a few classes and noting that despite my lack of experience I wouldn't be less effective than other teachers, I signed on. The idea of meeting more Russians and trying something new was exciting. I also wanted to meet other English-speaking teachers. The loneliness of living abroad was catching up to me, and I yearned to connect with Westerners in my own language.

On the first day, I showed up with nothing but my enthusiasm and a desire to teach. For better or worse, I had complete control over content, pace, and approach to learning. When I looked at my list of "advanced intermediate" students, I noticed it consisted of ten people whose ages spanned four decades. Misha, an experienced engineer in his fifties, needed to learn English to read work-related documents. And, while Tatiana was fifteen and simply wanting to learn English to meet Americans, a second young Tatiana was hoping to apply to go to college in the US. Inexperienced as I was, I looked at the list with delight, thinking the mix of students would help make our conversation lively and fluid. Galina encouraged me to approach the class casually and to simply bring my experience as an American to the classroom. Not knowing what this meant, I walked into the first class feeling a bit apprehensive. I hoped that my "Americaness" would pull me through.

It didn't. The first class was a challenge. I started off easy, asking each of them to introduce themselves and tell the class why they were here. I expected this exercise to eat up significant time.

"My name is Misha and I here to learn English."

"Is there a reason you are interested in learning English, Misha?"

"Yes, *da*, yes. I learn English to speak."

"Okay, thank you. How about you, Tatiana? Why are you here and how do you want to use the English language?" I asked the girl as gently as I could.

A blank stare. The younger Tatiana was very shy.

I quickly learned that while "advanced-intermediate" meant conversant for some students, for others it was knowing a few sentences, but having a limited vocabulary and a very basic knowledge of grammar. In this class, I had students at both ends of the spectrum, including those who refused to speak at all.

Their brief responses to my questions and general guardedness made this first class seem endless. I had prepared a few exercises to get to know my class—asking them to describe themselves, their families, and why they wanted to learn English. I had them ask each other questions while I sporadically corrected grammar, sentence structure, and word choice wherever I knew what I was talking about. On other occasions, when sentence structure was incorrect and I couldn't explain why, I'd remain quiet, convincing myself it was better to let them talk without interruption to maintain the flow of the conversation. Yet the ninety-minute session dragged on, and as I engaged with one student, trying to extract words from their lips, I could tell others were uninterested or bored.

By the end of the class, I was drained. I walked out knowing I had a lot more work to do to make the course rewarding for them.

We were scheduled to meet twice a week, so I had to regroup fast. I wanted my students to be as expressive, passionate, and engaged as possible—and I wanted to avoid any groaning or sulking in class. I shared some tea with a few British colleagues and they admitted that teaching was not easy, and their success came only after they opened up to their students and discussed what it was like to live in England. This window into a foreign land was exciting to the students and allowed them to ask questions and learn about other cultures. They found that students of all ages were engaged by this type of conversation and class time became more enjoyable and productive. They also reminded me that many elder Russians clung to Soviet propaganda: believing that crime in America was out of control, that Soviet strength through a strong military was what kept imperialist enemies at bay, and that American materialism would be its downfall.

I approached the next class differently. Sitting in a circle, instead of in rows, I decided not to dictate what we were going to talk about, but instead, asked what they wanted to know about me. The room fell silent. Either they didn't fully understand the question or were simply not sure how to respond. The students checked their shoelaces, sat with blank stares, or looked at the wall behind me. So, I began talking. I started with a description of my family and where I'd grown up, and to my surprise, got no further. After just a few sentences, the eldest student of the group, Misha, furrowed his dark unibrow, uncrossed his arms, and raised his hand.

"How many rooms in the house you grew up in?" he asked in pretty good English, with a knowing smile. He, of course, didn't know the answer, but as he eyeballed me I knew where he was going. It seemed he wanted to prove to the group that Americans were spoiled by their grandiose lifestyle.

I didn't immediately respond. I knew a straight answer could alienate my students. The average number of rooms in an apartment in St. Petersburg was probably four or five, while my childhood house had four bedrooms alone. Describing my most recent college apartment was a better choice.

"Good question. My most recent apartment had seven rooms, and I lived there with four other people," I answered. They looked at each other, intrigued. "It was in a house that had two apartments. We had a small kitchen, a living room, and two bathrooms," I explained in simple English.

"Two bathrooms?" one student asked.

"Yes, two. I know it seems like one too many, but we had two."

"Why were there only two apartments in the house?" asked another.

"In America, the term house does not mean a large building complex with many apartments, as it does here. We call that an apartment building. In my situation, it was actually a house—not an apartment building, and was converted into two apartments."

"And you lived in one of them with four others, yes?"

"Yes."

They nodded in understanding. From there, we talked further about where it was located, who I lived with, and I gave them a basic overview of how it was furnished. It turned out to be a lively exchange and the start of something that would continue throughout the session.

For some reason, however, Misha did not relent on his first question. Privately after class, I showed him pictures of the twelve room house I grew up in, and he told me of his travels to the US, which helped me understand his perspective. After explaining why I didn't go into detail about this house in class, he seemed to respect me for not revealing too much.

☭

Working at the Yazeek Cooperative, I learned that teaching was far more challenging, time-consuming, and rewarding than I had ever expected. I hadn't realized the creativity required to make lessons resonate, or the level of commitment needed to really help a student make progress. I discovered conversation starters that I never expected to find. We spent one class with my showing a picture of myself in America, and having students write about what they saw and what they thought I was doing. In another, I asked them to describe their favorite hobby and answer questions from the class.

As the weeks passed, I discovered the benefit of a flexible curriculum and found a common bond that spanned the generations—music. We analyzed Beatles lyrics, either by listening to the words or reading them from a music book. While I could never explain why the submarine was yellow or some of the jargon used in the songs, we were able to connect on topics such as war, peace, love, and work. Having played guitar at many Russian parties and witnessing firsthand the affinity Russians had for the Beatles, this approach should have been obvious to me. But as with so many things, I overlooked it until a student raised their hand and asked for clarification on a lyric. Most important, I validated an old premise about people: Despite government policies, posturing, and rhetoric, people are good by nature, and with time, are drawn to understanding one another and to getting along.

At one point during a class, the elder Tatiana delved into a topic I had tried to avoid—politics. Not that I wasn't interested, but I knew it could be divisive in our newly bonded class. She asked what I thought of Gorbachev and the policies he had introduced. I had a point of view, but based on some recent conversations at parties and with Babushka, I was worried about offending people.

"This is a delicate question and tough for me to answer," I said calmly and slowly. "As you well know, I look at Gorbachev from an outsider's standpoint." I looked each student in the eye to ensure they all understood. "To me, he is a new breed of Soviet leader. He is a smart, shrewd politician who sees the Soviet Empire for what it was—an array of cultures, states, and peoples who were forced by the communists to live as one."

I paused for reaction, but got none.

"I believe he understands that the ongoing dedication of resources to the arms race, instead of to Soviet infrastructure, has created an unsustainable situation."

I saw confused faces.

"You see, pouring money into weaponry instead of into roads, buildings, and transportation is hurting the country. So, he is doing what he thinks best—break it apart, slow the arms race to reinvest dollars internally, and institute real change."

I stopped. Did they understand me? Were they angry, in agreement, or would I have to continue in silence? A little desperate, I asked, "Does anyone have anything to say? Anything at all?"

Alexander, a middle-aged man with carefully combed salt-and-pepper hair, raised his hand.

"Alex?"

"*Da*, I mean yes, I will talk. I understand, but think you wrong. Gorbachev is not patriotic. He lets Soviet Union look like weak child and is too friendly with Bush. I don't like this. We had strong country and could stand up for ourselves." He spoke plainly, articulating sentiments I had heard before. Many believed Gorbachev was turning his back on Lenin and the communists. He was considered unpatriotic by those who fought or lost loved ones in World War II, and was thought of to be "in the pocket" of the Americans.

"Because of this, I am angry!" Alex was beginning to get emotional as he stomped one foot on the ground and slapped his knee. His voice rose. "I am not angry at you, but angry that he allow mafia to grow and food prices to rise. It is like we have no police anymore and now, to make my life worse, do you know how hard it is being to afford food? Gorbachev does not look out for me, my children, or the country. It is not good. This is not good leader."

At that, I looked around and saw multiple hands go up. I knew this could get ugly, but wanted to encourage discussion.

"I am in agreement with Alex, but our situation is confusing, I feel." Misha stood up to address the class. His demeanor was, thankfully, very calm. "I do agree with Gorbachev and you, David, that our country must stop buying weapons. This is no good to our people. I also think the idea of privatization of businesses is good. It is difficult for many people, especially my age, to understand. But, I think in long run, it will be good for our country."

He paused and looked at Alex.

"But I also agree with Alex. While this privatization is good, things seem to be moving quickly, very quickly. Or, without control. Yes, things seem out of control. This is what scares me. It is not only the inflation that makes life hard, but as Alex mentioned, where are the police? Who is deciding right from wrong? It seems nobody!"

"Do others agree with the idea that things are out of control?" I asked.

Many sullen faces looked at me and said, "Da," in unison.

"This is good way to put it, moving too quickly so things are out of control," responded Alex, a bit more soft-spoken now. "I must say that I know where police are. I think they are all now hired by mafia."

Holding his hand up as if to say "hold on a minute," it was clear he wanted to say something more, but was struggling to find the words.

"I am glad Misha bring up privatization. It is something I don't understand well. But, I see mafia and corrupt politicians grabbing businesses. I read about it every day in newspaper. How can this be right? I do not think this is right for our country. It is hard for me to watch," he said, sounding defeated.

This was a sobering discussion for me, but more so, a reality check. My students were passionate about their country and brought up real, relevant issues. I had not fully considered the notion of progress and economic development without the rule of law. Babushka had mentioned similar concerns, but now I realized how prevalent they were. I began to question the role of the police in Russian society and wanted to know more about how the privatization process was being implemented. I wondered, without government oversight and institutions to support business growth, what would the results of reform-minded policies be? Would capitalism flourish or would the country experience renegade, unregulated growth?

I looked at my students with admiration and respect. "Any other opinions?" I asked, looking at the younger Tatiana.

She shuffled in her seat and looked around. "I like new dance places I see now, so things not all bad." Her eyes darted to the floor, embarrassed. Her peers smiled knowing that the many entrepreneurs who were opening discos, bars, and restaurants were doing so in part due to the increased freedoms provided by Gorbachev's policies.

"Thank you, Tatiana. That is a valid opinion and well-spoken."

That day, everyone in the class had an opinion about Gorbachev's policies, Yeltsin's rise to power, and the future of their country. Each also had his or her own particular frustrations. While the younger students felt good about where their country was headed, the elder students were angry at what they considered an alteration of the social contract they'd grown up with. Their personal identities were deeply tied to their image of the Soviet Union—a strong, influential, and relevant country. They yearned for policies they could understand and a leader who maintained the Soviet Union's power and prestige.

Our class spent the next few sessions discussing Gorbachev, his policies, and Russia's future. My students began to trust that the classroom was a safe environment to complain, disparage leaders, and express their innermost frustrations. I helped them find the vocabulary to express their opinions, argue with each other respect-fully, and at times agree to disagree.

By the time the course was over, I felt proud of my students for learning how to articulate their positions in English. On the last day of class, I packed up my books and stepped out into the wintry air. Darkness was falling as I walked home amid the flakes of a fresh December snow squall. Already whitened, the city streets, rooftops, and parked cars glistened.

Returning to the apartment, I heard voices in the kitchen, I hung up my wet snowy jacket. Babushka and Zhanna sat around the table with three new faces. Zhanna introduced me to her friends, Svet-lana, Natasha, and Igor. All were about Zhanna's age, well-dressed, and had an intellectual air. Two bottles of vodka were open and shot glasses, partially filled, sat on the tabletop. As if on cue, Babushka encouraged me to come to the table and eat. Sitting quietly, I lis-tened to the conversation, knowing full well that none of Zhanna's friends thought I could understand them. They said hello, but continued talking in Russian without so much as a glance over to me or an invitation into the conversation. I ate my borscht, brown bread, and boiled potatoes. I soon realized that I was listening to a conversation similar to the one we were having in class.

Svetlana, a bubbly brunette with sparkling eyes and a loud voice, argued vehemently that Gorbachev was bad for Russia and that the country looked weak compared to its former self and to the US.

"Isn't it true that we now have problems greater than we have seen in the past?" Svetlana asked, directing her question to Babushka. "The lines for food are long, the inflation is maddening, the growing mafia threaten people, and now I hear that our government officials are corrupt. The only good thing I see are those imported Bush chickens (referring to an American food aid program), and they are not even widely available." She poured herself another shot.

"Yes, yes," said Zhanna calmly, slurring a little. "But things are slow to open up. We need to let capitalism run its course and see what happens. Just today, I had an interview with a German company who is looking to do business here in St. Petersburg, so I support what is happening." She spoke as if admitting a minor crime, and looked at me. Noticing I didn't have a shot glass, she got up and retrieved one, set it down in front of me, and poured.

I didn't really want a shot, but didn't refuse it.

"David," she said, "I can see you've had a hard day. Drink up!"

All eyes shifted to me, surprised that I understood.

She was correct. I needed some help relaxing. I didn't see my customary, college-taught beer chaser anywhere. As if on cue, Svetlana pushed the plate of pickles over to me.

"Try those," she said warmly, looking at my confused face. "After the shot, eat a pickle," she clarified. "It helps."

Curious, I downed the shot and ate a pickle. "That's good," I said in Russian, smiling.

"That's how we drink our vodka in Russia," Svetlana responded proudly, looking at her friends around the table. Then she continued. "But tell me, you are not angry when you wait in line and they run out of bread, meat, or eggs just before your turn? I wait in these lines not knowing if I'm wasting my time or will be able to put food on the table!"

"You have a very good point," interjected Babushka. "With Brezhnev we had these same lines and food was scarcer than today. But at least we knew what to expect. I support the changes taking place, but the hard thing is not knowing whether food has arrived for sale, is on its way, or will not arrive at all. And, of course, at what price? Even for me, this is the hardest thing right now."

"And what about his politics? I feel like in the eyes of the world, we look like fools!" Svetlana continued, unable to stop herself.

Nobody responded, afraid to feed her rage.

I looked up to catch Svetlana rubbing her bloodshot, tired eyes. Who was this woman? She certainly had some strong opinions. I helped myself to a few of the meat patties Babushka had left in the frying pan and sat back down at the table. I didn't realize it would get Svetlana going even more.

"Just look at what your guest is eating." She nodded at me slightly. "Boiled potatoes, meat that is indistinguishable, and some borscht. Is that it? He must think we are living in another time—certainly not approaching the year 2000. It's embarrassing."

"I don't consider it embarrassing, whatsoever," I retorted. I'd had enough of her complaining and self-deprecation.

She looked startled and I continued with my thought as best I could, using all the Russian I had learned over the months. "First, it is an honor for me to be here, sharing a meal with people that are supposed to be my Cold War enemy. Second, this is traditional Russian food and nothing to be embarrassed about. Sure, it is a simple meal lacking in some of the more diverse foods Russia could offer, but if I wanted the best, I could go to an expensive restaurant or even a foreign country. This is the 'real Russia' of today and what I want to experience. Third, I meet new Russians every day both on the street and at school. They are passionate, caring, and nationalistic. They believe in their country and its future and are proud to be Russian. It's refreshing. You, too, should be proud. Not of the simple food, of course. But on a personal level, your display of hospitality, friendship, and warmth has been wonderful. I understand that politically things are changing, and that your leaders are taking risks and are making decisions that are hard to understand. Is everything perfect? Of course not. But, let things work themselves out. It will take time, and I know this is frustrating. But be patient. I find it incredible to be living through a watershed time in the country. Really, it is something to be proud of."

I finished, smiling inside, proud of my feelings and of my Russian. I had said exactly what I wanted to say.

Svetlana looked at me blankly, obviously surprised. She said nothing, but filled everyone's glasses once more and stood up.

"That is a toast if I've ever heard one," she muttered.

THE SNOW CAVE

As the year 1991 ended, Gorbachev, who had resigned months before from his post as General Secretary of the Communist Party, also stepped down as President of the Soviet Union. His resignation signaled the end of close to seventy-five years of Kremlin-based rule and the formal end of the Soviet Union. In its place, eleven of the former fifteen Soviet states formed a new organization, the Commonwealth of Independent States (CIS). These included Russia, Ukraine, Kazakhstan, Uzbekistan, Tajikistan, Kyrgyzstan, Armenia, Azerbaijan, Moldova, Belarus, and Turkmenistan.[5] They began working together to improve their collective situation, but were no longer beholden to the Kremlin. Other former Soviet Republics, including Georgia, Latvia, Lithuania, and Estonia each formed their own independent nation.[6]

For me, the year ended on a positive note. Zhanna's many groups of friends had welcomed me into their circles. We shared common interests, and I was grateful to them for embracing a foreigner. We attended dinner parties and shared perspectives, allowing me to continuously improve my Russian and gain more insight into Russian life. This window helped me better see how people in their early twenties viewed their world.

They had many important concerns. Would privatization provide an opportunity to speculate in real estate? Was the growing mafia presence simply the maturation of the KGB, and how far would its influence reach? Was the growth of prostitution in Russia a sign that Glasnost was working, or was it an export of American capitalism that would cause an AIDS epidemic throughout Eastern Europe? Despite Russia's massive stockpile of weapons, could the combination of the collapsing infrastructure, the lack of an enforced legal system, and rampant inflation classify the country as Third World?

We enjoyed discussing these questions at length, typically over a bottle or two, without ever solving anything.

As it turned out, Svetlana, the opinionated brunette from that night at the apartment, was one of Zhanna's closest friends, and ended up becoming one of mine. She was a sharp, witty realist, and we agreed on more matters than not. She had a round face, pale skin, and big brown eyes that sparkled during arguments. Always smiling and ready to debate any topic, she was never passive and always passionate. Prone to exaggeration, Svetlana could be overly dogmatic, yet she was aware of her flaws and was able to consider other people's views. I was drawn to her, and we often exchanged ideas in both Russian and English for practice.

One day in January, she invited me and another friend, an expat named John, to visit her dacha—country house—located on the outskirts of St. Petersburg. She was going with her friend Tania so we could make it a foursome. I had heard that Russians eagerly and regularly visited their dachas, and when I found out that Svetlana owned one, I wasn't surprised. She was a successful professional in her early twenties, well educated, and from a politically connected family.

Having never visited a dacha, I initially imagined it to be similar to a summer beach house or winter ski house in New England—a place to relax, enjoy nice restaurants, revel in nature, and escape city life. But Russians talked of gathering mushrooms, planting gardens, and performing odd jobs and repair work on their homes. Meals were enjoyed at home, and the nightlife either included a good book or conversations with friends over a bottle of vodka. Of course, the experience probably depended on the dacha. I had visited the Czar's Summer Palace, a tourist spot of architectural beauty known as his "dacha," so in my head I conjured up three categories of dachas: the opulent mansion with manicured gardens and gold-laden intricate wall designs, the multiple-room comfortable estate, and the one-room wooden structure. I gathered that Svetlana did not own a palace, but based on her adoration for her dacha, we seemed to be in for something special.

I was also intrigued by the possibility of meeting rural Russians. While the people in major Russian cities accepted foreigners into society, albeit with the skepticism ingrained by years of skewed political messaging, the countryside was different. Few foreigners traveled outside the major Russian cities: in other words, loud-voiced, colorfully dressed, forthright, educated visitors were unusual in the countryside. My Russian language college professor's lesson on social cues floated up as a warning in my mind. He let us know that between cultures, misperception and misunderstanding was common but avoidable. He told us that when he traveled to Russia his tendency was to walk in the middle of the sidewalk, whereas his Russian friends hovered along the perimeter. Noticing this, he asked his friends why that was. They told him that from their perspective, walking in the middle of the sidewalk was considered pushy and snobbish. To me, it was such an odd story that it remained with me, as a lesson to remember.

Country folk were also known to be less politically savvy, and with opinions shaped by local communist newspapers and media, their view of the world was inevitably biased. Some households did receive national TV and radio, but the Soviet media was still strongly anti-West, especially during this time of radical change. Universities, museums, and newly formed competing newspapers in major Russian cities encouraged discussion, debate, and education on internal as well as world issues. These institutions, however, didn't exist in the countryside. Everyday Russians had no choice but to live with the remnants of a society in transition.

Erected in the mid-1800s, the *Moscovsky Vokzal*—St. Petersburg train station—was a massive structure.[7] It served as a gateway to the St. Petersburg suburbs, but was also a bustling Metro station. In appearance, it reminded me of the station in Moscow, but was far larger. Like much of St. Petersburg, its architecture had strong Italian roots. With ornate columns and high archways at the entrance, large, rectangular windows on the second level, and a two-story clock tower extending high above the main structure, it was a striking building.[8] I walked into its dimly lit, immense hall and searched for the doors to the outdoor platform where my friends were to meet me. It was a cold, mid-winter night but people bustled about, running to catch trains or meet loved ones. A thin layer of wet muck covered the floor—melting snow and dirty ice—and I caught the faint smell of urine, garbage, and vomit. Looking through one of the doors, I saw a few idling trains, waiting for the barrage of passengers to arrive. I searched the platforms and found my friends standing next to the train. They had already bought tickets, so we got onboard and settled in.

John, with his chiseled jaw, perfectly placed blonde hair, and great sense of adventure, was good to hang around with. We'd met as teachers and shared interests in culture and experiential learning. He was always up for exploring something new, and was overall very positive. Tania, on the other hand, was a petite, quiet brunette with curious eyes. She always seemed to be on the cusp of saying or doing something interesting, but had yet to rise much above the level of boring. I was hopeful there was more to her and this would be the weekend to find out.

The train itself was not unlike an older American commuter rail train with its long bench-style cushioned seats, stability rails throughout, and a dusty, grooved rubber floor. Finding two open benches opposite each other, John and I sat facing the girls. Without warning, I felt the familiar lurch of the train moving forward, and within a few seconds the wheels began to roll.

"David, you'll love my dacha!" Svetlana announced, smiling proudly from plump cheek to cheek. "It is so cute—just one room—but in such a beautiful area, and the mushrooms are of the best variety. We'll have to figure out our sleeping arrangement—we won't have beds for everyone—but I'm not concerned, are you?" Her description was in typical Svetlana fashion—positive and energetic, but lacking in detail.

I didn't like mushrooms but put on a positive face. "Sounds great," I responded, trying to hide my apprehension. "And is it still beautiful in the winter?"

"Oh, yes. The snow covers everything, and it will be fun to look for wood to heat the house and find fresh mushrooms to eat. There is nothing like fresh mushrooms from the area around the dacha."

"But we won't be looking for mushrooms in the snow, right?"

"No, no," she laughed. "I am bringing some. I meant in the summer they are terrific!"

"Oh, okay—does it have running water?" I asked.

"Well, not really. But we will get water from a nearby stream. That reminds me, I hope you brought boots for when we walk through the snow. Also, I packed a few bottles of vodka—they'll help us stay warm and in a good mood." Somehow, she had a way of making everything sound fun.

"Great!" I said with a grin. *Oh, G-d. What am I getting myself into? Should I be excited about going to the stream to get water?* So many things about the trip were unappealing, yet I couldn't imagine declining the invitation. I wanted the cultural immersion and the time with friends. But the mere thought of taking the train to what sounded like an under-equipped dacha in the dead of a Russian winter seemed crazy. I swallowed hard and hoped for the best.

☭

We arrived in the village at five o'clock. As we stepped off the train it was hard not to lose heart at the sheer volume of snow on the ground. Yet it was beautiful: A fresh coat glistened atop the tiny depot and covered the lampposts. Unlike the snowdrifts in St. Petersburg, many of these were piled high above my head. With no food stands, vendors, or taxis around, the evening felt serene. We walked into the pale blue, concrete outpost of a station. It was in dire need of repair. Faded, dirty walls surrounded well-worn, chipped tile flooring. Aged benches had broken arms, legs, and sagging wood.

A lonely agent dressed in a winter coat and fur hat sat behind the ticket window.

With backpack in hand and boots on, I followed Svetlana through the building and down some stairs that led outside. The snow-piled sidewalks were impassable, so we gravitated to the street.

"How far is it?" I asked her, knowing full well what her answer would be. I shared a running joke with my expat friends that when asking a Russian about walking any distance they always replied, "Not far, just around the corner." They may add a "down the street" or a "past the bread store," but rarely were they time-specific. And, despite their claims of close proximity, destinations were always farther than expected.

"Not far. We'll walk down this street and it will wind around over there past the edge of that forest. That's where we'll turn and head into my neighborhood."

John and I looked at each other and smiled. We knew we were in for at least a thirty minute walk.

We passed what Svetlana described as the village center—a few crumbling buildings, operational, but heavily weathered. Painted either yellow, light blue, or gray, each was nondescript, without signs marking their purpose, and were completely dark. She pointed out the police station. There were no police cars parked out front, and no prison bars in the windows.

Never completely plowed to the asphalt, the road grew more treacherous as we made our way out of town. There were no sidewalks to speak of, just snow. Our boots sank deeper, and the trudging took effort. But the trees thickened, became a forest, and eventually we turned the bend as Svetlana had promised we would.

The forest extended as far as I could see, and following the road into its mouth, we came upon a street lined with small wooden cottages. While most were set back from the road and screened by trees, those that I could see were quaint, log cabins with two or three rooms. The snow around them was untouched. The forest was mystical and silent. We didn't talk much, hearing only our boots crunching against the packed snow. There were no cars to speak of: In fact, since we'd arrived I saw no one driving. The air was see-your-breath cold, fresh and unpolluted. The scent of burning firewood carried on the breeze, and I imagined myself being in a ski house in Vermont, all cozy and warm. I couldn't wait to get to the house and warm up with a bottle of vodka and of course, some food.

After forty-five minutes of walking, Svetlana veered off the road and proceeded down a long driveway. The house before us was small and looked like the other cottages we'd passed along the way. Icicles hung from the snow-covered roof. I rubbed my hands together and looked at John. His nose and cheeks were bright red, but he smiled hopefully—we were both anticipating some relief from the cold.

We climbed up the snow-covered wood stairs, onto the porch, and made our way inside. Unfortunately, the difference in temperature between the outside and inside of the house was zero. The cloud of my breath drifted into the living room.

The interior of the dacha was as simple as the exterior. With one large room, a table, a few benches, and a couch–futon, it was functional. A large wood stove protruded from one corner of the square room, and instinctively, Svetlana and Tania began shuttling back and forth, feeding it with wood from the outside pile. John and I were still kicking snow off our boots when the flames caught, and the women were sitting down comfortably, looking at us. John and I were dumbfounded by their efficiency.

With plenty of wood in the stove, it wasn't long before the fire began emitting noticeable heat. A one-room dacha made sense. Without any central heating system, and only a stove as a heat source, the room warmed quickly. We relaxed, and sat around talking about plans for the evening. It was, after all, a Friday night, and despite the appearance that everything was closed, maybe this town had some sort of entertainment we'd missed on the way through.

I explored the small kitchen area to the left of the stove, opening and closing cabinets, looking through drawers for food.

"Svetlana, what should we do about dinner?" I asked, a bit concerned. "I don't see anything here to eat."

"I brought mushrooms and other ingredients from the market in St. Petersburg," she said proudly. "I'll get them cooking—they will help warm us up!"

"That sounds great," I replied with an artificial smile. This was going to be difficult. Mom always told me to try new foods, to expand my horizons. I should have listened. I had yet to experiment much with mushrooms, but from past circumstances, found them inedible. There was something about the consistency that made me queasy. To make matters worse, tonight the mushrooms were not the typical side dish. They were our only dish.

But tired, hungry, and without alternatives, I dug into the mushroom soup and pretended to enjoy it. "Mmmm," I muttered. "This is exactly what I needed!" Svetlana had been so excited about making mushroom soup that I didn't want to hurt her feelings. To some extent, it did hit the spot. It was warm and thick, which was satisfying. The taste, on the other hand, was barely tolerable.

During dinner we shared a bottle of vodka, exchanging toasts in both Russian and English. While Svetlana had spent time abroad and was always looking for occasions to speak English, Tania had mastered only a few words. Svetlana was methodical about speaking English and getting practice. She told us about how she would look for foreigners on the Metro, "pick them up," and end up developing friendships that turned into English practice. We were her latest targets, and for our part were grateful for a chance to practice Russian. That night we developed a simple system where John and I would speak Russian, while Svetlana replied in English, and Tania in Russian. We corrected each other as we went and pointed out idiosyncrasies of the language, compared sentence structure, and tried to find synonyms of words to help build our vocabularies. As far as I was concerned, language was the window into the Russian soul, and improving my skills was something of an obsession. The more I learned, the better I could acclimate and understand, and the more I could establish a foundation from which I could build stronger friendships with Russians.

Around 10:30, we decided to go explore the village. With low expectations, Svetlana visited a neighbor to get the lay of the land, and upon returning, reported that a popular new disco had opened. We were impressed, and credited Gorbachev for his long-armed changes. Despite the nation's economic malaise, the youth were taking advantage of their newfound freedoms. And sparked by curiosity, I was fully awake and ready to see this new island of entrepreneurship for myself.

Emerging from the dacha all bundled up, I tried to preserve a shred of warmth in my coat. No such luck. Standing on the porch, I silently admired the star-filled sky and silhouetted tree line, feeling the cold tingle over my bare face. And as we trudged through the snow down the road toward town, the cold was palpable. To our right, the forest was thick but half-revealed a still, shimmering pond. On our left, I noticed a snowy road hidden among high snow banks behind Svetlana's dacha, and periodically, as we walked along, I could see the lights in the distance. The center of town wasn't as far as I had thought.

As the forest around us thinned and the center of town became visible, we noticed bright flashes coming from one corner of what appeared to be an older office building. Soon, we could hear music and saw splashes of different colored lights on the snow outside—red, blue, green—reminiscent of a multi-colored strobe light. Walking closer, we now saw that the door to the disco was a back entrance or basement of a larger office building. This wasn't unusual considering what I had seen happening in St. Petersburg. By merely adding lighting, decorations, and music to community and office buildings, uninspired spaces were being transformed into popular nighttime discos.

I didn't expect much in terms of interior decor, but just hoped for some good music, drinks, and dancing.

Unlike in St. Petersburg, where bouncers hovered near the entrances of these new clubs, here, there was no one at the door. There was no line and nobody was outside collecting an entrance fee. Except for the loud music and strobe lights, all indications were that this place was dead. We paused outside, debating if we really wanted to go in, or return to the dacha. As we stood around, I kept warm by putting my hands in my jacket pockets and jumping up and down. I felt something hard and cylindrical in my front right pocket, and remembered it was the bottle of mace I'd carried since being followed. I had never used it and doubted if I ever would, but grasped it, glad it was there.

With no line and an open door in front of us, we decided to check it out. We proceeded down the steps into an unexpected world. The room was extraordinarily dark, and except for a small light coming from the flashing corner strobe, we could see very little. Cigarette smoke engulfed us. Walking in, I bounced from person to person trying to find a table big enough for the four of us to sit down. It was hard to tell, but the place seemed packed. Then suddenly, I heard the rustling of winter jackets and footsteps. Without warning or reason, and before our eyes could fully adjust to the room, a pack of men surrounded us.

Russian obscenities filled the nightclub. Their menacing tone was nothing compared to the sudden deluge of punches being thrown from all sides. With a bang, the door slammed shut behind us, making the room even darker. I strained my eyes looking for my friends, but the confusion overwhelmed me. The girls screamed. In a room so dark, I couldn't see who was punching whom, and without warning I received a blow to the head and a kick to my stomach. I stumbled back, reeling in pain, gasping for breath, shocked. Someone grabbed my head and pulled me down. A knee brushed me, barely missing my face. In the miscue, I could tell my aggressor was off balance and I had a minute to regroup. I ducked lower and remembered I had the mace in my pocket. I grabbed it, stood up, and raised it to where I thought my attacker's face would be. I pressed down on the button, hoping something would come out.

"AAAGGHHH! *Ny, blyet, shto eto?!*" Shit, what is that?

The loud yell by my attacker caught everyone by surprise and the fighting stopped.

"Move back and leave us alone," I yelled in both Russian and English. I directed my friends to stand behind me, closer to the door.

Now, eyes adjusted to the lack of light, I could see nine twenty-something guys, grimacing with hatred. Why were they so mad? What did we do? They seemed completely enraged and had absolutely no intention of backing down. They weren't using weapons, so with the mace holding them at bay, I shouted to my friends, "Get outta here!" Not needing to be told twice, they ran for the door, swung it open, and took off. The light from the outside spilled inside and I could tell these guys were all drunk, and that their friend's screams startled and confused them. I backed my way to the open door, turned, and ran to what I hoped would be safety.

Outside, I caught up with Svetlana and Tania who were not hurt, just frightened. John had taken the brunt of the beating, and the look on his face told us he was in real pain. One of his eyes was bruised and beginning to swell. We got to the main street and rested, knowing it could be a while before the police or anyone else would come to our aid. Small towns were close-knit communities, and if these guys were connected to the mafia, nobody, not even the police, would risk betraying them to help a few visiting foreigners.

"Svetlana, Tania, run back to the house and stay there. Call the police if you think that might help, but we don't want you in the middle of this. Go now—before they see you and can follow!"

As soon as Svetlana and Tania were out of sight, three guys emerged from the disco. Coming our way, they looked drunk, angry, and hungry for a drawn-out fight. They were dressed in what I thought was odd disco attire—Adidas sweatpants, sweatshirts, and leather jackets. Cigarettes hung from the lips of two of them and their large frames made it clear that we needed an alternative to actual fighting. We had no chance against these guys.

"What the hell is going on here?" I asked John under my breath. "This is insane. Why are they fighting us?"

"I have no idea!" he answered, spitting blood on the ground. "This is out of control!" We trotted backwards, scared of what was coming next.

John and I decided to split up and ran in separate directions. Two of the thugs chased John, while the other had his sights set on me. I ran down the main street, glancing over my shoulder. John was slow, probably hindered by injuries, and was quickly nabbed and thrust into another fight he couldn't win. Hands covering his face, he was doing his best to defend himself, but the two thugs were throwing reckless punches all over his body.

I was frozen in my tracks—uncertain how to handle the situation. I watched John being pummeled off the road near the trees and felt helpless. Meanwhile, the other thug was looking at me like a hungry carnivore eyeing a juicy steak. Time seemed to stop for an instant. I watched my exhalation float into the night as I questioned if this was really happening.

It was, and as quickly as time stopped, it picked back up.

I reviewed my options: join the fight to defend John and get beaten up badly, take off and meet the girls to look for help, or simply fight the thug approaching me, and in doing so, leave John to fend for himself. Or, possibly, could I somehow distract his attackers long enough for him to escape? They *were* drunk. I scanned the landscape to see if there was anything I could use to my advantage. Nothing. Standing in the middle of the road about one hundred yards from John, I had to create my own diversion.

I started yelling both Russian and English obscenities into the night. The two that were throwing punches at John stopped and looked up. The guy approaching me also paused, cocked his head, glanced at his friends, and peering back at me, yelled something. I hollered again, taunting them, asking them to come get me. While one of them stayed and held John, the other approached the road, shouting back at me. He was screaming in Russian, and beyond the curse words, it seemed he was angry that I had used mace on them. He was wildly exclaiming that in their town, when they fight, no weapons were allowed. Given such a ridiculous statement, I thought I was misunderstanding him.

Nobody was punching John; instead, they were focused on me. As my attacker slowly approached, his swaying gait confirmed just how drunk he was. I considered how I could use this to my advantage, but nothing came to me. The second of John's attackers left him and approached the road, hoping to see a good fight. This was John's opportunity to run, but he was lying on the ground, too hurt to move.

I volleyed back with more curses as my guy picked up speed and burst into a charge. Instead of fleeing, I felt my body running towards him. As we closed in, I realized he was even larger than I thought, and was barreling toward me like a Russian bear. I couldn't let him catch me. But, I still had to buy John more time. Even closer now, I could see my attacker's contorted face, squared-off buzz cut, and huge hands. *What the hell am I doing playing chicken with someone who wants to kill me in the freezing cold of the Russian countryside? How did I get here?* Out of the corner of my eye, I noticed John standing up, limping slowly to the forest. He disappeared into the nearby trees.

My attacker and I bore down on each other. I started bellowing in English, trying to sound like a crazed animal. Almost on top of each other, I watched as he committed his body to a tackle. I sidestepped to the left, spraying mace into his passing face. His big arms reached for me, but grabbed air, as he struggled in a cloud of mace. His knees buckled. He was screaming in pain, and I continued running, following the path John had made through the snowy trees.

I sped away, hearing my attacker's friends trying to console him. They were livid, and promised they'd find me.

I high-stepped as fast as I could through the deep snow. Not thinking straight, I lost John's tracks. Surrounded by trees on three sides, a meadow of pristine snow lay in front of me. *Don't run, think. Be smart here, but hurry up and do something!* Hearing no one behind me, I figured I had some time. I ran in circles, creating multiple lines of footprints, hoping to throw them off. Soon, voices reached me in the quiet.

I panicked. Dashing from the flat snow line to the trees, I scanned the area, desperately searching for a good hiding spot. But just as I was about to enter the forest, I tripped and fell down a large snow bank, landing on a narrow, concealed road. Brushing myself off, I stumbled across the snow-packed surface, climbed the large bank on the other side, and entered the forest.

I had heard of foreigners being killed by mafia in Moscow and St. Petersburg, but here? Unlikely as it was, I wasn't stupid. I picked a snowdrift behind a tree trunk and began digging. I climbed in the hole. Not deep enough. I dug more. Again, too shallow. I dug deeper and sideways to make more room. If I could just hide for a few hours, maybe they would give up and leave me alone.

I crawled into the expanded hole, sat up against one wall, and continued working, digging snow from beneath me to seal the entrance. Finally, I was fully hidden, but couldn't escape my thoughts. *What happens if they find me? Is hiding here the best option or should I keep running? Where did my friends run to and are they okay?* The night was eerily quiet. Ominous scenarios spun themselves in my head. My heart beat rapidly, my head throbbed, and my body sweated profusely.

And what about the police? Rumors said they were on the take as much as the mafia. Russians had little respect for the police to begin with, and often warned me never to trust them.

My thoughts raced until I heard muffled noises. It was them, looking for me.

"Where is he? Where could he go?" one said.

"I have no fuckin' idea, but who cares? Let's go back to the bar! We can find him tomorrow," the other replied.

Then a third chimed in, "I bet he just kept running! Let's go. Enough of this! We got his friend good. Come on, Misha."

Misha did not respond. The footsteps were getting louder. Someone was walking on the road, very close to my snow cave. Did he see my footprints going up the snow bank or did I cover them? I couldn't remember. Then, I heard him stop a few feet in front of me, and plop his body onto the snow bank.

The sweat now dripped from my forehead onto my glasses. In my head I was running through various options of how I would respond if they found me—none ended well. I held my breath, and resorted to the last refuge of helpless prey: praying for them to leave.

"I want to get the fucker tonight," he growled. "Stupid vodka. Stupid mace. I'm tired and can barely see straight." He then yelled angrily into the night, "I'm going to find you! I will find you!" The snow creaked as he got up, but no footsteps followed.

"Let's go," Misha said, sounding tired and defeated.

They walked away, boots crunching softer and softer on the snow. I heard grumbling, a few shouts, and then silence.

The forest was quiet and peaceful. I didn't dare move.

After what seemed like an eternity, I let out a measured breath. I checked my watch—1:30. I wanted to get up and find the dacha, but that wasn't a good idea. Maybe I was being paranoid, but terrible scenarios preoccupied my mind. *What if I was being delirious when I thought I heard them walk away? Could one of them still be out there waiting, watching, and ready to pounce at any mistake?* I decided to stay put. There was nothing to do but wait.

But wait for what—I had no idea. The police? My friends? The light of day? I had no plan and was frozen with fear. There was snow above and beneath me, snow on my left and right—so close that I could lick it. Yet I wasn't cold in the least. I had sweated so much that my long underwear stuck to my arms and legs.

Time passed, and I dozed off a few times, waking to reposition myself. My muscles were screaming at me, cramped in these tight quarters.

At one point, I thought about my predicament and how I'd ended up hiding in a snow bank. I had never felt so thrown into a dangerous situation with no clear-cut way out. During my college years I had no concept of how completely I relied on an extensive safety net to help me through life. It only felt like I was on my own, but college campus was in fact an incubator, providing support whenever I stumbled. Mistakes were easy to fix, and consequences were limited. If I chose a class but suddenly became disinterested, I could change classes. If I fell ill, a nurse was right there. If I was followed, intimidated, or assaulted on campus, an emergency phone was always nearby. Even if I did poorly on an exam, there was extra credit work. This, however, was *real*.

Blind trust had been a luxury. I was now vulnerable, and without a backup plan. I knew I had to stay vigilant. I checked my watch—3:20. Time was creeping by. Then, from afar, I heard something. Was I dreaming or was a vehicle approaching? And was that a loudspeaker saying something in Russian? Yes! There was a truck approaching slowly and the voice on the loudspeaker grew progressively louder. Headlights on, the truck's bright light illuminated the cave. I moved just enough to peek out of my bunker to see it was the police. They were speaking slowly, making sure to enunciate, obviously trying to ensure they were understood by a foreigner.

"We are here to help. If you are out there, this is the police. Come out and we can help you..." the voice repeated.

My gut reminded me of what I had heard: Do not to trust the police. I decided to wait.

The vehicle passed. It slowed down a few times, but never stopped. Four o'clock turned to five and five to six. Silence. Close to seven a.m., the gray of a cloudy day brightened the thinly sealed entrance. It was time to find my way back to the dacha.

I crawled out, stood up slowly, and glanced all around to ensure I was alone. My body was exhausted, my muscles tight. I resurrected myself from hours of being unable to move. I looked proudly at my crumbling snow cave. What a night! Sliding down the snow bank to the nearby road, I took several fresh breaths of air and followed the road away from town.

Briefly stopping to dump snow out of my boots, I took a longer look around. Drifts of stark white snow skirted the trees before me. I caught glimpses of the frozen pond. I trudged along thinking that at least I was going in the right direction. At a nearby intersection, I continued straight, following the road towards the pond. Soon, I was walking alongside small dachas, all with smoke dancing gently from their chimneys. From where I was, all the dachas looked alike.

As I got closer, I noticed a police car driving away from one of them. Maybe Svetlana had called them to look for me. As they pulled out of the driveway, I hid behind a tree. Just then a woman stepped onto the porch to have a cigarette—Svetlana.

Slowly, I made my way to Svetlana, who, when she saw me, started yelling my name and running towards me.

"You're here!" She hugged me. Her eyes were bloodshot, puffy.

"And I'm okay," I sighed. "Where is John? Is he okay? Are you okay?"

"Yes, we are fine." Svetlana stepped back to look at me. "John went to the hospital with the police. They are helping him, but we need to leave as soon as we can. The police told me we are not safe here now and they cannot help any more than they already have. Between you and me, I think they are scared."

"But, will John be okay?"

"Yes, yes. They said he might need stitches, but that's all."

"What the hell happened last night?"

"Remember what I said when we were doing shots at Zhanna's? They're protective. Embarrassed. They feel that Russia should be able to take care of her own. I can understand it. The dependence on other countries is not a good thing for the Russian people, and foreigners seem threatening," she said. "Those animals took it too far."

There was not much I could say. We walked quietly to the door.

"And, you, where were you and why are you so wet?"

☭

On the train ride back, my friends' faces were somber. John had stitches near his eye and lip as well as a splint holding two fingers together. Tania was quiet and gazed out the window. Svetlana felt bad about the entire trip. Even she was surprised by the extent to which ordinary Russians were internalizing the changes occurring in their country. None of us held a grudge against her, though—how was she to know? John and I were just in the wrong place at the wrong time.

IMAGES

The Russian White House, barricaded during the 1991 coup d'état.

View from the top of the Soviet tank I climbed.

I jumped off the moving tank and snapped this photo.

At the Press Club, me with former President Gorbachev in the background.

Four babushkas that Yuri and I met in Shepetovka.

Feeding a goat in Shepetovka, near the sugar factory.

We stumbled upon an unmarked building, the synagogue of Shepetovka.

Reviewing the cemetery plot list in Shepetovka.

My view of the White House from across the river.

One of the Russian tanks targeting the White House.

My grandmother and grandfather, Lee and Nate Spiegel in 1984.

ZA DOLGOLETYE!
TO LONG LIFE!

CONVINCING CHARLIE

John and I still went to the local jazz club, saw each other at friends' parties and dinners, and often hung out. But, emotionally, John wasn't the same after the beating. He was tentative at night, untrusting, and always on guard. He left Russia a few weeks later, leaving me wondering if his departure was related to that night in the country, or if his journey to Russia had simply run its course. I was disappointed but not surprised. I knew many expats who had made friends in Russia, but for one reason or another, left without notice. Others had major going-away parties, but in general, friendships in the community were often a matter of convenience.

With John gone, none of my friends in Russia spoke English as a first language. At times I just needed a break, and that's where he fit in. I didn't have to struggle for words, check for tenses, or optimize sentence structure. With this new void, I felt the exhaustion of constantly thinking in a foreign language, exerting mental effort with every Russian I met. His absence inspired me to try to meet more expats, reassess what I was doing in Russia, and explore other avenues. I recalled my dad telling me not to worry, but now that I was relaxed and enjoying my time, I wondered, what was I missing? Before graduating college I had done a lot of research on companies operating in Russia and expended a lot of energy worrying about my future. Now, life was just happening and I wasn't sure how to feel.

These thoughts brought me back to the fact that my last interview had been in Moscow, the day of the attempted coup. Teaching was fine, but inflation hurt everyone earning rubles. With my rent obligation depleting my bank account back home and the need to extend my visa again, it was time to find a more lucrative position. As I combed the newspapers and fished for job leads, I learned quickly that Moscow was the place to be. Foreign businesses were drawn to

Moscow, knowing that establishing a presence there was somewhat of a prerequisite to building a credible business in Russia.

I sat around the small Formica table with Babushka and Zhanna, drinking tea and glancing through job openings. They knew what I was doing, and weren't pleased. Beyond the bond of friendship we had established, I paid them for room and board, so it wasn't surprising that they begrudged my job search.

"*Nu?*" inquired Babushka.

"Nothing much. There is one opening that seems possible, but it depends what they are actually looking for." Actually, I felt no confidence in it whatsoever.

"Doing what?"

"It looks like marketing for a—" I had to use my dictionary to find the word *real estate*, which I had never needed in Russian until now—"real estate development company."

"What is that?" she said blankly.

I wasn't surprised that she had never heard of such a firm. Without private ownership of property, real estate development was an unusual profession in St. Petersburg.

"It looks like a company has come to Moscow and built office space and apartments that they now need to rent or sell. I did work like this in college, so my background might fit, at least a little."

"Who would buy an apartment here? I don't understand," mumbled Babushka to herself.

"It's in Moscow?" Zhanna asked, sullen.

"It is." I tried to appear neutral, answering Zhanna's question, but I was excited. I was starting to think that Moscow might be a great change of scenery.

Although Zhanna and I got along well, she had recently made things uncomfortable by trying to kiss me. I wasn't looking for a relationship, and especially not with her—she had a son who needed a father. I wasn't ready for that.

The next day, I called the firm and set up an interview. The hiring manager spent half his time in Texas and half in Moscow, and since he was in Russia right now, it made sense to meet soon. I called a college friend who had just moved to the city, and he immediately helped me find a place to stay. Within a few days of seeing the ad, I was on my way back to Moscow for another interview.

☭

My preparation for this meeting was not as extensive as the last one. My Russian was better, so while I practiced on the train from St. Petersburg to Moscow, I didn't obsess. I was already comfortable with the answers I'd prepared for the previous interview, which had seemed to go well. But as I exited the Metro station and walked up to the large real estate complex, a sense of self-doubt overtook me.

One look at the building and I realized this was the real thing. The massive, architecturally modern, sleek, white structure stood out against Moscow's old stone and brick buildings. Set on the corner of a busy thoroughfare, it stood at least two stories taller than any building around it, and its glass entrance and sheer size were striking.

Having not seen such a modern building since coming to Russia, I found myself gawking. It looked out of place, but reflected progress. Distracted, I stepped off of the curb into a wintry mess of slush and ice. *Damn! Pay attention!* The cold water penetrated my left shoe and sock, biting at my ankle. I looked down to notice that both black dress shoes were a mess, covered with white specks of salt and dirty snow. The brilliance of trying to save a few rubles by taking the Metro instead of a cab was lost.

Walking through the only revolving door I had seen in Russia, I approached a security guard who pointed me to the nearest bathroom. All of my attention was focused on solving my wet shoe issue. I squelched across the entranceway.

The bathroom was a relief. Unlike most public Russian bathrooms, this one was stocked with tissues, toilet paper, and enough paper towels to help me clean off my shoes. Once clean, I tended to my ankle by shoving paper towels into my sock to create a buffer between the icy, wet fabric and my skin. I looked at myself in the mirror, hoping that my trousers kept the ankle-stuffing hidden.

They did, and to my surprise, the distraction had eased my nerves. I set out in search of my interviewer, Charles.

With polished beige tile floors, beautiful bright lighting, high ceilings with skylights, and an escalator to the second floor, the well-appointed lobby felt—well, American. I noticed a sign pointing to a tennis court and gym, and meandered through the aisles of a small food market and gift shop. A restaurant with tables set out into the lobby looked inviting. A new, working Otis elevator operated beside the escalator. Large flowerpots softened hard edges and added color. Farther down the hallway across from the tennis courts and workout area, an office space was being built out from the inside, and adjacent to it a flower store appeared to be on the verge of opening. The ad didn't mention it, but I quickly realized that this was the first of its kind in Russia. A modern, mixed-use real estate project that offered foreigners amenities that were available nowhere else in Russia. As I wandered in awe, a security guard approached me.

"Can I help you, sir," he asked in English. I was taken aback. Not only was I impressed with his tidy appearance, dressed in a blue suit with a red tie, but this Russian security guard was obviously trained in approaching and speaking with foreigners. He was cordial, yet not overbearing, and allowed for personal space—the absence of which was a pet peeve of mine since coming to Russia.

"Yes, I'm looking for Charles Rourke. I'm here for an interview," I answered in English to see if he could understand me.

"Yes, that's him sitting over there, in the reception area leading to the tennis court," he said, pointing to a middle-aged man sitting in a chair on the other side of two glass doors.

Sliding behind a column in the foyer, I gathered my bearings. When I was ready, I approached Charles. Alone in the room, he looked at me, talking on a phone, engrossed in his conversation. I wondered why he wasn't in his office, but figured the call was unexpected and had been forwarded here. We had never met before, but I assumed he knew he had an interview scheduled for this time and would acknowledge me after a moment with a nod. Nothing of the sort. His eyes looked right through me. He made no attempt to say hello, so I just sat next to him on a bench and waited.

He was clearly on a business call, trying to close a deal that seemed to be near completion. Listening intently, Charles periodically murmured "a-huhs" and "gotchas." He seemed skillfully cheerful, but genuine at the same time. Something about his mannerisms and tone led me to believe he was always this friendly, especially with clients. As the conversation continued and seemed to be turning his way, my thoughts were confirmed, but still, he didn't acknowledge me. His perma-smile was plastered to his round face, and he habitually, ever-so-slightly, patted his product-enhanced hair as if to make sure everything was in place.

After five minutes of waiting, I began pacing in front of Charles. His level of energy was not only infectious, but intimidating, so I wanted to keep mine up as well. I checked my watch a few times. No reaction. Finally I sat next to him and pulled out my resume so it was visible to both of us. When he looked over and saw it, his mouth pursed, and his eyebrows shot up his forehead. It was clear he had forgotten about our appointment.

He was quick to end his call. In one swift motion he checked his scheduling book, closed it again, put on a smile, and shook my hand. "You must be David Kalis—great to meet you. I'm sorry about the call. I, uh, it just went far too long and was a deal I couldn't lose. Did you get here okay? What are you doing in Russia? What do you think of the space we have here—quite nice, huh? Let's go into the foyer so we can sit and talk." He spoke as if he was being rewarded for speed.

"It's incredible! I had no idea buildings like this existed here." I followed him out of the room and into the main hallway. We sat on a bench, and as I eased in and relaxed, he continued moving; putting pens away, looking through his briefcase, moving his knee up and down. He seemed more nervous than I. Or was he manic? I couldn't tell. But as our conversation continued it became clear that Charlie, as he asked me to call him, had more energy and passion than anyone I'd met in Russia.

"Well, this is the first of its kind and we couldn't have made it possible without our partnership with Yeltsin. You know, he was here a few months ago. Stood right over there and has been helping us work through the red tape." He pointed proudly to the second floor café.

"It's a unique project we have here," he continued. "And I'm looking for another piece of the puzzle—a marketing representative—to help us fill the residential and retail spaces with tenants. It's not an easy job, and the person I hire will have to be able to meet with executives, negotiate and close deals, and work with our Russian staff to build out the properties and ensure that move-in is flawless. I want someone who has a lot of different skills, and in the end, just gets things done." He'd grown serious, and was looking directly at me, almost challenging me to look away. I wasn't about to lose a contest of strength or commitment.

As he talked, I got a clear sense of what he was looking for. Essentially, he wanted a younger version of himself. I thought about what he must have been like twenty years ago, and what attributes he would respect. He continued talking about his travel schedule to the US, and needing someone who could not only stand on their own two feet while he was away, but also who could interact with business leaders from around the world. Putting myself in his shoes, I figured I had to come across as a confident, seasoned professional who had outstanding interpersonal skills and could be tough when required. I sat there, ready to respond, but had the sensation of creating a whole new persona for myself. Was this how most people felt in job interviews? Did it all come down to understanding the role and playing the part?

"So, David, now that you know more about the company and what I'm looking for, can you help? Tell me about your background."

Running through responses I had practiced over and over, I improvised, adding some buzzwords I thought would appeal to Charlie, like "having the dedication to get things done" and "ability to initiate and close deals" and "experience with multi-nationals"— and tried to do it in a genuine way. I talked about my ability to relate to people of all ages and ethnicities, and gave him examples of past successes working in real estate. As I talked, however, his eyes glazed over. Little did I know that Charlie had come into the interview thinking he didn't really need to hire anyone. He was testing the market to see what kind of talent was available, and had little intention of even giving me a chance. His reaction to my narrative was tepid.

As my mouth chattered away on autopilot, my mind was working overtime trying to read his body language and figuring out how to turn this around. I didn't want to let this opportunity slip away.

"So, on a day-to-day basis, what will the job entail?" I asked, hoping to buy time.

Charlie began talking and I immediately thought about the snow cave and what I learned about my support network. Here, in this interview, just as in the snow cave, this was up to me and nobody else. No recommendations, no strings to be pulled, no support system to help me get this job. Just me. I had to come up with something. He was winding down his response and I knew if I wanted the job, I would need his full attention. I had to be more aggressive and hit him over the head with something compelling. But, before I could even start, Charlie was done.

"Well, Dave, can I call you that? Good. We have all the marketing representation we need at this time—"

"What about the ad in the paper?" I said. "Has it been filled already?"

"Well, we were anticipating some changes that just didn't happen, so that job isn't available anymore." But then, Charlie changed his story. "You see, I'm looking for someone a bit more experienced. This is a tough market and you need to really be strong in your ability to relate to people, gain their trust, and sell them on our property. I'm just not sure you have that ability." He organized his papers, eyes darting everywhere except at me.

It was now or never. My parents had instilled in me that accepting no for an answer was fine, but if you wanted something badly enough, there was always room to negotiate.

"Charlie, okay, you know about my work experience, but what you don't know is why I'm uniquely qualified for this job." I began taking his initial response as a personal challenge. I stood up, and was now just a bit taller than him.

He looked at me, and seemed resigned to giving me another shot. "I'm listening."

I was more fired up than expected and that's when I realized how much I wanted this job. Without thinking it through, and for the first time in my life, I talked about my height in a professional setting. I told him that as a short kid, teen, and now adult, I'd experienced challenges that other candidates probably had not. I was teased, ridiculed, and perceived to be physically weak. His reaction was absolutely startling. He was no longer looking through me, but now, he was glued to his seat, eyes alert.

I was doing better, but now had to relate this short man's soapbox to the business at hand. How was it an asset?

"You see, Charlie, this challenge of being shorter than others actually helped me as I grew up. Sure it was difficult sometimes, but I'm also a strong athlete, so I know what it's like to win, feel good about myself, and develop an ego. I found some great friends and developed a very positive and confident approach on life. The combination of being ridiculed, yet personally confident and sure of myself, allowed me to appreciate different perspectives and groups of people. If a friend was sad or feeling ostracized, I could understand them, but if someone was overconfident or full of themselves, I could relate to that, too. Because I can see both sides, I have the interpersonal skills required to excel in your business in ways others can't."

"Well, I didn't know this," said Charlie, looking a bit surprised by my openness. I wanted to continue pushing, but didn't know what else to say. He was still there, so I was encouraged.

"And Charlie," I continued grasping at straws. "You are looking for someone with the interpersonal skills I just described, but also the skills to make things happen, correct? Well, what you don't see on my resume is that I was a top ranked state gymnast. I'm sure you recognize that to achieve success at that level, it takes hard work, dedication, and perseverance. I did it then, and I can do it now, in this role."

I was going overboard, bragging, even.

"Interesting, what else?" He looked genuinely curious.

"Charlie, you interact with professionals from around the world. I speak English, Russian, and some Spanish. I can relate to these people and I can help your organization. Give me a chance."

He paused, leaned back and crossed his arms. I could tell he was thinking about what to say.

"Well, Dave, I like what you are saying and it's true, I do like your drive and the maturity you seem to bring."

Finally, he was open to at least considering me.

"But, so you know, I currently do have three other Americans in this role, but none with your passion and unique experience. Let's say I took you on board, how do you feel about being paid in rubles?"

He was fishing to see how desperate I was. Expats hired by multi-nationals rarely worked for rubles. Companies like his could pay dollars by simply wiring funds to an American bank account from their US-based accounts.

I gave him what I hoped was a suitably stern look. "I'm not op-posed to a trial period where you pay me a below-market rate, but it has to be in dollars. I'm a US citizen with a US bank account and I understand what's going on in this country. Let's agree on a decent trial salary and go from there."

"I like you, Dave, and I think you are going to be successful here. Okay."

With that, we agreed on a yearly salary of $22,000, a visa extension, and a rent-free apartment in the complex to offset housing costs. It was a good deal for both of us, but I was particularly pleased. I want-ed a professional experience where I could meet other Americans, use my Russian language skills, and bank some money. I was also excited about moving into the complex; I would avoid the periodic and sometimes sustained loss of hot water, the smell of urine in the hallways, and the single-pane, drafty windows. On top of that, with accommodations taken care of, and the dollar strong compared to the ruble, I would have some newfound money to spend on the Moscow nightlife.

Leaving St. Petersburg was difficult. Although my relationship with Zhanna had become strained, I still felt close to her, and to Babushka. At least I had the future to look forward to—a new city to explore, new friends to make, and a new job to master. I promised I would stay in touch, and as I boarded the train to Moscow, prayed they would be all right. They would have it far tougher than me. Social, political, and economic change would force them to adapt, and while I thought they would do fine, was concerned for their days ahead.

MEETING OF THE MINDS

Convincing Charlie that I was the right man for the job turned out to be a good thing. Not only did he end up being a terrific boss, but my newfound, work-based support system helped me adapt to life in Moscow. Moving from the shared apartment with Zhanna and Babushka to my own two-bedroom duplex in a secure Western style apartment complex gave me a sort of reverse–culture shock. Built to attract wealthy foreigners, the units were appointed with hardwood floors, a full kitchen, a balcony, washer–dryer units, and even a backup hot water system. With the workout facility, tennis courts, restaurant, and a minimart downstairs, I was completely spoiled. No longer did I worry about the elevator working, or if the bathroom down the hall was free, or even waiting in lines for essentials like bread and milk. There was no staircase to ascend, but instead, a clean, new Otis elevator delivered me to my floor. In fact, due to the strength of the dollar, I had never lived so well—I hired a maid and a personal cook whom I paid a dollar each per hour.

Very quickly, the company became my new family away from home. Of the nine Americans, over half were from Texas; the rest were East Coasters. All except one were single, and the friendships we formed grew out of our need for camaraderie in a foreign country. War stories of life here—the challenges of losing hot water for weeks on end, the inability to find fresh fruits or vegetables, coping with rising street violence, the endless winters—were so commonplace that we often started each morning at work bonding over shared hardships. It was cathartic. We knew that friends and family back home couldn't relate to these experiences, so we depended on each other for empathy.

Of my friends from the company, Ashley and Julie, both American, were local hires like me and had also recently graduated from college, so we gravitated to one another. Julie, the group's social guru, had a large circle of friends outside work. Her sunny personality coupled with her long brown hair and wide smile made her an immediate object of guys' desires, and she often seemed busy with something or someone. I was a little guarded around her, however. While her smile was warm and friendly, the affection didn't always seem to reach her eyes. Ashley, short in stature with large, eager brown eyes, was genuine and down-to-earth, and she relished the burgeoning Moscow nightlife. Her neat Dorothy Hamill hairstyle and reserved demeanor often set people up for a shock—she had a strong wit and her remarks could be cutting.

Charlie, Clay, and Ted, the project leaders, were sponsored employees—sent overseas by the company—and were here to work. They didn't care to learn the language or culture, but had an international corporate reputation to build. If I thought my new lifestyle pampered me, they put it to shame: Each had a driver, a cook, a security detail when necessary, lived in the complex, and took advantage of corporate-sponsored trips home. They managed more than twenty employees each, and with expectations high, were focused on nothing but the bottom line.

Ted, always neatly groomed, impeccably dressed, and calculating, was responsible for the real estate partnership with the Russian government and was married to his work. A young guy in his early thirties, he had jumped up the corporate ladder due to his aggressive style and get-it-done-at-all-costs attitude. Clay was more relaxed in his approach. Outspoken and not afraid to get dirty, he was tasked with managing the operations of the complex—the Russian workers, construction, and security detail. All of these groups had their complexities, but because he had hired good people, many of these areas ran themselves.

As for Charlie, my boss, he was the most tenured of the group and thus knew the players in the Russian government, the business landscape, and most important, how to manage the necessary relationship with corporate headquarters. Colleagues back in Texas didn't always understand how or why things in Moscow were done the way they were, and he had an uncanny way of quickly and easily securing approval when needed. Charlie was also the eldest, and with his wife and two kids back home, he filled the role not only of a supervisor, but also of a father figure. He knew when to push for results but also when to back off, understanding that everybody missed home, had a few tough days, and sometimes struggled with living in Russia. As I'd learn quickly, Charlie handled almost any situation calmly, and with charisma.

On one occasion early in my time at the company, Charlie and Julie invited me to attend a press club event where former President Gorbachev would be speaking. Apparently these gatherings were good networking events and it was important for us to meet people and talk up the property we were managing. Little did they know that thanks to my particular college degree, I had elevated Gorbachev to rock-star status.

Leading me down a staircase to the basement, Julie brought me to the garage to meet the drivers. The company provided drivers for their foreign staff because they felt it was safer than hailing random taxis on the street. Living on my own in St. Petersburg, I had grown accustomed to standing outside, extending my arm, and hailing a car. It was a common practice among my Russian and foreign friends alike, and I thought of it as a way of meeting people and getting the pulse on the city. Official cab or not, as long as the driver was alone and sober, I'd hop in.

"Where is the Press Club?" I asked Julie as our driver weaved in and out of traffic on Leninsky Prospekt.

"You don't know?" she asked with a subtle hint of condescension.

How would I know? I'd never been there!

Charlie interjected, explaining that we weren't actually going to the Press Club headquarters but that the event was sponsored by the Press Club and was being held at a new hotel near the Russian parliament building.

While they continued chatting about business, I daydreamed, looking through the window. Babushkas were everywhere—carrying satchels of groceries, trudging down the sidewalks, seemingly immune to the winter cold. I thought of Babushka and wondered how she and Zhanna were doing, unsure if they had found another boarder. Closer to downtown, we made our way through a maze of streets. On one, I noticed a large yellow building with towering, white columns and a dome towards the back.

"What's that building?" I asked nobody in particular.

"That's the main synagogue of Moscow. Looks nice, huh?" Charlie answered.

"Yeah," I muttered. I turned to look as we passed it to get my bearings. Maybe I'll stop by later to meet some of the local congregants, I thought. Then again, maybe not. In my heart, I wanted to. I was proud to be Jewish and was pleasantly surprised that despite the history of prejudice in Russia, here was an open synagogue in the heart of Moscow. But, I was a bit embarrassed. Despite my upbringing, I wasn't an observant Jew. What if I stopped by and couldn't answer questions about Judaism or couldn't recite the prayers? Would they even ask? I knew I was being ridiculous, but still, I felt uncomfortable.

When we arrived I was shocked at how similar the look and feel of the hotel was to a four-star hotel in the US; it had a spacious and clean foyer, a neutral-colored carpet throughout the hallways, well-stocked stores, a concierge desk, and a well-appointed staff. I realized that while I had been living like a Russian on local wages with a Russian family, I had missed the fact that an entire dollar-based economy was emerging. I had heard about new hotels and bars opening up, but had yet to visit any of them. We walked briskly to the presentation room, passing a small gift shop, and sat down in comfortable, armless chairs. A variety of lackluster paintings hung on the beige, papered walls. A few unimpressive chandeliers hung from the ceiling, but overall it could have been any hotel conference room in America. On stage at the front of the room, a few men sat at a long table, talking quietly, leaving a center-stage podium empty.

The room quickly filled up and soon there was standing room only. I heard a lot of English, Spanish, and Asian languages being spoken around the room—it was primarily a non-Russian audience. Julie and Charlie seemed to know a number of people, waving and smiling as they settled in. I sat and watched the podium, trying to temper my excitement. I wondered if Gorbachev would look like he did on TV. What did that spot on his head actually look like up close? Was speaking with him even remotely possible? Daydreaming, I built up expectations of a hypothetical meeting, inventing some intelligent questions. By the time he was scheduled to take the stage, I had concocted and rehearsed an entire conversation in my head. I was convinced we would hit it off.

Without announcement or fanfare, his entourage entered from the front of the room, the back left side of the podium. Six large men surrounded him, three on each side, as he ascended two stairs to the makeshift stage. He walked slowly, waving and nodding in response to the audience's standing ovation. I admit it: I was star struck, smiling from ear to ear. Gorbachev was shorter than I'd expected and the discoloration on his forehead appeared larger and redder. He sat down behind a long rectangular table, and shook hands with those seated next to him. I stood and watched intently until it was time for everyone to sit down.

After a brief welcome message from the Press Club president, Gorbachev was introduced. He must have talked for twenty minutes, but I heard very little, catching a few phrases here and there. I was amazed at how similar he was to his image on TV and all my energy was focused on his presentation style. I guess I should have expected it, yet I thought somehow he might be different in person. His oratory skills were impeccable. He spoke slowly, almost ploddingly, waving his arms, using his hands, and making eye contact with the audience. He knew when to pause, as a mechanism to emphasize points or to hold the audience in suspense, almost like a song might do when moving away from its root chord but eventually returning so the song feels complete. His Russian was precise but effortless, and the audience hung on his every word, eager to understand this man's views on business growth in the former Soviet Union.

Before I knew it, his remarks were winding down. I was elated to be there, but disappointed that it was coming to an end. As I watched his arms wave and his tone soften, I noticed people on the sides of the room casually making their way to the front. Most were trying to get good photos of him, but some were hovering near the stage, hoping to shake his hand.

When he did finish, a standing ovation erupted. Julie was applauding next to me. We'd been silent during the speech but as if on cue, we both began approaching the podium. I gave her my camera and slithered through the crowd, hoping to get close enough so that she could snap a photo of me with Gorby in the frame. I made my way all the way to the front row and watched as he held up a T-shirt with the logo of the Press Club on the front. I turned and saw multiple flashes from my camera. She got something! I then ran to her to reciprocate and as she walked in front of the podium, I excitedly snapped a variety of shots.

With his speech over, and the crowd in front of the podium thinning, I noticed Gorbachev standing alone. In limbo between a series of handshakes from important looking men, he looked around for papers to shuffle or something to occupy his hands and look busy. Without warning or thought, I walked briskly toward the stage. I was conflicted. On one hand I knew this was a unique opportunity. I would probably never be so close to him again, and given that I had prepared what I would say, this was my chance to connect. On the other hand, I was afraid of what a Russian jail might look like.

I walked through the last group of people chatting at the edge of the podium and hopped up onto the makeshift stage. Nobody noticed me. I looked back at Julie and Charlie who mouthed encouragement. Gorbachev's guards weren't expecting someone to just walk on stage and were relaxed, peering out into the audience. I extended my hand towards the focus of my attention.

"President Gorbachev, very nice to meet you," I stammered in Russian, trying to sound as native as possible to help him understand me.

He had been bending over his chair with his back towards me and when I spoke he turned around to look at me. "*Zdrastvooytyeh,*" he replied in greeting, looking around as if to see if I had been cleared or someone was there to introduce me. His hand met mine. His rounded face appeared calm and kind, his glasses large for his face, and his hair receded more than expected.

His guards quickly realized what was happening and briskly approached and separated us. They didn't shove me away, but cautiously set up a wall-like perimeter around Gorbachev.

At that, I continued talking, trying to act unfazed although whatever plan I had developed was gone. I was flustered and now had to work around some very large men whose goal was to remove me from the podium, if not the room.

I spoke louder so he could hear me. "I'm an American working here and I want to let you know I believe in what you started and think it will work out for the best. It is an honor to meet you," I said in Russian, giving him two thumbs up, knowing he needed no such praise from a twenty-three year old American. The guards held my shoulders to keep me in place.

But Gorbachev heard me and asked his guards to make way. He walked up, looked at me, and took my hand to complete the handshake I had initiated. "Thank you," he responded appreciatively.

At that moment, I realized that I was standing in front of someone I'd studied, respected, and in some ways idolized for his courage, foresight, and ability to bring about change. He had singlehandedly been the catalyst that recognized the flaws of the Soviet Union and implemented policies to address them. For better or worse, Russia was on a path that valued law over fear, drive and ingenuity over planned development, and people over weaponry. Significant challenges lay ahead, but his aptitude for standing strong and fighting for his beliefs had a tremendous effect on his country's future.

Now was my chance to say things I had planned to say. But with so much swirling in my head about the man and his impact on Russia, I froze. I looked at him, half smiling. He looked at me, serious. An uncomfortable pause ensued. As our handshake ended without me saying anything coherent, his guards stepped in and this time politely asked me to leave. Gorbachev didn't say anything, but instead looked away to someone else who was following my lead trying to meet him. My thirty seconds with him were over. I stepped down and was escorted out of the room where I met Julie and Charlie.

"Nice move, Dave," Charlie said, patting me on the back. "That took guts!"

"What did you say? How could you do that? Did you speak with him?" Julie asked, barraging me with questions.

"I don't know—I just did it," I responded robotically, feeling a bit dazed and disappointed.

"Did he respond? What did he say? What did his bodyguards say?"

"Yes, he was great. Very nice." It was then I realized how angry and disappointed I was with myself. "I didn't say anything of substance! I...I basically said nothing." In my impressionable head, I had hoped he would have taken some interest in me, resulting in a thoughtful discussion on foreign affairs.

"At least you did *something*, and you got to meet him. How cool is that?" Julie said, not expecting a response. "Oh, and here's your camera. I got what I could but who knows what will come out."

"Thanks," I muttered. The three of us walked to our driver and made our way back to the development. As Charlie and Julie bantered back and forth about how to approach a deal they were putting together, I brooded. The encounter with Gorbachev replayed over and over in my head. I considered the many directions the conversation could have gone, yet none of them happened. It was frustrating to know how foolish I must have come across just standing there, shaking his hand, looking at him, silent.

Over time, as I told and retold the story to friends, I grew more comfortable with my naïve approach to the Gorbachev encounter. I understood there was very little I could have expected from such an interaction. At least I took action and didn't stand there aimlessly. I made something happen.

MIXING WORK WITH THE MAFIA

In my role as a marketing representative, I met with business leaders from all over the world. I was their first point of contact with the firm, and portrayed our property as the best in the country. Any firm that was interested in the Russian market checked in with us, if only to get our perspective on real estate development in Moscow. While our property was not the only game in town, there were few others that offered the combination of security, modern amenities, and both office and residential space. Visiting executives were decision-makers and came from some of the top companies in the world, including Pepsi, Lukoil, Daewoo, and Daimler. They were polished, tough, and seasoned, and because of this, I learned a lot from their experience and approach.

I also interacted with local businesses, some Russian and others from former Soviet bloc countries, which weren't as savvy. They sought a respectable location that would make it difficult for mafia tentacles to reach them. Businesses, both foreign and domestic, were paying exorbitant "protection" fees and those who could not pay sometimes found their offices firebombed or worse. The complex, with its twenty-four-hour security personnel, provided some measure of protection against property damage, and was a strong deterrent against more aggressive action such as homicide.

Many of these post-Soviet bloc business people had never traveled abroad and were thus astonished at the prices and requisite long lease terms. Some were mafia themselves who wanted to appear legitimate and enjoy the luxuries our complex provided. Others weren't mafia per se, but were new to the business world and were involved in questionable activities. The bottom line was that they viewed the law as for sale, and contracts as breakable. These visitors presented challenges to Julie, Ashley, and me. They didn't approach us and say, "Hey, we're mafia," so it often took time for us to fully understand the realities of how they made money and if they were financially qualified for our units. Some weren't savvy enough to follow basic accounting practices and thus didn't have income statements or balance sheets that we could review. Others dealt primarily in cash, so were close to impossible to evaluate.

The three of us worked as a team, helping each other when necessary, translating unfamiliar words in documents, and standing in for each other when appointments ran late. Working in one large, rectangular room with multiple phones, open desks, and a printer to share, we didn't have much privacy, but we made it work. Instead of hanging wall art, we covered the stark white walls with pictures of family and friends, livening up the space as best we could.

One day, Julie was overbooked and needed help.

"Dave, I am swamped with back-to-back clients. Can you take this Russian company for me? I'm sorry but I don't have much background on them."

"Sure, when are they coming?" I asked, hanging up the phone. I'd just completed my cold calls for the day and was free.

"They're in the waiting room—so, now would be good." And then she was out the door.

I was slightly irritated that it was so last minute. I walked into the lobby and saw two middle-aged men with gray, wrinkled suits, whispering to each other, waiting for someone to help them. Both had mustaches and hair that needed trimming, and carried professional-looking, but worn briefcases.

"Hello, how can I help you today?" I inquired in a professional, welcoming voice.

They looked at each other. One took the lead. "You know to speak Russian?" he asked in broken English.

"Yes."

"*Prekrasno*," he said, pleased. "My name is Sergei and this is Igor. We have a business and are looking for an office. We heard you have offices to rent. Is this correct?"

"Absolutely. How large a space do you need?" I answered looking at Sergei's eyes. He wore extraordinarily large, black-rimmed glasses.

The lenses were some of the thickest I'd ever seen, and it wasn't completely clear that he was looking at me.

"Not big. We just need it for back-office type work. We will have a secretary there and possibly hold a few client meetings, but a small space will be fine."

It was typical for a small firm to want a professional office space in an impressive building for clients to visit. I showed them around and we chatted about their company's success, what they were looking for in an office, and the prices and terms we offered. Their business was in import–export and I showed them a space that had a basic kitchen, a meeting room–office, and an area that could be made into a waiting room or conference area. I didn't get a great feeling about their interest level, and on their way out, when they said they would be back for a second look, I didn't give it much thought. As I always did, I let them know we would need to see letters of incorporation, income statements, and other background data to ensure they qualified for the space. They assured me this would be no problem, and went on their way.

The next day, Sergei of the large glasses showed up unannounced. On my way down from my apartment and over to the office, he found me in the hall.

"Hello, Mr. Kalis. Do you mind if I take another look at the office space?" he asked, peering through those impossible lenses.

I greeted him as if he was expected. "Let me get the keys and we'll go right up."

Walking through the complex to get to the office, we said very little, but I noticed he was wearing the same suit as the day before, and his disheveled hair had a greasy look. I kept my expectations low.

When we entered the office, he headed straight to the far end of the room. "Come step outside," he asked softly, pointing to the door leading to the balcony.

An odd request, but I obliged. The use of bugs was so prevalent in the former Soviet Union that many people were skeptical that the practice had ended. Given that the complex was new construction,

I had never considered it here, but didn't know for sure. I stepped outside.

"We like the office space you offered us yesterday, but are looking for a discount on the price or on the length of the lease," explained Sergei, looking directly at me, trying to read my response. "I'm wondering if this can be negotiated."

I was glad he was so interested in the office, but surprised that they had decided in just one day. Because we were offering units that came with a minimum seven-year lease term at a premium price, most tenants needed at least a few weeks to consider the terms.

"We don't usually negotiate, but it can depend on how qualified the company is. It will be important to get those documents I mentioned yesterday."

He looked away into the bright blue Moscow sky, gazing at nothing, but obviously considering what he was going to say next. "Yes, I understand about the papers you need, but our company is quite new, so we don't have everything you require. On the other hand, we do have money, and can reward you nicely for a deal." His magnified eyes turned back to me.

I wasn't sure what he was saying, but blurted, "You know we don't accept cash, correct?"

"Yes, I understand," he replied. "But, if you would, please take a look in here." He brought his carrying case closer to me and opened it. I didn't get a clear view, but from what I saw, it was filled with neatly organized bundles of hundred-dollar bills. "What do you say we meet at a restaurant tonight for dinner to discuss a deal? When we finish eating, I'll leave this bag for you," he said, smiling broadly, as if he knew he had done a good job. "There's ten thousand dollars for you and ten thousand dollars for your boss. How does that sound?"

I paused, stunned. I had never seen that much cash in one place.

"Uh, well, it sounds okay, but let me check with my boss on how to handle this," I said, trying to extract myself from the situation, knowing full well there was no way we would accept the offer. Given the shady circumstances, however, I didn't want to reject it outright. "My boss is in the US right now, but I'll speak with him tonight."

"Okay, you do that and let me know something as soon as you can. We are eager to move in."

"I understand."

As we parted ways at the revolving front door, I let security know they should watch for this guy and his partner. Anytime they were on premises, we wanted to know. I then called Charlie and walked him through what had happened. As expected, he immediately rejected the idea. The entire situation was ludicrous. Not only did their proposal totally disregard our policy, but he reminded me that our real estate company was fighting an uphill battle. Our goal was to be viewed as an honest, above-board firm, in a society that had fallen into an abyss of corruption.

The next day, I called Sergei to let him know our decision.

"Sergei, thank you for your offer, but we are not interested," I said calmly.

"Really? Are you sure?" I could tell this was not the response he was expecting. For his company, bribes must have been commonplace, simply a part of doing business. He continued, "You know, I can increase our offer to fifteen thousand each, but that is as high as we can go."

"I'm sorry, but we don't operate this way. It's our policy," I stated firmly.

"Well, if that is that, then okay. There is nothing more I can do."

And there wasn't. That was that. Interestingly enough, interactions like this were not uncommon for us. Bribery and intimidation, even outright threats—we faced many unscrupulous situations, and somehow treated them all with shared humor. When we thought we had seen it all, an even more outrageous situation would come along.

A few days later, Mikhail, a middle-age CEO of a growing oil company, showed up wanting to discuss a property. He was tall and had dark hair and high cheekbones. His look, coupled with his solid, athletic build immediately reminded me of James Bond. Not uptight, but certainly not relaxed, his mannerisms were calculated and intentional. He stroked his hair to make sure it remained in place, gently touched his hand to my elbow as he talked, and stood directly in front of me, emphasizing his large physique when trying to make a point. Dressed impeccably in a designer suit, he was prepared to talk business, and as I led him on a tour he asked many good questions, and listened intently to the answers.

He paid attention to every detail. As we talked, I could tell that he also preferred to be in control. He had a tendency to answer his own questions or rephrase my answers, if my responses weren't to his liking. He comfortably interrupted at will, and led the conversation if the anticipated outcome was potentially not to his benefit.

"I understand you have lease terms including years and prices, but I'm sure exceptions can be made for certain clients?" he asked, raising his eyebrows.

"We stick with our policy, as it has served us well."

"But, for valuable clients, I would think something could be done, yes?"

"We haven't made exceptions yet, so I don't think it's an option. I hope you understand," I responded. I wanted to be firm yet conciliatory.

"Let's keep it on the table for a discussion to be had later, shall we?" It was more of a statement than a question.

Following the tour he suggested we meet in a conference room. I told him I would get some floor plans and papers to review but that he should sit down and relax—I'd be in shortly. When I returned, Mikhail was sitting at the table with two tall, burly men standing alertly behind him, one over each shoulder. Unfamiliar to me, they were dressed well, in ties and blazers. I was puzzled.

"Mikhail, do you know these men?" I asked, looking at them.

"Oh, yes, of course. I forgot to introduce you," he said casually. "These are my associates and are accompanying me today."

"Would you like to see the property?" I asked the men, standing up, addressing them directly.

"They are fine, thank you," interjected Mikhail, waving me to sit down. "They already know about the property and are satisfied."

I had no idea what he meant by satisfied, or how they knew about the property, but their silence made it clear that Mikhail was in charge. Sitting back down, I looked at one of the men again. He avoided eye contact but at the same time seemed to intentionally open his jacket gently. I noticed a black, shiny object and immediately was at a loss for words. I glanced at the other man, who opened his jacket, and as if on cue, blatantly revealed his gun. Not wanting to overreact, I fixed my eyes on the papers in front of me, shuffling them as if I were organizing the stack. Nervous but not afraid, I paused and looked at Mikhail. His calm demeanor, relaxed posture, and nonchalant approach made the entire situation even more unsettling. Did I miss a signal from him? Was he upset with some of my answers to his questions? I knew intimidation was part of his game, but I was prepared to hold my ground.

I shifted my weight to find a comfortable spot, but knew it was impossible on the hard wooden seats. Did I really just see what I thought I saw? Here, in the conference room? Really? He leaned back in his chair, blowing smoke rings into the air.

This seemed like the stuff of movies, not real life. I was upset with their approach, but balanced my frustration with pragmatism. Moscow was not a safe place. Businessmen were threatened daily, and with the environment becoming more dangerous, I had to temper my reaction. I grabbed hold of my senses, and met Mikhail's gaze.

"I'm glad you're interested in our property and pleased we were able to meet today, but we don't do business this way." I pointed to the two men and their guns. "If you'd like to meet to discuss what we can offer you, I'd be happy to, but not like this."

"But I am interested in your apartments. You don't want to help me?"

"Mikhail, it's not that. But I can't allow guns on the premises and will not talk business under these conditions. If this is how you conduct your affairs, this might not be the right place for you."

"You don't want to continue the meeting?" he asked, sounding surprised, not mentioning the guns or his men.

"No, I don't," I responded, unsure how he might respond to my candor.

He looked at his men, and then back at me. He seemed a bit confused, and looked again at his men.

My heart was pounding and I was more fearful now that he may respond as in the movies—by nodding at his henchmen, and leaving the room while they disposed of me. Or, worse yet, he may wait until nightfall when I was least expecting it. My mind was racing. Did he understand my point of view or was he offended by this conversation and the tone I was using? Grinding his teeth, jaw protruding, he gazed at me. His fingers danced on the table slowly, as he thought through what he wanted to say. Finally, with temples pulsing, he looked at me sternly, leaned over, and spoke.

"Fine. Then how about this? You come and meet me at my offices and we will continue these discussions," he suggested. "I now understand how you do business and it's refreshing. I respect it. I meet many businessmen who only respond to this." He waved his arms and pointed at his men. "But you, and...it seems your firm, is different, which is a good thing."

"I'm glad you said that. I will set up time for next week."

He and his men left the building and I breathed a sigh of relief.

That week, Charlie and I went back and forth about whether I should even attend the follow-up meeting. While our information about his company indicated it was a legitimate provider of energy solutions in Russia, we remained wary. Rumors swirled about how the company became so powerful so quickly; it was linked to various unscrupulous activities, including bribery and extortion, but nothing stuck. Without any concrete findings against it, and because it clearly had the profits to afford the property, we decided to overlook the hearsay and continue.

That following week, sitting in Mikhail's lavish office, I fidgeted in my chair. Fortunately, his bodyguards were nowhere to be seen. Seated behind a large mahogany desk in a room appointed with flowing window coverings, colorful wall tapestries, matching mahogany furniture, and an exquisite chandelier, he seemed more at ease. He walked over to a sideboard and poured himself some coffee.

He motioned to me. I had never tried coffee, but took his lead. I took a sip and pursed my lips. Bitter—very bitter. But I shook it off and smiled. For the good of the relationship I had to show appreciation for his hospitality. Having reflected on my earlier encounter with Mikhail a bit more, I decided it was important to defer to him, offer respect, and make sure he felt he had an edge on the relationship.

We chatted for a while, and wanting to walk away with a deal, I offered him a break on the length of the contract in exchange for paying a premium on the unit. He agreed and we established a good working relationship. He even apologized for his behavior at our first meeting, but explained that given the uncertain times in Russia, he sometimes did what he had to do to get the deal done. He realized he'd made a mistake with us. I had a feeling that this client would end up being one of our best tenants.

☭

On the way back from Mikhail's office, my driver, Vladimir, and I were pulled over by the police. It wasn't the first time this had happened, and I knew the drill. We weren't speeding and didn't violate any traffic laws, but because Vladimir drove a foreign car—the ultimate sign of wealth in the new Russia—he was a target. He pulled the car over, reached into his glove compartment to grab his driving documents, and then looked at me. Often, a $5 or a $10 bill would do the trick, and we would be on our way. I handed Vladimir a ten, watched him bribe the officer, and listened to them chitchat. It bothered me to see such a blatant disregard for the law, but I sat silently, knowing it was not my place to intercede. As we were pulling away I realized once again that things in Russia were not always as they appeared.

Mikhail's first impression was of an underworld baron who muscled his way through the business world. On the contrary, from what we found, he had built a good business; and while he was a bit rough around the edges, he was actually a pleasant and reasonable person. The police, on the other hand, tried to appear lawful, but weren't. They reinforced the city's rampant corruption, and given the uncertainty of their allegiances, made it even harder for legitimate businesses to flourish.

DAVE THE AMERICAN

Russia's new President, Boris Yeltsin, was an outspoken, boisterous, former legislator who attempted unsuccessfully to bring economic stability to his country. The old Soviet economy dictated by government mandate had become unreliable and overrun with people taking advantage of their positions. What many in the West thought to be progress toward capitalism was better described as a hoarding of assets for the very few who had power. Government officials and the mafia built their fiefdoms based on loyalty and relationships. It was a "land grab" mentality similar to the Wild West in America years prior, complete with overwhelming business risk.

Once it became clear that the mafia was as disorganized and ineffective as the government, rival groups emerged. Driven by greed, dueling mafia groups who initially claimed specific territories ended up battling for power. For new businesses, this maze of conflicting mafia entities made the operating landscape difficult to navigate. Even when a business felt safe or "protected" there was always the risk that a new mafia group would move in, making the protection money they'd been paying irrelevant.

As the mafia grew, so did the amount of discretionary money flowing into the hands of society's elite—mafia, businesspeople, foreigners, and government officials. While it was only select groups of Russians and foreigners who suddenly became wealthy, it was enough to sustain a burgeoning restaurant and nightclub industry. Moscow was becoming an international hot spot, and I was enjoying the ride.

One evening I went to a dinner party with a group of American friends. Most were expats, but many had their own circles of Russian friends, whom they brought and introduced. That night I met Oleg, Anton, and Nikolai. Oleg, a gregarious twenty-year-old who had perfectly parted brown hair and dressed like an American pretty-boy, had lived in Pennsylvania on an exchange program. He spoke fluent English and was an avid sports fan. His friends, Anton and Nikolai, spoke very little English, but my Russian had improved to the point where we could communicate easily. As the vodka shots flowed, we had a great time toasting, singing, and exchanging stories.

Coincidentally, Anton and Nikolai had just opened a nightclub that was doing very well. Over the next few months I got to know them by visiting the club often, and came to understand how they managed their business—far better than I wanted to, actually.

Thanks to boyish looks and a thin frame, Anton could pass for sixteen. He was known to be a nice guy, very strong in school, and more than anything, decent and fair. He managed the entertainment portion of the business, setting up performers, coordinating the DJs, and creating the ambiance. Based on the crowds he attracted, their club became one of the more popular nightspots for local teens and twenty-somethings, even though the building itself was a bit odd. By day it was a community center where young kids learned about former communist leaders, and where teens could get involved in athletics, politics, and music. The large meeting hall was adorned with paintings of Vladimir Lenin and other communist propaganda, and Anton's job was to turn it into a hip nighttime destination spot where young people could relax. He did what he could by dimming the lights, adding colorful strobe lights and decorations, and bringing in food to create an energetic atmosphere. The key to his success, however, was being able to attract some of Russia's up-and-coming musical talent, including bands, singers, and other artists who agreed to perform well into the night.

Nikolai, on the other hand, was a shrewd businessman who ran the operations and managed its relationships. His unshaven jaw, deep-set dark eyes, and pockmarked skin made him the better guy for dealing with the mafia. He paid protection bribes weekly, and simply considered these payments as a built-in tax, the cost of doing business. He also negotiated rent with the owner and hired guards to watch over the club. I found it interesting that the guards weren't mafia, just a collection of larger men who acted as bouncers. At first,

I didn't understand why the bouncers were there given that the mafia was paid to "protect" the establishment. In time, I'd understand.

I enjoyed the nightclub and was practically a fixture there on weekends. Typically, I'd go out with some expats for dinner and then try to convince them to join me at the club. All too often, however, I'd end up alone, as my friends found it easier and more comfortable to go back to their apartments to party with other English-speaking friends. I didn't blame them. The disco was extremely smoky and loud with a clientele that was mostly Russian. The food and drink was primarily Russian snacks and beers, and while the live music was good, it was all unfamiliar Russian artists.

To some extent, I liked the challenge the club represented; I had to speak Russian exclusively, try new Russian foods, decipher Russian lyrics, and make Russian friends. But, deep down I was a bit scared of the place. When I was there, I rarely looked men in the eye. Most of the guys who visited the club seemed volatile and were generally rude to others. They'd stand around in packs glaring at people, occupy tables not reserved for them, and cut the lines for food and drink. Although I hadn't had any dangerous run-ins with anyone, I was always cautious. Despite my western clothes, glasses, and of course, developing Russian, I tried to blend in as much as possible.

I wasn't fooling myself, however. I knew it was impossible to hide my true identity and that the clientele included a lot of mafia. Find a sweat suit, and you would find the mafia. They were partial to Adidas sweatpants and matching hoodies. Other brands were also popular, but the sweat suit was the identifying factor. Not surprisingly, one Saturday night I watched Nikolai and some of the bouncers drag a man from the bathroom. He was bleeding badly from his head, and wasn't moving.

"What's going on?" I asked Nikolai as he helped carry the unconscious body into the backseat of someone's car.

"Payback."

"Mafia?" I whispered.

"Yes. He must have done something they didn't like. It's ugly, but it's the Russian way right now," he said without remorse.

"Should you call the police?"

Nikolai chuckled. "The police? No, they would fine the club but do nothing to implicate any mafia group. They are afraid of the mafia, too, and want no problems."

He walked silently back into the disco, and the car sped away.

☭

A few weeks later, Oleg, Anton, and I were at another dinner party, where I was playing guitar and singing—typical for a Russian get-together. Having performed many times in college as a street performer in Harvard Square, I knew a number of songs and loved getting everyone involved. My Russian friends were well versed in Beatles songs, so we'd sing, dance and drink into the night. I was astonished at how much these guys smoked and drank. My fraternity drank a lot of beer, sure, but Russians drank straight vodka with a pickle chaser. And, when doing shots, there was a custom to follow. As my Russian friends explained, I was supposed to drink each shot in its entirety, prior to setting it back down on the table. It showed respect to the host. For me, however, it was like asking me to intentionally get sick. My small body simply couldn't handle shot after shot, and a few in succession would land me face down on the floor. To avoid offending, I got in the habit of drinking half the shot and keeping the glass elevated until I could down the remainder, or in some circumstances, drop it into the nearest plant. Although ridiculed at first, my Russian friends eventually accepted this approach.

Still, though, it was vodka, not beer.

Following a drunken rendition of one of my original songs, Anton put his arm around me and announced that I would be singing at the disco every Saturday night. Without thinking about it, and distracted by the party, I slurred that I loved the idea. It was cause for another toast, which I soon forgot.

The following Saturday afternoon I stopped by the disco to say hello. Before I could utter a word, Anton came running out of the front entrance, screaming with excitement.

"Look here! Look what I have done! I hope this is okay." He had printed out that evening's version of the set list, and scanning it I noticed "Dave the American" was performing at 3 a.m. Seeing this in print, it conjured up a faint recollection of the previous weekend. *Oh, shit.*

"Where did you come up with 'Dave the American?' And, why didn't you ask if I was even available to perform tonight?"

"Last week you said it was okay," replied an impassioned Anton. "I wanted to get you going quickly—what can you sing? And I thought the name was good because it describes you."

"It's fine. But I'm not sure tonight is good. I don't have a song, I haven't rehearsed..."

"No problem. I've heard what you can do. You are ready. Go home and find a song and do what you need to prepare yourself. See you tonight?"

I acquiesced.

Sitting at home, flipping through the international TV channels, I thought about what I was signing up for. The disco was popular and attracted great talent—including, Lada Dance (the Russian version of Madonna), and others who were so popular in Russia that they were cutting record deals, selling CDs, and performing at large venues. They would light up the stage with acts that included a full band, dancers, and terrific lead vocalists that the Russian audience recognized.

And then there was me.

I imagined being up there alone, singing an unfamiliar American song. I had no band, no choreography, and no dazzling outfits. And, to top it off, I'd be betraying my low-key profile. Yes, I was waffling. I loved singing and knew I wasn't afraid to entertain, but my deeper concerns about the place had the ring of common sense.

I called Anton mid-afternoon. "Are you sure you want me to do this?"

"*Da, konechno!* Yes, of course!" he said, flippantly.

"Okay—you have a tape player, right?" I asked, grasping at an idea I thought could actually work.

"*Da.*"

"And can you wire things so that the sound of the tape player can go through the large speaker system in the disco?"

"*Da.*"

"Great. How about I sing live, but with the karaoke track? That way, I can perform without the band I don't have, and can just focus on learning some words for tonight?"

"No backup vocal track? Are you sure?" Despite the level of talent he hired, most of them preferred to lip sync.

"Absolutely. I can't do it any other way."

"Okay."

"But why 3 a.m.?" I asked.

"It's perfect," Anton continued. "You'll go on right after Slava climbs the rope to the ceiling and before the break at 3:15. We'll have fewer people in the audience in case they don't like you." A wry smile had entered his voice.

"Sounds like a good plan," I said, just as sarcastically.

We hung up the phone and I told myself it would be fine. I'd enjoy it—I just had to finish preparing. What would I wear? Could I sing any of the songs on my tapes well enough? I was to follow Slava—was this good or bad? His act was a staple in the program. He was a big, burly, muscular Russian man with long blond hair and an attractive face who every night ascended a rope to the ceiling half-naked. Although his hairy, bare-chested gymnastics routine seemed a bit over the top, the way his muscles flexed as he climbed the rope mesmerized the crowd. After he descended, the women would regularly throw themselves at him, hoping for a smile or a hug. He would oblige by walking through the audience, meeting people and socializing. Tonight, however, instead of getting more of large, muscular Slava, they would get the short guy with glasses, "Dave the American."

Meanwhile, I stood in front of my closet and chose an outfit. Jeans and a button-down. I struggled to understand why Anton had such confidence in me. He knew the crowd. What was he thinking? My concerns returned, deeper than before. First, the disco was a dance hall, blaring heavy bass-driven techno music. I had two karaoke tapes with me in Russia—Billy Joel and Elton John. Second, the nightclub was packed with low-level mafia who had no interest in the outside world, let alone "Dave the American." Third, well, so much for blending in. And finally, I would be up there alone, singing a song in English, trying to relate to a group of horny, drunk Russians.

But just like when we drank shots of vodka at the table during a party and there was no putting the shot down until it was empty, I couldn't back out now. Rummaging through my tapes I found two songs that were somewhat usable—the moderately paced Billy Joel song, "Italian Restaurant," and the slower Elton John ballad, "Don't Let the Sun Go Down On Me." Both were classics to me, but chances were high that very few in the audience would recognize them. I knew most of the words to both songs, so I began practicing to ensure I could hit all the notes.

I tried to control my nerves. I paced in my apartment and mapped out some dance moves I used to do when singing with The Beelzebubs. I loved performing in front of sold-out college crowds with the Bubs. The preparation and rehearsals were intense, but what I remembered most fondly was road tripping and meeting people from different schools, running on stage to inexplicably wild and admiring fans, and partying well into the night with my brothers in song. It was an incredible experience.

As I reminisced, I heated up some leftover borscht and potatoes for dinner. I knew this show would be very different from those. I had moved on from college, but still, my mind took me back to the days before I arrived in Russia. I had been a nervous college senior who wasn't sure where my life was headed. More than anything, I recalled the pressure that the last few months of college presented and realized that in many ways, I ran away. I didn't think of it in those terms back then. But now I saw that's what really happened.

Tonight's performance could go well or it could flop. Faced with such uncertainty, I recognized that familiar feeling of worry creeping into my psyche. Gazing into my hallway mirror, bowl of borsht in hand, I took a deep breath and studied the specks in my hazel green eyes. Perhaps it was time to learn from my own actions. Just like my life in Russia, which had begun as a month-long immersion,

I had to trust that things would work out because I was capable of making them work out. Instead of being about anxiety, tonight was simply a night to enjoy.

When I got to the club later that evening, nobody was there. I waited outside. Anton and Nikolai arrived soon thereafter and I helped them set up. By midnight, the place began filling up. I found some friends, sat at a table, and did some shots to relax. Later, I caught up with Anton and Nikolai. They were sitting at one end of the downstairs room smoking cigarettes, keeping an eye on the place with deadpan faces. Both nodded at me, barely smiling, and asked if I was ready for my debut.

"I am. But what's going on with you guys?"

Anton just looked at me and nodded, inviting me to take a seat next to him.

"Don't look over there," he answered, "but that guy in the blue Adidas behind you near the entrance was in a fight last week with the guy in the black hooded pullover to your left."

"And?"

"They are from two rival mafia groups so we're concerned about having them both here tonight. Each mafia has its specific territory, so this is unusual. They typically stay out of each other's business. We pay the blue Adidas guys for protection, so they can come and go here as they please. But the other group is kind of meddling. We don't know if it means anything so we're just watching for now."

"Good thing you have security here," I said.

Anton looked at me as if I had said something ridiculous. Maybe my Russian pronunciation was off, or maybe I'd mixed up my vocabulary.

As the night progressed I ran into more and more expat friends who had heard I'd be singing. The support was great but, by 2:30, most of them had gone home. Still, by 2:45, I was standing backstage ready for my entrance. Dirty, old, and overlooking a large, dust-covered dance floor, the stage was just that—no props, no instruments. It would just be me singing to the audience, trying to relate to them, with nowhere to hide. As I watched Slava descend the rope that extended from the ceiling, my nerves clamored. When he finally touched down on stage, screams from female teens filled the room as they waited for him to greet them. Instead, Slava's theme music faded and he exited towards me. His fan based gawked.

He and I exchanged smiling glances and over the crowd I could hear the loudspeaker announce the newest act: "Dave the American."

Expecting the music to immediately play, I ran out on stage hoping to make a great first impression. Unfortunately, Anton and I had never discussed the technical details of my entrance. So, despite the fact that I had a working microphone, the backstage guys were fumbling with the tape. Over one hundred eyes were looking at me, wondering who I was. Wearing jeans, a long-sleeve button-down shirt and black shoes, I wasn't much to look at compared to Slava. I felt naked and embarrassed, and instinctively began retreating towards the back wall.

After what seemed like an eternity, the music finally came on. With that, I put my failed entrance behind me and did my best to sing and get the audience into the music. I pointed to people, sang to them, and tried to be as animated as possible. No reaction.

My first song, "Italian Restaurant," fell flat. Either they weren't familiar with it, didn't like it, or didn't like me, but the dance floor began to empty. From the stage, I could see them chatting, peering at me, and eventually deciding it would be more interesting downstairs. It was painful to watch. The second song went a bit better. It was a slow ballad and those who remained upstairs danced. It was apparent that the lack of a dance beat could easily be compensated for with a slow song that naturally brought people together. For a few minutes I actually thought it was going well.

Suddenly, however, the ambiance in the room changed. Halfway through the song, people started whispering and heading towards the large staircase that led down to the first floor. What was going on? As more people rushed to the stairs I looked backstage to find the stagehand. Nobody was there. I looked at the few stragglers in the audience and realized Anton and Nikolai were gone, too. I was alone, basically singing to myself.

I turned the microphone off and ran over to the stairs. Peering over someone's shoulder I noticed the wide concrete staircase was packed with people looking onto the first floor, straining to see over each other. I squeezed between people to get a better look, but halfway down the stairs I still couldn't see anything. I pushed through the onlookers and reached the bottom step.

Anton yelled, and when a body landed in front of me, I realized I'd gotten too close to the melee. There were multiple fistfights in front of me and I was unintentionally pushed to the ground. I quickly crawled back up the steps into the crowd for safety. I shoved my way up a few steps and turned around.

Anton's fears had come to fruition; a fierce brawl had broken out.

The mafia guy in the blue Adidas sweat suit was conscious, but barely. He was sprawled halfway through the disco's broken front window, his bloody torso resting on glass, and he slowly began to fall. He was writhing in pain, anguish on his face, and unable to defend himself. Someone grabbed him, lifted him off his feet, and moved the fight outside. With a sudden fist to his stomach and a knee to his head, he stumbled and collapsed into a snow bank, unconscious. His aggressor looked around, and with nobody near him to fight, fled.

Through the smoke I could see at least three other brutal fights in progress. Women, probably girlfriends, were trying to break things up as best they could. Jumping on the men, pulling them away, and finally crying, shrieking, and screaming, they couldn't stop the battle. Thrown to the ground and pushed aside, they backed off as their boyfriends continued to pummel each other. Unabashed, desperate punches were being thrown wildly. Arms and legs were getting twisted and bent in painful ways. Aggressors were throwing each other against walls, trying to inflict injury in any way possible. Anton and Nikolai frantically tried to push the brawl outside, as they couldn't afford any further damage to the club. I watched in horror; I had never seen a fight of this magnitude up close and in such detail. The anger on everyone's face was intense, the effort in every punch visible, and the agony and distress, palpable. It reminded me that at our core, humans are animals.

At one point both Anton and Nikolai were hit with stray punches, and wisely retreated to a corner away from the action. They continued yelling for the fighters to move outside, and somehow it worked. Once outside, the cold doused the aggression. One fight ended with a bloody, roughed-up youth running off into the night. In another, an overweight, bearded guy collapsed halfway inside the foyer, while his aggressor immediately tended to his friend in the blue Adidas sweat suit. It was clear he was hurt badly, so his comrade rushed him into a waiting car. Given the blood coming from his face and torso, I presumed they were off to the hospital.

A final battle continued in the street. It was between the hooded leader of the rival gang and a member of the blue Adidas group. Both were bloodied and exhausted by previous fights. The disco crowd emptied into the parking lot, but I stayed inside, watching from a window. After my experience at the dacha, I knew I should stay out of it.

I found myself standing next to a security guard whom I had seen regularly at the club. Like the rest of the security detail, he stood with an empty, blank expression, having sidestepped combatants. He had remained silent for the entire fight. I noticed his jaw muscles twitching as he ground his teeth. We nodded in recognition and looked straight ahead, through a window, as the drama unfolded before us.

"This is unbelievable. I've never seen anything like this," I said in a faint voice.

"It's not unusual these days."

"Things are that bad?"

"Oh, yes. This is not the worst I've seen." His voice was casual. "You know, before, under Brezhnev and strong party leadership, this would not happen. The police and KGB would enforce rules. In fact, they would have done something to avert such foolishness! Now we have these hooligans running around ruining our country. They drink too much, get in fights or worse yet, they shoot each other.

Good for them—kill each other, shit!" he exclaimed, starting to get agitated.

He continued, "These young hooligans call themselves mafia, but what do they know? They are only kids playing games and terrorizing neighborhoods. Meanwhile, the former KGB and other communists are robbing the country. Now look—where are the police, where are the KGB, where is the order? This country is out of control."

"Did anyone call the police?" I asked.

"*Da, nyet. Ne nado! Nu, shto tee!* No, no need. C'mon, don't be silly!" he said, incredulous. "They know this region, they know this disco, and they know it is better not to get involved. They'll show up later, when these hooligans have either worked things out or killed each other."

"And you, the security team, should you be involved?" I asked, gently broaching the obvious.

"Security team?" he chuckled. I sensed a lecture coming on. "This is my second job and I do it only because I can't make ends meet in my first job. I am a doctor at the hospital."

"You are?" I was stunned. All of this was happening in the presence of a doctor who was too intimidated to help.

"Oh yes. But this is mafia—I know not to get involved. You see, good people, teachers and scientists, don't get paid enough in Russia now," he continued. "I am a forty-four year-old man and need to support my family. It's impossible with the hyper inflation we have! So, I work here, too. This is why so many Russians want to leave the country. If they are not leaving the country, they are being pushed around by these hooligans. I myself have applied to leave the country, but we are waiting for visas. I want to leave quickly, but it is hard if you don't have money for a bribe or don't have a connection."

I'd read about the frustrations of everyday Russians in the newspapers and Western press, and in St. Petersburg got some flavor of the anger, but not like this. If society had reached a level so low that the best and brightest were fleeing, no wonder people were scared. The lack of an authoritarian hand plus this unregulated capitalism had unleashed a human phenomenon that was, in a sense, barbaric.

The strong took what they wanted while others fled or suffered. This was not the capitalism I knew and not the system I hoped would replace communism. For many Russians, however, this was all they knew.

The more we talked, the more I felt for Anton and Nikolai. They had no insurance on the building, were still obligated to pay the mafia, and would have to prove to their clientele that the disco was a safe place to enjoy an evening. They had to run a business, knowing that a fight like this one could break out at any time.

A loud thud came from outside. The man in the hoodie grabbed the other guy's hair and smashed his face into the headlight of a parked car. He was the stronger of the two and after a few painful blows to the head, the other man collapsed into the snow bank. As the glistening white snow slowly turned red, the man with the hoodie paused to talk with his buddies. I hoped it was over. It wasn't. The crumpled man got up and pressed on, waving at the hooded man in a way that seemed to say "bring it on."

The hooded man stepped forward and without warning pulled a knife and stabbed the man in the stomach. He cried out in pain, startling onlookers who turned and ran. It was hard to watch and even harder to believe the cruelty of what was happening. He removed the knife and jabbed at the crumbled man one final time and then ran off. Anton, Nikolai and the security detail approached the man lying in the snow. He wasn't moving. They didn't dare touch him and went to call the police.

Meanwhile, the security guard—the *doctor*—watched from the window.

The man lay there bleeding for about ten minutes before the police and an ambulance arrived. By now it was 4:30 a.m., and there were only a few of us left at the disco. He was lifted into the ambulance and taken to the nearest hospital. The police questioned Anton, Nikolai and the security staff. I listened as closely as I could to their renditions of what happened, but nobody mentioned specific names and they kept their responses vague. The police must have interviewed ten people but all anyone did was report what he was wearing, and that he had friends with him. Nobody wanted to risk acknowledging that they knew the aggressor, and the police didn't push for details.

As the officers wrapped up their inquiry, I asked Anton what he had told them. "What I knew and what I saw," he replied blandly.

"So you think they'll catch the guys?"

"No. They look into the crime, they take their notes, and they go home. They play the part. They have families, too, and want no part of mafia warfare. He will not be caught. In fact, you will see him here next weekend, if we open. This is Russia now."

I didn't ask any more questions. By the time I left the disco, the sun was coming up. I walked slowly on an icy, snow-covered road leading to the Metro—eventually meeting up with the security guard I had talked with earlier. He was on his way home, too. We were both tired and just wanted to get some sleep, so we didn't talk much.

"That was a horrible night," I said to him.

"Yes, very upsetting. It is a sad country right now."

"Will it get better?" I asked, filling the silence with nervous words.

"I have to think so—but I don't know. It is impossible to say."

We fell quiet for the rest of the journey, kept company only by the intermittent sound of our shoes crunching in the snow.

DIPLOMATIC IMMUNITY

The next day I woke up around 2 p.m. and called Anton to see if he wanted to meet me at the McDonald's near the Kremlin. The largest in the world, and one of the first symbols of capitalism in Russia, this McDonald's was clean, comfortable and staffed with smiling, courteous employees. They seemed to relish working behind the counter, especially with food they loved. To ensure we'd find each other through the crowds we planned to meet at a nearby milk store on Tverskaya. When I arrived, however, it wasn't there. I knew I was in the right place, but for some reason I couldn't find it. I stood in front of an unfamiliar European clothing store, scouring my memory for cues.

"What's up?" a smiling Anton asked as he walked up to me. I hadn't seen him coming.

"Nothing. But, uh, are we in the right place?" I asked, looking at the new entrance.

Anton looked around. "I think it must have been remodeled, and this is it," he said, pointing to the new storefront. "Wow, this looks a lot nicer."

Once deteriorating and colorless, the retail space was now full of life and color, remodeled and reminiscent of stores back home. This was happening all over Moscow, with chains such as Pizza Hut suddenly appearing and changing the downtown landscape.

"It happened so fast," I said, a bit surprised. I watched as a few elderly Russians walked up to the new store, paused, and turned around, seemingly confused. One smiled and admired the colorful coats on display, but the others looked bewildered and uncomfortable. Another walked away, cursing out loud that the products inside were too expensive.

"A familiar story," chimed in Anton, as we crossed the street to get in the long line for McDonald's. "Where I live, one of those markets that only accepts dollars is replacing an old hair salon. By the way, you did great last night, but the fight kind of took over—sorry about that."

The downtrodden feeling of the night before settled over me.

"I had heard so much about the mafia and how evil they could be, but to see it so close was...frightening and disappointing," I lamented.

He put his hand on my shoulder. "As much as I can, I feel bad for the guy who got stabbed, but he chose his lot," he said without emotion.

We stood in line for thirty minutes and finally scarfed down some food. Our conversation was limited as I struggled to think of anything but the events of the previous night.

On my way back to the Metro I passed the old milk store. Deep down, I harbored guilt. The dollars I earned afforded luxuries and a lifestyle most honest Russians only dreamed about. At times like these, I felt ashamed, knowing that they wouldn't be able to enjoy their country as I did, at least not until some semblance of political and economic stability returned. I lingered for a moment in front of the renovated store window, reflecting on the fact that the face of Russia was changing in front of me, and we were all paying the price.

☭

One evening after work, Charlie convinced a bunch of us to go to a downtown restaurant that had recently opened across the river from the White House. It was a Friday night and with two drivers still on call, it seemed like a great idea. Julie vouched for the restaurant, having heard it was an American-style Chinese place, the first of its kind in Moscow. Our driver, Vladimir, however, had a different opinion.

When a few of us piled into the back seat of his car and told him where we were going, he uncharacteristically turned to look at me.

"*Nu, shto?*" he mumbled, almost grunting, asking me what I thought I was doing.

"What's up?" I continued in Russian. I could see he wanted to say something. He looked at Charlie and Clay, who understood only basic Russian, and then back at me. While he often switched from Russian to English depending on who was in the car, this time Vladimir continued in Russian.

"I haven't heard good things about this place."

"Meaning what?"

"Meaning the food is okay, but it is connected to the mafia. It's known for this."

"What level of mafia?" I asked, not sure it really mattered.

"What level? Shit, they are all bad. I don't know. I wouldn't go there, but if you want to go, fine, I'll take you," he muttered, as if he couldn't care less about our well-being.

This got me thinking, especially coming from Vladimir. He was one of our best drivers, and was the one I trusted the most. Not that I didn't trust the others, but Vladimir was unique. When I'd first met him, he was hard to read. He had a quiet demeanor, and a tall, lanky frame that hunched into itself when he walked—and he seemed obsessed with his black leather jacket. Coupled with his lack of eye contact, he seemed a little shady. Yet once Vladimir realized I could speak the language, he opened up. He didn't speak much English, so could hardly connect with the three managers, but we became good friends. He supported a family and had an optimistic outlook on life amidst the chaos that was Russia. He kept his head down, did his work, learned from the people around him, and tried not to get involved in politics or anything related to the mafia.

"Can you speak English so Charlie and Clay can understand what you're saying?" I asked. If we were going to this new place I wanted them to know what we were walking in to.

"They won't understand. You know Russians and have seen what the mafia can do. *They* are clueless," he responded, nodding in the direction of Clay and Charlie. He was annoyed by the situation and wanted no part. He continued, "This is a new place so only mafia and corrupt politicians can afford it. I don't think foreigners go there yet."

"It's okay, we'll be fine. But just tell them. It's more convincing coming from you."

He looked at me and shook his head as if I'd stabbed him in the heart. He hated having to think about structuring sentences in English, but he did his best to describe what he knew. It was no use. Charlie's mind was set.

"We'll be fine. I've heard this place is great. Oh, and I called Jim Minkowski on the way out of the office and he's coming downstairs. He loves the idea of Chinese. You know Jim, right?" Charlie responded, smiling and hitting me playfully on the arm.

I nodded. Jim was a tenant at the complex who had befriended Charlie. A jolly, chubby American, Jim was in Moscow to open a regional office. I had actually spent some time with him and considered him somewhat of a mentor. He was down-to-earth, and the more I ran into him in the complex, the more I realized that he was not only a good listener, but also had a great perspective on career development. I valued his advice and insight.

We pulled up to the restaurant fifteen minutes later. The outside appeared classy, with illuminated red Chinese lettering, a simple rock garden, and a few Asian-style outdoor lamps and benches. In Moscow, even the slightest outdoor décor was unheard of. We had high hopes for a good meal. As I exited the car, Vladimir turned and told me to be careful.

"Thanks, Vladimir. Are you going to wait for us tonight?" I asked, hopefully.

"I wasn't going to, but now I think I will," he responded, looking around at the restaurant. "I need to get some bread and will be back soon."

"Sure, take your time." I tried to keep my usual, confident tone, but since the night in Anton and Nikolai's club, that tone was beginning to sound foolish to my own ears. I knew exactly what Vladimir was afraid of, and for some reason I was pretending it didn't matter.

Upon entering, we were not disappointed. Unlike most restaurants I had visited in Russia, the interior was clean, bright, and welcoming. The floors were newly carpeted, and we were greeted by an outgoing and friendly wait staff. New linens, framed wall art, and small, contained waterfalls added to the overall ambiance. The only problem was that most of the tables were empty. As the maître d' led us farther inside, we noticed only one other table with diners, and of the four men sitting there, chatting quietly, two gave us the once-over as if we were not invited. They wore dark leather jackets, and their companions wore Adidas sweat suits.

We avoided eye contact and kept to ourselves, but their presence was a bit worrisome. We made our way to the table and sat down.

At first glance, the menu looked great. They appeared to have everything I could want from a Chinese restaurant, including Szechuan chicken, fried rice, soups, and great beef dishes. And because good restaurants were a rarity in Moscow, we decided to order a lot. The only remaining question was, would they have the food? Historically, Russians ate meals at home, and without private enterprise and the competitive fire that encouraged continuous improvement, restaurants weren't well run. Now, with capitalism merely taking root, the idea of exceptional customer service was new. Not only were rude waiters common, but often half the menu would be "sold out." Food availability was at the mercy of the distributors, who often were government or mafia controlled, and thus inefficient and undependable.

"Chicken lo-mein, please," Ashley ordered. She was perpetually hungry and wanted to get things moving.

"Sure," responded the waiter. Definitely a good start.

"Shrimp with peapods and a side of wonton soup to start," said Charlie. Seafood was always a challenge in Moscow, so he was testing them.

"Good—rice with your shrimp?" asked the waiter.

Seven of us ordered, and seven of us got the same positive reaction. We were flabbergasted. Restaurants simply didn't operate this way in Moscow. When the food arrived, we were equally impressed with the quality. The vegetables were crunchy and fresh, the sauces were flavorful, and the noodles were cooked to perfection. It turned out to be well-run; the owners had thought through the details and offered what they knew could be supplied. Good décor, a great wait staff, and tasty food. We spent a few hours savoring the meal, downing shots of vodka, and relaxing.

Then we got the bill.

We knew the prices of the dishes; they'd been plainly listed on the menu in rubles. We were used to converting rubles to dollars, but this time, were shocked. We expected a bill of approximately $350, including all appetizers, entrees, and drinks. The restaurant said we owed about $722. They must have made a mistake.

"Waiter, can we ask a few questions, here? It seems we've been double charged for a few items," I called out, trying to sound pleasant, thinking it was an innocent oversight.

He came over and took the check from me. "Hmmm, looks like everything is in order. I don't see any double charges and these *are* the dishes you ordered, are they not?"

"Yes, we ordered these, but let me see one of your menus again," I said, straining to see where the menus were set down. "Can you grab one?"

Ashley spoke up. "Sir, this bill is not right. There must be some kind of mistake."

I noticed Charlie and Jim whispering and got a bad feeling about where this was going. They were both looking at the front entrance, watching the guys from the other table talking with the maître d' as they walked out the door. Meanwhile the waiter walked away in search of a menu we could review together—or so I thought.

Charlie leaned over to me from across the table. "I think we better get out of here as quickly as possible. Those guys from the other table were taking a good look at us and I don't think it's because of the company we are keeping." He tried to joke, referencing the women that were at the table.

"What are you thinking?" I asked.

Julie intervened. "David, this is crazy. There is no way we owe this much! Where is Vladimir? Is he coming back for us? Can't we all cram into his car and get out of here. This looks like a bad situation."

"He had some things to do but planned on coming back for us. If he's not outside, he should be here any minute," I said. "Let's just see what the waiter says when he comes back with a menu. Maybe he will see the error and we'll be fine."

Charlie and Julie didn't look convinced. Again, I heard the false naivety in my voice. I wanted to believe this was an honest mistake. The familiar malaise of disappointment settled over me again. I looked over and saw the waiter whispering with restaurant staff and someone who appeared to be the owner. They looked serious. I waited. They glanced over at us periodically, and made no attempt to find a menu. Finally, one of the waiters approached and said, "Thank you for coming, but we are closing now. I can take your payment when you are ready." He turned and walked away.

We just looked at each other, dumbfounded.

Ashley was obviously concerned. "Unless we do something, this is not going to end well. Those people that were at that other table were not just visitors. Did you see how they were looking at us? I think they have some kind of interest in this place and there is something going on."

Charlie motioned for all of us to huddle closer around the table. "Let's just pay what we think is fair and get out of here—fast," he said emphatically. "Julie, go outside and see if Vladimir is back—now. In the meantime, let's gather the money. Clay and Ashley—you go with Julie and see if you can catch a cab. I know we are in a remote area, but you never know who might be driving by. We could use some luck."

We agreed and began searching our pockets for money. Appeased seeing money on the table, the wait staff backed off. Smiling and acting cordial, the other three walked past them through the front doors.

Together we didn't have the $722 the restaurant was claiming we owed, so we slowly gathered up $435 and in our own heads called it even. We left a pile of cash on the table. There wasn't a waiter nearby, so we had a minute or so until they picked up the cash and counted. We got up from our seats, put our coats on, and shuffled out.

Unfortunately, Vladimir was nowhere to be found. Instead, the mafia guys were now outside, lurking in the parking lot. The four of them were nonchalantly leaning up against their black Volgas, smoking cigarettes and chatting. With their quick glances our way, it was clear they had us on their radar. We walked down the steps and followed a paved path toward the parking area and the street. Their casual appearance turned more focused. They seemed to be looking past us, possibly waiting for some sort of signal.

It appeared they got it. Suddenly, they jumped into action and strode up to us. We tried not to look at them. Our heads forward, eyes looking beyond them, we hoped that one of the oncoming cars in the distance was Vladimir. Before we knew it, these men had blocked our way. When we moved to walk around them, we noticed a few of the waiters had followed us out of the restaurant. We were quickly surrounded by unfriendly Russians.

"You owe us more money," snarled the approaching waiter, following us down the path from behind. "You think you can just walk out on our restaurant without paying? That is not how we do business."

My blood started to steam. I thought about the frustrating growth of the mafia, the pain and fear they imposed on society, and the ruthlessness with which they treated others. I replayed the scene outside Anton's club in my head, seeing the mafia guy stabbing a man twice in the stomach, the man's blood turning the surrounding snow red. My patience for the mafia and how they bullied people was wearing thin, and having drunk too many vodka shots, tonight I was not afraid. I was sick of seeing these ruthless criminals lie, cheat, and steal to impose their will. And the worst of it was that the entire public system seemed corrupt.

"Well, in civilized countries we don't charge guests double what they owe," I yelled in Russian, looking at no one in particular. The waiter caught up to me and I turned to look at him. "You think that because we are foreigners we can't add and don't know what our bill should be?"

"Give us the money! Now!" He was toe to toe with me, and his breath stank from alcohol.

"I'll give you nothing," I retorted, glaring into his eyes, which were at least six inches above mine.

He bellowed something over his shoulder to the owner behind him who slowly approached the both of us.

I knew we had no chance in a fight. Not only was he tall, but he was built like a tank. We had no next move or plan, but in a stroke of luck, three cars pulled up simultaneously, including Vladimir. He was the first to get out, and being smart enough to read the situation, immediately began pleading in Russian, asking for some flexibility from the restaurant owners, arguing respectfully that we didn't understand how things worked in Russia. He was smart to make us look dumb—it was a tactic often used by foreigners who knew they had either broken the law or betrayed a custom, but here it didn't seem to be working. We had already spoken too much Russian.

The other cars that arrived were police officers—but they drove up without sirens or lights flashing. And as they ambled out of their cars, it was clear where their allegiances lay.

By now, the four mafia men had surrounded Clay, Ashley, and Julie, while Ted, Charlie, Jim and I were facing off with the restaurant personnel.

As the police approached all eyes were on them. Nobody said a word and time seemed to stand still as we waited for them to speak.

"Leave them alone," one officer barked, looking at the guys near Ashley and Clay. He hoisted his belt over his rotund belly. "What's going on here?"

The restaurant waiter explained his side of the story in rapid Russian, making it difficult for me to fully understand how he framed the situation. Then the officer looked at me and I explained our side of the story.

"Enough!" The officer cut me off before hearing what I had to say. He was flustered by my drunken Russian. "Pay the bill," he stated, calmly but firmly.

"They overcharged us and there is no way we are paying this bill," I responded, digging in. I was not going to be another victim of the mafia. "You look at their menu and then at our bill, and tell me if there is any way we could owe $700. There isn't!"

The officer wasn't sure how to handle me. He wasn't angry, but raised an eyebrow and had an uncertain, confused look on his round, pudgy face. I don't think he expected my aggressive defense.

"Wait one moment," he finally said in English, holding up his hand like a guard at a crosswalk. He turned away from me, took off his police cap, and slowly approached the restaurant owner, probably mapping out his next steps. Nobody wanted this to escalate into an international incident. As he did this, Jim and I motioned for our friends to get in the car with Vladimir so we would be ready to leave. The meeting broke up and the policeman came right up to me and looked me in the eyes.

"Pay the money or you are coming with us," he said definitively.

"With you? What do you mean 'with you'—I've done nothing wrong!"

"You pay the money, yes or no?" he asked, his face flushing with anger.

"Fuck no!" I retorted. Somewhere deep down I knew the drinks I'd had at dinner were helping with my bravado. But there was something else too: We had done nothing wrong! As an American, I had grown up with a strong sense of justice, ingrained in my being since before I could remember. Intellectually, I knew the world didn't work according to this same sense of right and wrong, but in my heart, I expected it to. Coming face to face with such barefaced criminality set me off.

Without warning, I was flanked by both officers and had a hand-cuff on one wrist. I struggled wildly to escape, but to no avail.

"You can't do this to me!" I screamed. "I'm a diplomat and my government will have your ass for this! You let me go now, or I'll get both of you arrested." I had no idea where the bluff came from, but had no choice now. I was trapped in my own lie.

"Diplomat?" asked the policeman as he quickly released me and removed the cuff. His face softened, and he respectfully asked to see my passport.

I was screwed and I knew it. I didn't have a diplomatic passport on me or at my apartment. I looked at Jim and silently mouthed the word "help!" He ran to the car, where the others were watching. I wasn't sure what he was doing, but I briefly had an image of him jumping in the car and leaving me to rot in some Russian gulag somewhere. I had heard stories about foreigners being arrested for minor offenses but then being incarcerated for months on end. Whether these rumors were true or not, I didn't want to find out.

"I don't carry it with me," I scoffed, as if to say, who would do that? "It's in my apartment, and you can take me there for proof if you'd like." I had no idea where the story was coming from, or where it was going.

"Cuff him and let's go," yelled the other cop. "I don't have time for this." Fed up with me, he removed his pistol from his holster and pointed it at my head.

That's when I got really scared.

He had let his friend do most of the talking, but now, with a piercing look in his eyes, he was visibly angry. Just the sight of the gun made me practically piss in my pants. I couldn't help but think, what if his finger slips or he trips and the gun accidentally fires? As they began forcibly pushing me towards the police car, I broke down and pleaded with them to let me go.

"Hold on, officer, just wait a minute," I whined, trying and failing to stand my ground. "All right, all right, we'll pay. Let me go, and I'll get the money. Wait one minute—let me see what we have."

"No, we've had enough of you. This is it," the one with the gun drawn replied.

Just then Jim ran up to the officers with all our remaining money and practically threw it at them. Julie interpreted for Jim and explained that I was drunk and didn't mean to cause a problem. We would pay with what we had on us, and bring more money if they insisted. We were sorry and just wanted to make sure I wouldn't be thrown in jail.

Jim's conciliatory tone was exactly what the situation called for. The officers looked at each other and then at the restaurant owner, who nodded his approval.

"Put the gun away," one officer bellowed to his comrade.

"Here it is—it's all we have," Jim said, handing the money to one of the officers. "Thank you and we're sorry for any inconvenience," he continued, in his most deferential and sincere voice.

"Most of what they owe is here," said the cop as he approached the restaurant owner. "It's what they have and I think we should be done with this."

"Okay," said the owner and he quickly turned around and went back inside with his wait staff, as if nothing had happened. The police officers followed him inside, most likely to divvy up the proceeds. The fiasco was over.

Back in the car, Jim gave me an astounded look.

"Dave, what were you thinking?"

My shirt was soaked in sweat and my hands were shaking. I hardly recognized myself. "I didn't want to pay them and quite honestly, I wasn't thinking. I am just sick of the way the mafia rules the city. I know. I'm lucky. Thank you for saving me."

"Just keep your mouth shut next time, and think about taking a break from Moscow. We all get frustrated and fed up with how things operate here, but you have to control yourself."

☭

It wasn't the long winters or the distance from home that bothered me. I could tolerate the hardships that Moscow presented. But the mafia-induced corruption was getting to me. And because this was the first time I'd been caught on the wrong end of it, it hit me hard.

In the past, it had seemed almost like a game or an uncomfortable requirement for living here. I bribed an official to get into a museum, was offered cash from a client at work, paid my way out of traffic stops, and even went through the black market to get my visa renewed. As much as I tried to live like a native Russian, I always had my US passport and greenbacks to bail me out, and had consistently been able to use the corruption to my benefit.

For the first time in my life, I felt truly at the mercy of corruption. And in this feeling lingered a deep, lasting resonance with the ordinary Russian. Was this the deep understanding I'd been searching for? If it was, it hurt. Whether you paid an official to live in a specific apartment or for the protection of a start-up business venture, you had no choice but to play along. The Russian spirit was being crushed. Under communism, your fate was determined by who you knew in the Party. Under capitalism the situation had not changed, except now the thugs wore sweat suits.

MY UNCOMFORTABLE FIRST TIME

The struggle for ordinary Russians to provide for their families wasn't just financial, but ethical as well. It was the noose of corruption that drove Babushka to hoard food, my friends at the disco to pay for protection, and businessmen to offer me thousands of dollars in bribe money. The rules of Soviet society that had once been enforced by the government, the police, and the KGB, were gone. Everything was negotiable, and citizens no longer knew what to expect.

A few weeks after the incident at the restaurant, Charlie and I were closing a deal, working late on a Friday night. It was a significant client and took many rounds of negotiations to convince the lessees that the amenities in the complex were worth the price. I checked my watch—11:30. I was tired, but not enough to go to sleep.

"Charlie, what do you say we go get a beer?"

"Definitely. I already asked Vladimir to hang around, so he's downstairs."

"I'll go find him and let him know we'll be a few minutes. Do you have a place in mind?" I wondered aloud, knowing he was more familiar with the nighttime options.

"Um, yes. Tell him we'll be going to my apartment. I want to get some money and change out of these clothes. Do you have cash on hand? You might need it..."

"I'll go upstairs and get some." I kept a stash of dollars and American Express traveler's checks in my apartment. ATMs in Moscow were hard to find and fees were high. "See you downstairs."

Twenty minutes later, Vladimir dropped us off at Charlie's apartment. Charlie grabbed some cash and led the way. Walking silently through a dimly lit neighborhood on our way to the city center, we were lost in our own thoughts. In the distance I could see the walls of the Kremlin, standing tall, creating both a physical and an emotional barrier between the people and its government. The chill of the winter breeze reminded me that the cold Russian winter was ending, and with so much change happening throughout the city, it was an amazing time to be living here.

Our shared respect and common challenges had kept my new colleagues and me close, and more important, safe. These same friends had bailed me out of a bad situation just weeks before. And a deep gratitude for their help that night had settled into my bones, not only soothing away the frustration of the moment, but reinforcing that I had found a support group away from home once again. This notion of community satisfied my thirst for the familiar, even amidst foreign situations. Charlie had my respect, too. Jet-setting home for two weeks every month to see his family, he cared very much about them. Often, when his door was closed in the office, it was because he was on a long call with his wife, who rarely visited. She either didn't want to make the trek or was too busy. I didn't blame her. Moscow was cold in the winter and if you didn't speak the language or have a guide, was a dangerous place to live or visit.

Charlie was similar to many visiting businessmen who didn't have the time to learn the Russian language nor understand the nuances of the culture. He depended heavily on me and other multi-lingual staff to interpret, but he eventually learned some key words and phrases that helped him in day-to-day situations. Professionally, he taught me a lot about negotiating contracts, working with people, and how to navigate a multi-national company. Hands-on when required, Charlie also gave me plenty of leeway to make my own decisions and develop deals as I saw fit. He was my first mentor, and in the process, helped me understand the importance of learning from those with more experience, listening for growth opportunities, and asking questions to generate insightful answers.

With an apartment in the center of the city, Charlie had the flexibility to wander on the weekends, visit museums, and take advantage of what the city had to offer a wealthy American businessman. But unlike many others of his kind, he remained faithful to his wife. Prostitution, once unheard of in the Soviet Union, was becoming a staple of the Russian nightlife. Economic and social change bred all kinds of businesses. Pornographic magazines, both domestic and imported, quickly grew in popularity, gaining distribution even on street vendor shelves. As the market for magazines grew and the underworld saw the opportunity, other sex-based enterprises became commonplace. Many of the new nightclubs welcomed prostitutes or hired alluring waitresses as a means of attracting wealthy clientele. I was pretty pedestrian when it came to anything risqué, but even in my eyes, prostitution was a common, even trite, part of the nightlife here.

These nightclubs were primarily an import of foreign firms from Europe or former Soviet satellite states like Poland that understood the market and its potential profit. Often, they would partner with influential mafia or government groups to grease the skids, and open up businesses. The influence of these firms on Russian society created an uncomfortable reality for me. I believed in capitalism and democracy, but with prostitution and racy nightclubs the most immediate and obvious result, I wondered if it was right for the new Russia. I heard the grousing of friends who watched their society go from orderly and conservative to out-of-control and often in poor taste. I questioned whether this was typical of an emerging capitalist society and if this type of progress tarnished the economic and political maturation process.

Hence the ethical dilemma of the new Russia. As Russian friends explained it, with so many families struggling to make ends meet amid soaring inflation, quite often daughters, sisters, and mothers would strip or prostitute themselves to help the family get by. Most of these women abhorred the work, but felt they had no choice. That's where the money and jobs were, so much so that many women ended up becoming the primary breadwinners in their family.

Charlie and I continued walking silently, and I followed him down the street. "Where are we going, Charlie? Or are we just walking?"

"Jim told me about a new club that opened a few weeks ago down here," he said, pointing farther down the street. "It's around the corner. I've never been but we're meeting him there. He says it's great, so we'll see."

As soon as we turned the corner I couldn't believe what I saw. It was as if I had been transported to New York City. Bright lights and well-dressed people surrounded a new club. Unlike others I had seen in Moscow, this club shed the hard, stone, overbearing Soviet look and welcomed a sleek, Western approach. The façade looked out of place with its shiny, smooth granite next to the older, weathered buildings. The entrance had four symmetrical, square windows built into the front outside wall around the door and a posh, maroon awning. A curtain kept the cold, and voyeurs, out. And similar to most hip clubs in New York or L.A., but new to Moscow, this club had velvet ropes to ensure orderly lines. I was caught off guard.

"Dave, stop looking at the building! I'm right here," laughed Jim, approaching Charlie and me. Last time I saw Jim was at the Chinese restaurant. I hoped he wouldn't bring it up.

"It's just not what I expected, but it looks great!" I replied, mouth agape.

"It is," Jim replied, shaking our hands. "Let's go inside."

Fortunately, there was no line so we walked right in. Most clubs I visited featured typical Russian nightclub décor—dirty, dusty floors, a limited assortment of alcohol, no atmosphere, poor lighting, and an unattended or makeshift bar. But here, it was different. The place was dark, but had just enough funky, colorful lighting that we had no trouble walking around. The music was loud, but not too loud, and the rectangular bar was large, new, and made of fine wood. Clean wine and beer glasses were hanging upside down behind the bartenders, a full complement of liquor sitting behind the bar was visible to all patrons, and the staff was dressed in casual, sexy attire. In fact, as I looked around, all of the employees were female, except for a few large men, whose role was clear.

As we proceeded further into the bar a tidal wave of cigarette smoke rushed towards us. Jim led us past the main dance floor to the back of the bar area to get some beers. As he and Charlie tried to get the attention of the bartender, my eyes acclimated to both the smoke and the darkness. Looking around, I noticed that behind us, even further back into the bar, was a section of several smaller rooms occupied by a few lively groups of patrons. The area we walked through had a few tables set up, but the main attraction was a large square dance floor featuring walled mirrors and a hanging disco ball. Since it was late, the place wasn't all that crowded, and from our vantage point we observed other guys along the edges of the room doing exactly what we were—ogling girls on the dance floor, sipping drinks, and making small talk to pass the time.

I had never seen such an upscale bar in Moscow. And, to top it off, I was surprised to see that all of the women were Russian, while most of the men were foreign. Maybe I was a bit tired, but it took a while for me to figure out that this was the exact type of place I had discussed with friends—a new bar catering to wealthy businessmen. And based on the attire and movements of the women, it became abundantly clear that fun was for sale.

Most were scantily clad, wore heavy make-up, and flirted with us the minute we walked in. Others seemed out of place, standing off to the side, looking uncomfortable and lost. These women weren't dressed as provocatively, and I wondered if they were the mothers and sisters I had heard about. The entire scene struck me as odd. Charlie finally got our drinks and we sat down at a nearby table.

"Quite a place you've found, Jim," I said, hoping for him to expand on how he found it, what he thought of it, and why we were here and not somewhere more conventional.

"Yeah, it's nice and I find it kind of relaxing," he answered.

"Relaxing?"

"Yes. Everyone knows their place. In other words, they know why they're here. There's no games or chasing, it's just fun," he explained grinning from ear to ear.

"I guess," I said, thinking that this was definitely not his second visit. "Are they all prostitutes? It seems like some definitely are, but others don't look the part." I looked at a young woman in jeans and a short-sleeve shirt.

"You know, I'm not sure, but I think they're all available," he responded, looking around the room, evaluating what he saw. He waved hello to someone across the room.

"Her, for example," he said, pointing to the girl who was returning his smile from across the room. "She's a great girl. We met here last week. I just went up to her, started dancing, and we ended up in my apartment for the night. And you know, I can hardly speak Russian, so with her broken English, things just happened naturally." He was boasting now.

"You mean she went home with you last week?" I tried to hide my surprise. Even though I knew Jim to be gregarious and flirtatious, it was tough to get past the fact that he had a wife and kids he loved. But who was I to judge? I had heard about open marriages, so I tried to give him the benefit of the doubt.

"Oh yeah, and she was great in the sack," he answered, proudly leaning back, draining his first rum and Coke.

I had never heard him talk that way nor would I have ever expected it. I looked at Charlie and he at me. It seemed we were both trying to act as cool as possible. Just then, the very woman we were discussing approached.

"Hi, Jimmy," she said in English, smiling broadly and flopping her arm around his shoulders. She was about five-six, had dyed blonde hair, dark eyes heavy with make-up, long legs, and a curvaceous figure.

"Hello, Natasha," he answered in Russian, matching her smile and giving her a kiss on the cheek. "These are my friends, Dave and Charlie," he tried to say in Russian, but I ended up finishing his sentence so she could understand.

We exchanged pleasantries and she continued with Jim.

"Maybe tonight?" she asked, caressing his shoulders.

She got right to the point. You could tell she wanted to say more to reel him in but with their communication gap, it was difficult.

"No, no," he said, kind of laughing, glancing over at us, fishing for a reaction.

As she slithered away, Jim turned to us. "Pretty nice, huh?"

"I guess," I said, uncomfortably. I had respected Jim for his counsel and insights on business, for his career advice, and for his friendship. His choices now were out of character and hard for me to accept.

"So, what do you think of those two?" continued Jim, nodding in the direction of two women dancing with each other rather closely, almost fondling each other, obviously enjoying the attention they were attracting. "Charlie, I'm going to go talk to them. Want to join me?"

Charlie shook his head. "No, thanks. I'm fine." His voice was terse.

"And you?" Jim asked, looking at me.

"I'm not interested," I said. "It's fine for you, but I'm just not into it." In fact, I wasn't fine with it at all, and it quickly became clear that we had less and less in common. His capacity to please himself without any remorse or consideration for his family was shameful.

Jim gave me a mischievous look. "Listen, Natasha was great but I couldn't tell her what I liked or wanted so it was a bit uncomfortable for me. Come over and help me with these two girls. I need you to do some translating."

"I don't know. I mean, I'm not sure I even have the vocabulary you might be looking for," I said. "Are you sure I—"

"Come on!" he said. "All you have to do is talk!"

"Dave, give it a shot. It could be fun. Go do it." Charlie seemed to be enjoying my discomfort. "Go ahead, it's fine," he encouraged. "But, I'm more tired than I thought. You guys stay and I'll see you tomorrow."

I cringed knowing Charlie was leaving me here with Jim.

But Jim knew I wasn't interested so there would be no peer pressure to take the next step. It would simply be a new experience—I'd never spoken with a hooker before.

I looked at the brunette and the blonde Jim was eyeing. Both were thin, almost emaciated, swaying gently to the music, gazing at us, hoping we would approach. From afar they seemed like they could be regular people, but they wore skimpy outfits—one in nylons, a red miniskirt, and a white drop-neck top, and the other in a silvery miniskirt and a skin-tight, black blouse of sorts. They were wearing heels and had plenty of makeup caked on their faces. Their outfits left very little to the imagination, so it was no wonder Jim was drawn to them.

"Let's just try, okay?" he asked, almost pleading now. He didn't wait for a response and grabbed me by the arm, as he tended to do when he really wanted someone to do something, and we walked over.

"Hi," they both said as we walked up.

I introduced us, telling them in Russian that Jim was interested in talking with them, and I was only here to interpret. They immediately turned their eyes away from me to him—they knew who had the money. "Do you speak English?" I asked.

"Little bit," they said, giggling and looking at each other. These two were definitely young; maybe nineteen or twenty, and I wondered if they had done this before. I looked at Jim incredulously and wondered what he was thinking. He was a smart guy and knew HIV was prevalent in Russia. What was he doing? The four of us stood there, each uncomfortable for their own reason, each knowing what the end result could be, but very uncertain of how to take the next step.

"To work?" asked Jim, trying out his Russian and failing miserably.

I corrected him. "Are you both working tonight?" I didn't even consider that they might not be prostitutes, but as I asked the question I crossed my fingers, hoping they would understand.

"Yes." They looked at each other again and smiled.

"Who does he like?" one of the girls asked me.

I hadn't thought of this. "Jim, which one of the girls do you like?" I asked in English.

He looked at me and with a straight face just said, "Both, but let's see what kind of deal we can get."

Again, I was flabbergasted. He truly looked like a kid in a toy store—eyes wide open, smile plastered to his face, rosy cheeks. He was so casual that it became clear that this was like any other night on the town for him. There was no shame in what was happening. It was just business. And when he asked me about getting a deal, I feared I would be stuck here for a while. When Jim negotiated his deal at our complex, it was a long and arduous process. He spent a lot of time pressing on the details. I hoped this would be different.

It wasn't. Jim wanted to focus on the finer points. As always, he wanted to make sure he was getting what he paid for, so he fed me question after question.

"What does each of you like to do in bed?"

"What do you like done to you?"

"Do you mind using food or toys?"

"Is anything off limits?"

"Will you stay all night?"

"Are you interested in each other?"

"Would you perform together for him?"

"Do you know the English words for different body parts, in case it comes up?"

"What is the cost for one? What about both?"

As the conversation progressed, I grew increasingly impressed with my expanded vocabulary, using words I didn't know I knew. I was also delighted to learn a few new words and phrases. When I couldn't come up with the right one, I would either act it out or the girls would help finish the sentence. At one point, I had to bend over to describe a position to ensure we were all on the same page. In another case, I didn't know how to express what Jim was saying so I used an expression to help; friends had taught me how to say, "Suck my dick," but I had never asked anyone how to say blowjob. When Jim asked specifically for that, I simply looked at the girls and said, "Suck my dick" but pointed to him. They quickly put it together and laughed.

By about 1:30, I was exhausted. We had discussed every aspect of the interaction including price, length of time, and actual content of the activities. Jim's attention to detail in this circumstance was a bit over the top. Next thing I knew they were on their way.

Before I left, however, one girl caught my eye. I knew she was probably working, but I just couldn't believe it. Barely taller than me with dirty blonde shoulder-length hair and just a hint of lipstick, she looked like any of the girls that had grown up with me at home. She wasn't provocatively dressed, wasn't hitting on any guys, and was simply dancing alone. I danced with her for a song and then bought her a drink. As we sat down, I began speaking Russian, and her provocative demeanor immediately shifted. She was obviously disappointed. Her best clients were men who were in town for a just few days, didn't speak Russian, and were willing to spend a lot of money. I quickly divulged that I was not that, and let her know if she wanted to move on, I would understand.

We ended up talking for about thirty minutes at the bar. I learned that she was nineteen and was the only source of income for her family. Her dad had lost his job and her mom had never worked, so they were counting on her to make up the lost income. They knew what she was doing, and while they were ashamed, it was their only choice. She had been prostituting for about a month, and while she was upset with her current lot in life, I think the fact that she had friends doing the same thing helped her cope with the situation. She had dreams for a better future, but felt it was her responsibility to help her family now.

As I listened, my heart grew heavy, but I was grateful for her candor. I tried to reassure her that things would get better for her and her family. Her blank response to my empty words spoke volumes. She lived for each day, and simply got through it. That was it. Who was I to know what the future of Russia would hold? Nobody really knew.

I walked out of that bar alone at about 2:30 and made my way slowly down Tverskaya Street to Red Square. I strolled past Lenin's Tomb and followed the brick walls of the Kremlin, pondering the history of the Soviet Union and wondering if Lenin would recognize his country today. Even his people didn't. What would he, resting in his tomb, think of Russia's so-called progress? It seemed that within a few short years, everything was transformed. Development would be good for Russia in the long run—that's what everybody said. If enough of us believed it, would it become true?

As I started thinking about the future of Russia, I also began questioning my own. My original itinerary was for thirty days. Close to two years had passed, and my path seemed as uncertain as that of my adopted country. Both in Russia, and for me, something had to change.

SLEEPING WITH OKSANA

Frustrated with the dangers and complications of Moscow's night-life, Julie, Ashley, and I decided to take matters into our own hands. We planned to host a party. The apartment complex had a common lounge that tenants used for meetings, TV watching, and entertaining guests. With beige painted walls, no artwork, and basic furniture, it was an ordinary space, but had enough room to accommodate a party. Best of all, we wouldn't have to worry about mafia, security, or cost.

Holding a party in the complex meant that it would be open to invited guests and friends, but also to tenants. We had an intriguing mix of lessees. While some were quite accomplished in business, others were a bit rough around the edges. Would my shy friend, the Bangladeshi computer parts business owner, emerge from his shell? And what about the Koreans who tirelessly and annoyingly reviewed and re-reviewed the contract multiple times—would they find such an event appealing? We expected the Argentine business owners to come, as they were vocal about their disappointment with Moscow's scene. And then there were the awkward Russian tenants who supplied halfway-legitimate business papers, and kept curiously quiet, avoiding our Russian security guards at every turn. We knew that many of our more social Russian coworkers would attend, but would they loosen up in front of their American colleagues? The mix of cultures would be interesting to observe.

When the night arrived, we didn't focus much attention on decorating the room. We moved the uncomfortable couches to the sides, brought some tables in from the café, and dimmed the lights. Next, we hooked up a CD player and overloaded one table with bottles of vodka, soda, and beer, and another with pickles, random pastries, and salty snacks. And as the guests started arriving, we realized people liked the idea of an internal party. Not only did our Russian office workers come, but so did all our drivers and many of the off-duty Russian security staff.

As the music blared and the shots were poured, I looked around, thinking how wonderful it was to see so many cultures enjoying themselves together. I watched my Bangladeshi friend, hazy from too much vodka, doing some kind of drunken, hanging arm-type dance with a typically reserved Russian secretary who had become surprisingly seductive. In another area, Charlie was dancing with a young Russian woman, while on the couches, in the corner of the room, a group of off-duty security guards were beating a combined group of Finnish and American businessmen at a vodka-shot drinking game. American music blared, and despite the dull room, the party generated a festive atmosphere of its own.

With the vodka flowing and my inhibitions gone, I took full advantage of the familiar music and threw down some of my signature Michael Jackson dance moves, moonwalking and spinning into the night. And, as I danced, I couldn't help but notice an unfamiliar girl stealing glances at me. I was intrigued when the head of our security detail, a retired lieutenant named Ivan, informed me of her interest. He and I had bonded in the past, as he respected my drive to learn Russian and willingness to interact with his group as equals, not as "the Russians," which had a demeaning connotation. He was a bit long-winded, and despite his typical soliloquies about the danger the mafia posed to society, this time, he stood squarely in front of me and asked if I was interested in Oksana.

"Who?" I asked, concerned that it might be his daughter.

"Her," he said turning and overtly pointing to the girl who had been checking me out. "You don't know her? She started a few weeks ago. Have you not seen her on duty at the front entrance?" His tone implied that I should know everyone on his staff of about fifty. "She's a very nice girl, and has noticed you."

"Never seen her before, but she looks nice," I responded, noticing how red his face was and just how bulgy the veins in his head were. He was a goliath of a man and looked uncomfortably warm in his worn, faded green sweater vest.

He smiled and chuckled to himself. "Good, I'll go tell her."

I grabbed his huge biceps. "What do you mean? Tell her what?"

His overgrown eyebrows furrowed and I could tell he was annoyed. "Do you want to meet her or not?"

"I do. You stay here and I'll do it myself," I said firmly. He was obviously drunk and appeared uncomfortable with his role of matchmaker.

I left him alone and went to talk to Oksana. She didn't speak much English, so we spoke Russian, and she turned out to be quite grounded and kind. Her straight brown hair hung to shoulder length, accentuating her brown, almond-shaped eyes—an Asian influence, possibly Kazakhstani. We did some shots, talked, and danced until it was obvious the party was winding down. Without hesitation or any uncomfortable "what do we do now" moment, we left the party, meandered down the hall, and took the elevator to my apartment.

What ensued was a drunken, late-night bedroom scene not unusual for horny young adults. Once inside we immediately ripped at each other's clothes and landed in bed. Taking a few moments to kiss and explore each other's bodies, we searched for cultural differences that didn't appear. Her soft skin and full breasts were warm, and as she closed her eyes and began to breathe heavily, I could tell where she liked to be touched. As time passed, I could feel Oksana asserting herself with a directness that translated well to the bedroom. I let her lead, and soon it became clear that our sexual desire and passion crossed cultural boundaries. We eventually fell asleep beside each other.

☭

The next morning we woke up disheveled but lucid; neither one of us was hung over. The early summer sun streamed in through the blinds, lighting up the hardwood floors. We lazily sauntered out onto the deck to take in the view of Leninsky Prospekt. Although we weren't close enough to see downtown Moscow, the twelfth floor apartment did provide a nice view of the expansive forest that surrounded the complex. We watched as cars drove past our building towards the city, following the road into the trees, disappearing from sight. Each would end up in the center of Moscow.

Oksana looked at me as if something were on her mind. "So, tell me, why do Americans and other foreigners choose to come to Russia? Don't you know the danger? Why did you come? And, more important, why do you stay?"

I wasn't exactly sure how to answer. The short answer of "because I wanted to" was usually fine, but I decided to tell her the longer version: that I wanted to finish what I had started in learning the Russian language, that I wanted to better understand the people and culture, and that I wanted to learn more about the land where my grandparents came from. When I mentioned my grandparents, her interest grew.

"Where in Russia are they from? Are they alive?" she asked.

"I never knew my father's father, but both of my grandmothers and my grandfather now live in Boston. They were from Ukraine."

"All from the same part?"

"No. I think my father's parents were from Lvov, but I'm not totally certain. I do know that my mother's father, Nate, was from a small village named Shepetovka." I paused, but she was waiting for more. "He actually grew up in Ukraine and remembers a bit about his childhood, but is convinced that the village he once knew no longer exists."

"Have you ever been there, to Ukraine, I mean?" she asked.

"Yes. A few years ago I visited Kiev for a few days, but that's it. I'd like to go and see if Shepetovka is really gone, but I haven't figured out how to get there. You see, my grandfather is sick, so I've been thinking more seriously about trying to find the village he mentioned."

"Did he ask you to do this?"

"Whenever I ask him about the village, he tells me to forget it. I think he fears the worst so he doesn't encourage me to visit."

Oksana walked back into the apartment and plopped facedown on the bed. Her t-shirt rode up, exposing her rounded buttocks. I sat down next to her, expecting some response, but she was quiet.

"What are you thinking?"

She sat up, got dressed, and kissed me on the cheek. "Meet me downstairs at around 2:00 this afternoon." She gave me a cute smirk, as if she were hiding something. "I'll be working the front entrance. I have someone for you to meet."

☭

For me, Saturdays in Moscow were subdued. I kept them open so I could find time to relax alone, recover from a late night at the disco, shop for necessities, or just read. This one was no different. After Oksana left, I watched some TV, visited an open-air market to browse Russian trinkets like matryoshka dolls, lacquer boxes, and Soviet pins, waited in a typical hour long line at the recently opened Pizza Hut, and had a casual lunch. Oksana's 2 p.m. meeting puzzled me. She and I had just met—she hardly knew anything about me, but seemed excited to surprise me with something.

When the time came, I headed down the elevator to the main hallway and wandered to the front lobby. She sat behind the security desk with another guard whom I had seen a few times before. Her hair was pulled back in a ponytail and she looked very professional, but cute, in her blue uniform and red tie. She got all bubbly and excited as I neared the desk.

"David, do you know Yuri?" she asked, presenting him with a hand motion.

I extended my hand and shook Yuri's. "I've seen you around but I don't think we've spoken," I said. *"Ochen preyatno*—very nice to meet you."

He didn't appear to speak any English, so we had a brief conversation in Russian. Probably in his mid-twenties, Yuri had a dark complexion, moustache, and brownish-black wavy hair combed neatly back. He was approximately five-eight, and as we talked, he smiled a few times and noted how short I was. I'd grown accustomed to this in Russia—I was the shortest man most people had seen, and they didn't hold back.

I still felt as if I were missing some key part of Oksana's "surprise."

"So, Oksana tells me you have an interest in Ukraine. Is this true?" he asked more seriously.

"Yes, have you been there?"

"Sure, I am from a village near Lvov, southwest of Kiev. I take the train there a few times a year to visit my family." His voice was a soft mumble. I would learn later that Yuri was a subdued person, and this quiet demeanor was his version of normal.

"Interesting. I'm familiar with Kiev, but have never been to Lvov. You see, my grandfather is from Ukraine—but from a very small town that I'm hoping to find," I explained.

"Oh, yes. I hear there are many foreigners doing the same thing in Ukraine. My brother who lives there tells me this." His eyes glinted with humor. "What do you know about this village?"

"Not much except that at one time there were many Jews who lived there." I wanted to say the word Jew to gauge his response. My journey to Russia had been free of bigotry so far, but I still wanted to be careful.

"I know," he said sympathetically. "Years ago there were many Jews living in Ukraine—actually in my town. But things are different now."

"Do any live there now? I mean, in the city where you're from?" A familiar fear stirred in me, and I recognized it as the same one I'd felt when learning about the Holocaust.

"I don't know. If so, very few."

I explained, "My grandfather is convinced it was wiped out years ago around World War II. The other thing I remember him telling me was that there was a sugar factory in his village."

"A sugar factory?" he repeated. He then looked at Oksana. "What's the name of the town?"

"Shepetovka."

"Shepetovka?" He wanted me to confirm the pronunciation.

"Yes. Shepetovka. Do you know it?"

"Do I know it?" He smiled and looked at Oksana as he asked the question. "Do I know it? Of course, I do—I grew up there!" It then hit me that Oksana had already told him about my grandfather, and he was either trying to get to know me first, or he liked being a little theatrical.

I was surprised. "Is it still there? I mean I guess it must be, yes?" I couldn't believe it.

"Of course. In fact, there is an old town and now a more modern section—it is quite nice. Anyway, let me tell you up front. Oksana told me you might want to visit there and I'm going in a few weeks to visit my family. My brother is getting married, and if you'd like to come, you are welcome to travel with me. I'm sure we can find you a place to stay and you can come to the wedding!"

The discovery was so sudden, and the invitation so unexpected, that it seemed foolhardy to turn down such a stroke of good luck.

"Are you sure about this? Will it be okay—"

"Yes, yes, no problem," he said, waving his hand at me. "You will stay at my parents' house with me. Okay? *Dogovorilis?*—Are we agreed?"

I shook his hand. I turned to Oksana, kissed her on the cheek, and thanked her for making the introduction. Beyond excitement, I was touched at how she took just about the only piece of information she knew about me and gave me a gift not another soul on Earth could have imagined.

NA DOROSHKU!
ONE FOR THE ROAD!

TWO FEET ON THE GROUND

A few weeks quickly passed and before I knew it, I was on the train sitting beside Yuri, bound for Shepetovka. We shared a *cupet* with two other travelers. The four of us looked at each other awkwardly, anticipating a long trip. What would we talk about? I thought of Oksana, wondering if we'd share more time together when I returned. We were both busy but found time to see each other periodically—yet was it enough? I leaned back against the wall and felt an unexpected nudge from the wood paneling behind me. The walls were thinner than I realized.

Leaving the station, the train slowly swayed back and forth and the methodical clanking of the wheels underneath normalized into a steady rhythm. My thoughts drifted to the story my parents had told me a few days earlier over the phone. At first they were taken aback to hear that I was actually making the trek to Shepetovka, but quickly warmed to the idea. With my grandparents now living at my parents' house, my sister Sheryl, our family historian, had recently conducted a series of interviews with our grandfather, Nate. The information she uncovered had created more interest in his story.

As my parents explained over the phone, unlike my grandmothers, who were first-generation Americans born in Boston, Nate Fishbein was born in 1911 in Shepetovka. He had a sister and two brothers, and his father had a good job as a foreman at a sugar factory. Nate's uncle, Israel Spiegel, was a butcher, and whether it was because Nate took an interest in the business, or was named after Israel's father, Nate became his uncle's favorite.

The family lived well and spent a lot of time at synagogue. They considered themselves quite religious, attending Hebrew school, celebrating Jewish holidays, and centering their lives around religion and family. After the Russian Revolution in 1917, and with the growth of anti-Semitism in the region, their situation worsened. Nate's father was imprisoned by the communists for being a member of the so-called bourgeois class, and died in prison of influenza.

Pogroms were not uncommon. Out-of-town farmers would come to terrorize local Jews, often with the intent of injuring or even killing them. Whether condoned by the government or not, they involved fighting, throwing bombs, and burning houses. On one occasion, during Passover, an aggressive group of farmers formed a pogrom near my grandfather's house. As Nate's mother prepared the customary large pot of borscht, a handmade bomb flew through a window. Instead of detonating, the bomb landed in the soup, defused, and the family survived. What might have seemed like a miracle to the family back then was the stuff of legend to me. The way I saw it, my family, including my mother, brother, sister, and all of our future children, owed our lives to that pot of borscht.

Soon thereafter, with the situation deteriorating for the Jews, Uncle Israel and Aunt Sophie decided it was time to leave Shepetovka. They were fortunate to have the money and requisite visa invitation from Sophie's recently emigrated relatives—so, they were qualified to leave. The relationship formed between Nate and his uncle was special, and without hesitation, Nate, and only Nate, was asked to join them on their journey. After bribing a train official, and with only the clothes on their back and some money, the new family hid in a cattle car for two days on their way to Antwerp via Warsaw. There, they boarded a boat to New York where they were processed through Ellis Island and welcomed by friends and relatives. Taking the lead from those they knew, they settled in the Boston area, where a support system had already taken root. And while no formal adoption process was completed, Nate changed his last name from Fishbein to Spiegel, and was warmly welcomed into his new family. While he did hear from his siblings and parents following the move, the letters slowly stopped arriving, and following World War II, he never heard from them again.

As my parents ended the tale, I asked a few questions and learned that Nate rarely spoke of his time in Ukraine, and never of the adoption. I knew he was not an expressive man, and by the time I made my journey to the Soviet Union, he was eighty-two. In all that time, I had never heard him speak any Russian, and we had never broached the topic of his upbringing or his immigration. So upon my insistence, my parents handed the phone to him.

"Papa, listen," I began, enthusiastically, "I know a town named Shepetovka *does* exist. Someone confirmed it for me a few weeks ago!"

"Oh, okay," he responded, sounding apprehensive. I imagined him sitting in his worn easy chair with a newspaper on his lap, open to an article on the Red Sox, rubbing his bald head, or adjusting his oversized glasses as he spoke.

"So, assuming it's the same place where you grew up, if I were to visit this town, what should I look for? Was there a street that you remember?"

"A street?" He yelled into the phone, compensating for his poor hearing and the crackling phone line. "Back then, there were no streets, just dirt roads. I don't know if we called it anything. Why do you want to waste your time going there? I'm telling you, it was tiny and I'm sure the Nazis were there."

What he was saying was probably true, but I wanted to know for sure. I had no real expectation of finding any long-lost relatives, but he did leave behind two brothers and a sister, as well as his mother. When he stopped receiving letters from his siblings in the mid 1940s, everyone assumed the worst. But I wanted more information. And, I wanted to at least see the place where he grew up. Given his age and declining health, I was determined to do it now and to make the most of the visit.

"I know it's not the same as it used to be, I understand that. But if sections of it do exist, what should I be looking for?"

"You won't give up, will you?" he sighed. "Let me think. Yes, I suppose if you need a landmark, my father worked at the sugar factory right there in Shepetovka. It was one of the larger industries in town, so I would look for that."

"Okay—good. What else?"

He was opening up. "We lived across from the factory there, on a dirt road near the river. I don't know what the river was called, but it wasn't a large river, just some water—maybe a stream. We had chickens and goats walking around, but it was nothing special, nothing out of the ordinary..." His voice trailed off.

"I know that your family was religious. Is there anything about the synagogue that you recall? Was it close to your house?"

"Yes, we often spent time there. And I think we lived close, but tough to know for sure. I was young so it's hard for me to remember." He paused. "David, what you are doing is nice, but I don't want you to be disappointed."

"I know, and I won't be," I assured him. "Is there anything else you can remember that might help me?"

"No, it was so long ago."

I thanked him and we hung up. Whether it was the phone connection, the fact that he didn't want to recite his history over the phone, or his fear that Shepetovka didn't exist anymore, he had offered little more than I received from my parents. But at least it was something.

With a long train ride in front of me, I tried to relax and get some sleep. But thoughts of what could lie ahead in Shepetovka, mixed with a sense of what I was missing back home, kept my mind alert and racing.

☭

Since embarking on my trip to Russia, I had never really longed to return home. I was engrossed with a new culture, challenged by a new language, and energized by extraordinary experiences. Loneliness never really set in. I certainly missed the familiar; the people, foods, and easy conversations I was used to having with friends. But now, something about this trip to Shepetovka got me thinking about where I was in my life. Whether it was the long train ride calling up memories of my first weeks in the country or the personal nature of my investigation, I sat mired in thought. I wondered what my brother was up to at Tulane since his motorcycle accident last year. My sister was now working in New York, flying to and from

England on business. I spoke with my parents periodically, but the ocean between us was wide, and without visiting, it was impossible for them to understand or visualize my life. From my perspective, it was tough to really know how my grandfather was doing and how my parents were adjusting to having three kids in different areas of the globe.

I thought of my friends and wondered what they were doing. Many of them had chosen a career or gone back to school and had set their lives in motion toward a specific goal. Were they happy with their choices? Did they keep in touch with each other? And then there was me. Was I on the right track? Where was my life headed? I wasn't unhappy with the choices I had made, but wondered where I stood in comparison to them. This question of whether I was falling behind lingered. I tried to tell myself there was nothing to gain by judging myself, but sitting on the train with nothing else to do, I couldn't help it.

I gazed out the window. The sun was setting over a wooden barn surrounded by leafy trees, which swayed in the warm wind. The countryside looked serene; it was dotted with rotting wood shacks, unkempt and overgrown plots, and grazing animals. I considered the Russian farmers who lived here with no clear way to better their lives. Unlike me, they couldn't simply leave the country to travel, easily switch jobs, or afford the specialized education needed to get ahead. In many ways, they were held hostage by a government in transition and a growing mafia presence that threatened progress. In the near term, their future looked terribly bleak.

A sinking feeling came over me. I started to realize that any comparisons I was making to friends were completely shallow. I had my health, a support system, and the means to do anything I put my mind to. Moreover, my country allowed and enabled me to pursue my choices. Instead of comparing status, achievements, and lives, I needed to change my way of thinking. I had to appreciate the things that were working in my favor, and set a course for myself. I realized that although many of us grew up in similar circumstances, we each had to pursue our own paths to feel comfortable in our own skin. At some point, I surmised, we would reunite, review notes, and find that no track was wrong, just different.

This realization was liberating. Without knowing it, I had always compared my progress to others. Maybe it was natural, but it never felt right. Sitting on that train, on my way to trace my roots, I realized I wasn't lost. I was simply taking a circuitous route to wherever I belonged.

SHEPETOVKA

Although somewhat cathartic, the train ride was long and at times, unnerving. Throughout the journey, I straddled consciousness and was jolted awake by periodic creaking sounds and sudden train movements. Intoxicated passengers shouted from nearby *cupets*, arguing about everything and nothing. Many hours into the trip, while I slept, the train stopped at the Ukrainian border. I had a vague memory of Yuri telling me to remain quiet and still, informing me through my slumber that I was crossing the border illegally. Evidently, he had forgotten to tell me that I needed a travel visa to enter Ukraine. Alarmed but too tired to exert any energy on worry, I followed his direction and fell back asleep. Fortunately, the train conductor checked the neighboring *cupet,* not ours.

A few hours later, I felt something flicking at my head. I sensed the train had stopped and opened my eyes to Yuri hanging over me. "Dave, we're here," he whispered, his face close to mine. Exhausted from the intermittent sleep, I was slow to get up, deterred by his rancid breath. I turned away. If my breath was half as bad as his, I would spare him the torture. The problem with an overnight train was that you shared the few bathrooms on board with everyone, and tended to let personal hygiene slip.

"Okay, I'm up," I groaned, trying not to sound annoyed. I rolled up the window shade to reveal a beautiful, sunny morning. The platform was packed with people of all ages shuffling back and forth, carrying both large and small satchels of beets, potatoes, and other items. About thirty feet from my window was a sky blue building with large windows. The station wore its age in its cracked walls, chipped paint, and bare concrete patches. A constant stream of people flowed in and out of the entrance as people searched for relatives, asked questions of the conductors, and looked to see if this was their train to board. The black letters over the station doors declared, indeed, that Shepetovka existed and we were here. I snapped a picture for my grandfather.

☭

Yuri and I stepped outside, seeking shade from the bright August sunshine. Walking down a side street away from the station, headed for his house, I looked at everything around me yet saw very little. I wanted so desperately to take it all in, but was overwhelmed with emotion. I knew that the pavement we walked on was right here, in Shepetovka, but it felt like it could have been anywhere in the world.

It was close to eight o'clock when we arrived at Yuri's parents' house, a shingled white cottage. The setting reminded me of a Monet—flowers, overgrown vines, and bushes dangled through an old white picket fence along the house, and onto the covered wooden porch. From the outside it appeared small, but as we walked closer I noticed a back addition that doubled its size.

We walked in through the front screen door and were immediately surrounded by Yuri's family. Yuri's younger brother, Alex, came right up to me, gave me a huge bear hug, and began speaking to me in rapid Ukrainian. He was obviously excited about his upcoming wedding. Yuri's father stepped in to calm his youngest son. He was a tall, broad-shouldered man who greeted me with a wide grin and a firm handshake. His round face was rosy, and I felt comfortable with him right away. He introduced his wife, Yuri's mom, who had a pleasant, warm, and welcoming aura. She was more reserved than her husband, and resembled a younger version of a Ukrainian grandmother with her traditional patterned, colorful dress, white apron, and tightly bound hair. With introductions complete, Alex motioned for me to sit down next to him at the large wooden table, and we dug into a waiting breakfast.

That is, they began eating while I took a more cautious approach. I was curious about the food, but tentative. Many of the dishes were familiar. The pickles, brown bread, pastry, and fried potatoes looked appealing, but the mystery meat was different. In fact, I wasn't sure it was meat. It didn't appear to be red meat or chicken, the only proteins I had seen in Russia. It was, however, something meaty. It was whitish-clear, and I lifted a small piece of it with my fork. It was soft in places, hard in others, and very salty.

"What is this?" I asked Yuri's family.

"Pig."

"Really?" I figured it must be some variety of bacon.

"It's the fat part of the pig. We love the fatty sections. Much more flavorful than the meat," explained Yuri's dad.

"So, this is just fat?" I confirmed incredulously, taking a bite.

"Yes, very tasty, no?"

"A bit salty," I answered, smiling mildly.

I was being polite. The fat was just gross. I lifted my glass of water and in anticipation of both quenching my thirst and cleaning my palate, took a few gulps.

"What the—" I vaulted up and spit out the liquid. "*Shto eto?*" My mouth and throat began to burn, and my eyes welled up. I looked around and through my tears saw his dad and brother chuckling. Yuri motioned to his mom to bring me a real glass of water.

"That's not water," laughed Yuri's dad. He took a hearty sip of his own. "This is samogon. Have you heard of it?" He stuffed another bite of the pig fat into his mouth.

Coughing, I reached for a pickle and struggled to get the words out. "I've heard of it, but never tried it." I had heard that some country folk who couldn't afford vodka produced samogon, Russian moonshine.

"We make it here out back—isn't it good?" he asked.

It actually wasn't bad. It seemed somewhat smoother and less flavorful than store-bought vodka.

"I like it, but didn't expect it. Wow. Do you have more pickles?" I asked.

His mom flashed me a knowing smile. "Of course." Yuri proposed a toast to friendship and by 9:00 that morning, I was slurring my words and nicely lubricated for the wedding.

Because Ukrainian is similar enough to Russian, we were able to understand each other. Yuri's family was interested in where I grew up, why I was living in Russia, and what I thought of their country. I fielded so many questions that I felt like I was in an interview. I was their first American visitor and as the time passed, their questions extended to music, Hollywood, and my opinion of Yeltsin. They were hungry to understand what made the West so different and if it promised a better or worse life than the one they led. Ukraine was now an independent nation, and they acknowledged that with this freedom came responsibility. Similar to those I met in Russia, among Ukrainians there was a distant admiration for America, but also a prevailing skepticism. The unknown evoked fear, so it seemed the better they could understand me, where I came from, and what values I held, the more they could embrace what might lie ahead for their country.

I was glad I could allay some of their trepidation, but inside, even as I was trying to evoke positivity, I was afraid for them. These were good-natured people, honest and hardworking. I was scared to think how their perceptions of capitalism would change if they experienced the same growing pains as Russia's; mafia, prostitution, corruption, and fear. The feasibility of exporting the American way of life—one that perhaps didn't match the timeline and sensibilities of other nations—stirred doubts and questions in my mind. I had no answers, only a hope that the entire nation, not just the select few citizens with connections, would benefit from the transition. I wanted Ukrainians to take the very best that America had to offer, and discard the ideas, policies, and ways of life that didn't fit their culture. As the conversation turned to my reason for visiting, the family became animated, even excited for me. They promised to help me explore the town and trace my roots.

After an hour or so, breakfast was over and it was time to prepare for the day's wedding festivities. Before I could even get a good look at where I would be sleeping, a sudden influx of men crowded into the living room. Some were dressed in wrinkled suits, others in faded jeans with t-shirts. Eagerly, they introduced themselves as Yuri and Alex's cousins, uncles, and friends and began talking feverishly about an upcoming event they called "paying the ransom" for the bride. I had no idea what they were talking about, and as the men gathered in the house, they joked about the cash, goats, and other goods they would trade for the bride. I watched intently, trying to understand what was going on. Unable to follow the dialect and slang fully, I was a bit in the dark.

As more and more men showed up, they became rowdy, hugging each other, gesticulating, and giving the groom a hard time. With so many people in the house, it was hard to find room to stand, and many ended up falling onto the nearby chairs and couches. I ended up squished between two large men with thick salt-and-pepper beards who spoke no English, but from what I could understand, were shocked and excited to meet an American.

Soon thereafter, we left the house and made our way to the bride's parents' house. Yuri walked beside me and explained the tradition: As was done in earlier years, the groom had to pay a ransom to get his bride. It was all done in fun, and grooms often showed up with livestock, jewelry, or money to close the deal. The bridesmaids played a key role in the event by protecting the bride from being stolen, resulting in festive negotiations that increased the bride's value. It was apparently an amusing custom that had become a pre-marriage ritual, and anything given in the course of negotiations was eventually returned.

When we arrived, the front door was ajar and the entire horde of men struggled to be the first in and up the stairs. Shoulder to shoulder, they pushed and shoved to get in. Meanwhile, Yuri's father took a more subdued approach, observing quietly and smiling. Slowed by the breakfast samogon, I stood with him on the sidelines, waiting for the melee to subside.

Soon enough, he entered and ambled up the stairs. The other men stepped aside, creating a walkway, and it became quiet enough to hear the boards creak under his feet. Announcing his presence at what I surmised was a bedroom door, Yuri's father yelled for the bride, and instead of the groom, he was the one to commence negotiations. In response, the bride's father hollered back, indicating his refusal to open the door until satisfactory payment was made.

Without delay, chaos erupted. All of the men swarmed the door, and with shouts, calls, and screams of their own, demanded to see the bride.

When those inside again refused to open it, a surge of new pandemonium ensued. The screaming and banging grew louder. Amid shouts, the door would periodically open quickly and then slam shut. Each time it opened the men would throw rubles, kopeks, and American dollar bills through the crack, insisting on seeing the bride. The pushing and shoving seemed crazed—Yuri's dad was at one point pinned against the door, unable to move. This continued for about ten minutes until suddenly the bride's father opened the door, blocked the entrance, and looked sternly at Yuri's dad.

Silence befell the scene. Crossing his arms and standing tall, he sternly asked for more money and three goats to finalize the deal. Onlookers smirked and covered their mouths, trying desperately to suppress their laughter. A handful of rubles were thrown at him from somewhere, hitting his face and falling to the floor. At that, everyone's smiles and laughter could no longer be contained, and the horde rushed through the door. Both families celebrated together, shaking hands, embracing, and recounting the entire episode over shots of samogon.

The wedding itself was comparatively subdued and, in many ways, similar to the American tradition. Relatives from both sides filled a rented hall. The ceremony was brief yet touching, complete with an impeccably dressed wedding entourage, meaningful vows, and a beautiful ring. As we walked into the reception hall, my first sight was of vodka-bottle centerpieces, and I knew it would be a memorable evening.

But just as the traditional music began to play and the atmosphere was becoming festive and rowdy, I was introduced to another unfamiliar custom. Apparently, as soon as the bride and groom were married, they rushed outside, hopped into a car, and sped off. Unaware that the groomsmen and bridesmaids were racing to join them, I stood alone, in the reception hall, taking in the scene. Unexpectedly, Yuri grabbed me by my suit jacket, lifted me up, and within minutes I was in a car with five other groomsmen, on our way to an unidentified location.

"What's going on?' I asked frantically.

Yuri was focused on driving and didn't answer, but one of his brother's drunk groomsmen mumbled something about a forest.

"Huh? Where are we going? Shouldn't we stay at the wedding?"

"No, we're going to the forest. Don't worry, you'll see," another less intoxicated young man answered. "There's plenty of time for the reception later!"

"The forest? What's there?"

They laughed to themselves and didn't answer. Off in the distance a smattering of trees came into view. Yuri took side streets and unpaved roads confidently, and soon he turned onto a dirt path bordered by trees. This wasn't an official roadway, but was more like a grassy trail through the woods, wide and flat enough for a car. About three hundred yards in, the road opened to a clearing surrounded by tall trees. We parked on the edge alongside two other cars, one of them belonging to the bride and groom.

This must have been a secret spot they'd enjoyed as kids, I thought. It was secluded and beautiful—pine needles carpeted the ground and sweetened the air. In the middle was a large stump, and I immediately understood what was happening. Shot glasses were lined up side by each atop the stump, one for every person, with four or five vodka bottles leaning against a nearby tree. Next to the bottles was a jar of marinated pickles. In total, we were about twelve people, everyone smiling ear to ear, congratulating the bride and groom, anticipating what was to come next.

Standing near the shot glasses, Yuri opened the first bottle, poured the vodka and toasted his brother. We stood in a circle listening to his touching rant, which is what it became as he went on and on. All the while, he gazed proudly at his brother. Around the circle we went, toast after toast, drink after drink. When it was my turn, it took all the concentration I could muster to put together a coherent, simple thank you and congratulations. I was well on my way to being drunk. But, as I listened to them revel in their shared experiences, I remembered the good times I'd shared with my own longtime high school friends. No matter the country, these power-ful feelings of camaraderie were universal. The familiarity I felt with my new Ukrainian friends was surprising, and their willingness to include me in their circle, touching. Similar to how I was naturally included in the ransom ritual, nobody here looked at me as a for-eigner or an outsider. Experiencing this tradition, together with others from Shepetovka, was powerful. My grandfather's family might have followed different rituals, but I was able to get a glimpse into how things might have been, through a window of the current villagers' lives.

As the toasts continued, I couldn't keep up with the drinking. I began splitting one shot for two toasts. Pickles were my life preserv-er. Following each shot, I'd chase the vodka with a pickle, leaving a sour but pleasant tang in my mouth.

By the time the toasts were done and we were back in the cars, I was hammered beyond any point I had been in a long time. At the reception, I tried to fight the weight of my eyelids. For a while, I was able to watch relatives dancing to traditional music, forming circles by holding hands, high-stepping in unison, and celebrating together. My body felt heavy, my head was spinning, and it was dif-ficult to talk. Speaking Russian was always a challenge, but now it was unfair to anyone listening. Those who did want to engage in conversation were sorely disappointed. They'd ask a question about life in America or my impressions of Russia, and when I tried to respond, their faces would scrunch up, trying to understand, and when they couldn't, they'd just walk away. I had let myself go, and instead of worrying about sentence structure or word choice, had a great time slurring my words, being misunderstood, and laughing with other drunks. The last thing I remembered from that night was sitting in a chair, shot in hand, laughing at a Ukrainian joke I didn't understand.

The next morning I awoke on a couch in Yuri's parents' house, unsure of how I'd gotten there. I felt surprisingly okay and was excited about the prospect of exploring Shepetovka. Yuri and I planned to walk the city, find the sugar factory, and talk to people who might know something about the historic side of Shepetovka.

It was a glorious summer day, not too hot, with a slight breeze, perfect for walking, so we set out early in the direction of the old town. We made our way through the modern section of Shepetovka where paved roads and well-kept, freestanding houses like Yuri's were the norm. We turned the corner, and a wide, clean sidewalk led us alongside a four-lane road that looked newly paved. Off the edge of the sidewalk grew lush, green, manicured grass covered with bright yellow flowers. We passed what appeared to be a newly constructed red brick apartment building. Mature trees and white flowering bushes bloomed, and further down the street were more apartment buildings, new wooden benches, and a playground.

We reached a beautiful large pond surrounded by large, leafy trees and green brush. People walked hand in hand, frolicked on the wooden pier, or enjoyed the natural scenery from benches. The air was fresh and invigorating. Shepetovka seemed so vibrant, yet to my grandfather, this place had been lost forever. Could it be that he knew it still existed but because the people he knew and the places he frequented were gone, it was dead to him? Maybe he'd prefer I find nothing, allowing him to leave it in the past.

I grew more curious and intrigued as we approached the older section. When we came to the point where the road literally ended and became dirt, Yuri didn't need to tell me we'd arrived. While the broader surroundings didn't immediately change, the paved roads and sidewalks gave way to the dried, sun-cracked dirt of the historic district. This was the Shepetovka my grandfather knew.

We walked the empty road, looking for a sugar factory. Although not as beautiful and well-maintained as the new section, the old city, with its narrow roadways, older buildings, and overgrown shrubbery, had charm.

"Yuri," I said, "before my grandfather was adopted, his name was Fishbein. Is there any place here in Shepetovka where we can research the name to find out what might have happened to his relatives?"

"I don't think we have anything like that. The one thing I would say, however, is that this is a very small town, as you can see. We can ask people."

"Just ask people on the street?"

"Yes, I think that could work," he said, shrugging his shoulders. "People here are very nice."

"But just think of your family. They've lived here for a few generations, and when we spoke yesterday they had never heard of the name. You really think it might mean something to others?" I asked, looking at him and shielding my eyes from the sun.

"Yes, and remember, we are not Jewish. That's probably why the name was unfamiliar."

"True. Okay. I'll ask." Soon enough, amid the growing heat of the day, Yuri and I were stopping and talking to all sorts of people on the street. We chatted with young families, elderly residents out for a stroll, and people rushing to work. Encouragingly, they were all open to speaking with us, but nobody recognized the name. It was interesting to see how warm and friendly these people were in contrast to Muscovites. In the big city, eye contact was shunned and people rarely spoke to each other on the streets—and if they did, it was either to express anger or frustration with their lot in life. Here, they welcomed me with hugs, handshakes, and a simple joy that an outsider was visiting their village.

People listened, smiled, and I could tell they wanted to help, but no leads surfaced. At one point, I approached four elderly ladies sitting on a bench near the sidewalk in front of a lush area of bushes and trees. They appeared nice enough, each wearing a colorful, patterned dress, holding their worn satchels, quietly chatting amongst themselves in the summer sun. The lines on their faces intimated age and wisdom, while their eyes were welcoming. As I started talking they smiled wide, showing their priceless silver and gold teeth. I told them why we were here and what we were looking for. They seemed to listen intently, looking at me directly, but as I continued their faces appeared confused. When I finished my explanation, they just sat there looking at me blankly. I asked Yuri for help.

"Who are you?" one stoic lady blurted out in a tough, deep, challenging voice.

"As I said, my name is David, and I'm an American looking to trace my roots."

They looked at each other. "American?" they asked.

"Yes," I answered.

Then one lady stood up, approached me, and without warning hugged me close. Holding on for only a few seconds, she released me, stepped back, and sat back down on the bench.

"We've never met a live American. And you know, we couldn't understand what he was saying. He speaks Russian but his accent makes it hard for us to understand. You need to help him learn Ukrainian," she said laughing, looking at Yuri.

The ice was broken, and Yuri and the ladies began having a boisterous discussion. I caught a few words here and there, but nothing seemed to be relevant to our search until the quietest of the four ladies spoke up.

"I know a Fishbein. She lives in my complex behind us to the right," she said as she pointed behind her.

Yuri and I looked at each other.

"No, you don't," argued the loud overbearing one, motioning for her friend to stop talking.

"Sure, I do," said the quiet one. She acted demure, but seemed satisfied that she knew someone the others didn't.

"Maybe she does," chimed in the other two, looking at the defiant one, eyebrows elevated.

"Really? Can you take us to meet her or tell us which way to go?" asked Yuri.

"Of course I can," she said confidently, crossing her arms and looking down.

I couldn't believe it. I never thought I might meet a long-lost relative, so I approached this development with skepticism. Yuri and I listened to her directions and walked along through the grass behind the bench over to the nearest multi-story apartment building complex. As in Moscow and St. Petersburg, this one had high concrete archways that led into a poorly manicured grassy courtyard and parking area surrounded by four wings of the complex.

The building looked to be slowly crumbling: Windows were cracked, doors were coming off their hinges, and overall it appeared dilapidated. The lady on the bench was able to give us the exact wing the Fishbein she was thinking of lived in, so we searched for the correct entrance. True enough, we found the name on the buzzer, and because it was out of order, walked up a few flights of stairs and down a long hall to get to the front door. I knocked.

It didn't take long to hear someone shuffling around inside.

"Hello, who's there?" asked a tentative, older woman.

Yuri briefly explained who we were, and she unlocked the latches to her door. Standing in front of us was a middle-aged woman with short brown hair and brown eyes. Her appearance matched her apartment, clean and neat, and the terrific smell wafting through the room hinted that she was in the middle of cooking a meal. She stood about five-six, and asked us to come in and sit down. As I shook her hand I couldn't help my eyes from darting up and down her face, searching for some resemblance.

Her apartment was small but comfortable. I sat in a chair and looked around. Noticing her family pictures, I tried to find anything within them that could provide a familial link. Nothing. She had simple furniture in the living room, a nice wooden dining table, a curio cabinet filled with dishes and trinkets, and a divan with the traditional, colorful, hand-woven rug hanging behind it on her wall. I explained in more detail who I was and the circumstances of my visit. I described my grandfather by appearance and then explained when and why he came to America. I let her know that he had two brothers and a sister, and that his father worked at the sugar factory.

She listened quietly, processing the information. I could tell she was trying to determine if there was a connection besides a shared name. Her face was expressionless, not giving off any clue whether or not she was happy, sad, or indifferent to my explanation.

"You know, many people have come to my house. Mostly Americans. But, yes they've come. They ask questions and are looking for relatives just like you. Some come with families, others like you, alone. I have met many people, but, thus far, none has seemed to be a relative." She paused again and glanced at Yuri and then at me. "I don't know if Fishbein is a common name, but it seems many people are looking for relatives of this name."

As I listened, I thought of her age. She was too young to be my grandfather's sister, too old to be his grand-niece, but it was wholly plausible that she could be his niece.

She continued. "And, based on what you are saying, I don't think we are related."

With that, I began respectfully asking her about family lineage, religious affiliation, names, and memories. I couldn't just walk away without knowing for sure. But as we spoke, nothing seemed to line up.

"I'm sorry. You seem very nice, but the names you have mentioned are just not familiar to me."

"No need to be sorry," I said a bit frustrated, but knowing it had been a long shot. "It was nice meeting you. Do you know of any other Fishbeins here in Shepetovka?"

"No, no I don't. But you might try the synagogue near the sugar factory. They might know more there," she suggested.

"Synagogue? You mean there's still a synagogue here in Shepetovka?" I was in disbelief. I looked at Yuri, who shrugged his shoulders. It was a discovery to both of us. My grandfather had mentioned one, but I assumed that it, too, had perished in the war.

"There are far fewer Jews than there used to be, but there are some, and they might be able to help."

Excitedly, we thanked Mrs. Fishbein and went on our way towards the synagogue.

☭

Yuri and I walked deeper into old Shepetovka. Apartment buildings, once comparable to those in the newer section of town, were in need of fresh paint, spackle, and general maintenance. Untended bushes and grasses grew high and out of control. We passed a dilapidated bakery and stopped in to get directions. The employees were warm, open, and genuinely interested in helping. In fact, the ladies working there gave us a tour of their backroom, which was stuffed with huge bags of flour and sugar, stacks of pots and pans, and a few large, shiny ovens. They beamed with pride as they showed off a giant pink and white frosted cake. With refined directions and a loaf of fresh bread in hand, we were soon on our way.

Meandering along dirt roads, over small, grassy hills, through overgrown brush, and after passing a few older, crumbling storefronts, we found ourselves a bit lost. We stood in front of an unremarkable, faded red structure. Its facade had inlaid columns that had once been white. We walked around the side of the building looking for anyone who could help, but it seemed deserted. In fact, we couldn't find a door that opened—but finally, Yuri noticed a back door with a small blue sign. It bore a small Jewish star and read "Synagogue of Shepetovka." We had stumbled upon it, and without the sign, would never have known it was there. The building had no other stars of David, nor any other markings that would signify a Jewish establishment.

Next to the sign were a few stairs leading to a heavy metal door. We knocked, but nobody answered and we heard nothing. A bit dismayed, we hovered outside the door, uncertain how to proceed.

Without warning, someone banged against the door from inside. Stuck, the old door needed a few good kicks to get it moving. Soon enough, it was pushed open and out popped an elderly man. Like my grandfather, he must have been in his eighties. He wore dark-rimmed, oversized glasses and a small brown fedora that matched his suit. He had gentle, understanding eyes, and before he even uttered a word I could tell he was a nice man.

"Hello," he said questioningly, obviously a bit surprised at our presence.

Yuri explained who we were and asked if this indeed was the synagogue of Shepetovka.

"Yes, yes, this is the synagogue. Please come in." And he led us into a small room where three other old men were sitting around a beat-up wooden table. The small, rectangular room was set up as some kind of backroom meeting area. The floor was dusty and the room smelled mildewy, like it desperately needed an influx of fresh air. To the right of the table and against the wall stood a desk that had piles of papers, candles, yarmulkes, and prayer books on it. A few full bookshelves lined the opposite wall to my left and behind the seated men was a door that probably led to a larger room for community prayer. As I looked from face to face I saw that these men looked like my grandfather's contemporaries. The lines on their drooping faces were pronounced, their movements tentative, and their eyes curious. They sat wearing loose-fitting suit coats, slacks, fedoras, and button-down shirts. One had a white beard; the others were clean-shaven. Without saying a word, they motioned for us to sit down.

Their eyes gravitated toward me and I felt a bit uncomfortable. One reached over and gently touched my camera bag and backpack.

"Hi. My name is David Kalis and I am from the United States. I grew up in Boston, a town on the east coast," I stated tentatively.

They looked at each other, smiled, and nodded in approval. It was a good sign for me, as it meant they understood my Russian.

"My grandfather and his family came from Shepetovka. He lived here until he was nine years old and then immigrated to America in 1921. We've been looking for anyone that may know of the name Fishbein or Spiegel. From what I know, they were active in the synagogue and my grandfather's father worked at a sugar factory. Is there a sugar factory near here?"

I was hoping to see some spark of familiarity from any one of their faces. They began looking at the ceiling and down to the floor as if trying to browse through their library of memories, attempting to find a match. Watching them, I realized these men could have had a shared experience with my grandfather, could have known him or his father's family directly, or could know what happened to the family. One man looked at me. He didn't speak, but seemed to study my face.

"I do not remember your grandfather specifically, but if his father lived on the road across the street from the sugar factory, I think I knew this family. Of course, this was many years ago, but I recall a family with shorter men like you, and they were hard workers."

I was excited. My grandfather was a hard worker, always fixing and fiddling with things in the house. "Was there a river near the sugar factory? I was told that he lived beside the river and near the sugar factory."

"Yes, when you go look at the factory, across the street was a river. It is mostly dried up now, but it was there."

"Do you know what happened to that family or to anyone in it? Could there be relatives here or near here?"

"Young man," he responded respectfully, but with authority, "the synagogue you stand in today used to be filled with many worshipping Jews. It was a beautiful place with new scrolls, ornate walls, stained glass, and prayer books. You see what has happened? Today, we are a very small community. We once had forty thousand Jews in the region. Now, we have maybe five hundred. There was a long history here, and now it is gone."

He paused and I looked down, almost ashamed. They had lived through more than I could comprehend. What I had learned of the Holocaust in school was their reality. Their entire community was destroyed, and I came asking about one family. I should have done more research and found some way to help their community. Instead, I was asking for things from them.

He continued, "Many Americans come to Shepetovka looking for their roots. This is very common. I tell all of them about our town and what has happened. The Jews in this area were mostly killed in the Great War, and this synagogue and the few Jews that are still here remain. Unfortunately, soon we will be gone, too."

I paused as Yuri asked a few more questions, which didn't shed any more light on the situation, but gave me time to reflect. He then paused and looked at me.

"Thank you very much for sitting with me and talking. It means a lot. You look like you could have been friends of my grandfather's, so it's encouraging to see you here, at the synagogue and in Shepetovka," I said. I wasn't sure if they were bothered by me or appreciated my questions, but I knew I would not be visiting Shepetovka again anytime soon. I had only one more question, and then I would leave them alone. "I don't mean to take more of your time, but is there anything else I should see while here that may help me understand what happened to my grandfather's family or any way I could see where they might have lived?"

The man with the dark-rimmed glasses who greeted us at the door and the other man who had spoken up, looked at each other. They got up and slowly walked out the door. "Would you like to see the cemetery? We may be able to find some information there. I know there is a list of the plots, so it is worth a try," said the man with the glasses. Yuri and I looked at each other. Another lead?

Following our guides, we exited the back of the synagogue and walked onto a dirt path that led us into a wooded area. As the path narrowed, we walked single-file to avoid the heavy brush and damp, muddy patches on the ground. The path soon widened and we walked four across up the hill and around a bend. From our vantage point atop a ridge, we could look down into the distance and see a rolling field, tall trees, and even further on, some small houses.

Within a few minutes I noticed a white cement wall to our right. Portions of it were visible; others were covered with brush. It stood approximately five feet tall, so at times I could look over and see various shapes and sizes of headstones. We followed the wall for about ten minutes until we reached the main cemetery entrance, a white cement arch with a connecting iron gate. Passing under the arch, I realized we were at the top of a hill overlooking a cemetery that descended onto a field.

As I studied a few of the weathered headstones, a rotund elderly woman emerged from a small wooden hut, waddled over, and struck up a conversation with our guides. She was the cemetery caretaker and informed us that while we were welcome to stroll the grounds, we probably would do so for hours without any guarantee of find-ing a specific plot. She explained that half of the graves were actually under water from a flood that took place years ago. She didn't know of any Fishbein or Spiegel in the cemetery, but she admitted her knowledge of the cemetery was incomplete, and that they could, in fact, be there. We asked about a register or plot list, and without hesitation, she returned to her shack and brought it over to us for review.

As soon as we opened it, we knew it wouldn't be helpful. The register was a paper notebook that listed plots, years, and people buried in the cemetery in pencil. With many entries smudged, faded, or simply gone, it was difficult to decipher. In fact, as she admitted, it was not a complete list and was in no particular order. It did include the most recent years of burials in order, but the data earlier than the 1970s was essentially gone.

It was disappointing, but helped me realize that this was the reality of living in a rural town in Ukraine. What they lacked in data and resources, they made up for in hospitality. I walked a portion of the cemetery with these elderly men, each of us focusing intently on the headstones. Many were adorned with Star's of David and had familiar Jewish names, but we couldn't find a Fishbein. After about thirty minutes of searching, I glanced over at the hunched, aged gentlemen helping me. I could tell it wasn't physically easy for them to continue looking, so we stopped and headed back.

When we returned to the synagogue, we thanked them profusely and let them know we had one more stop: the sugar factory.

As if on cue, one of them immediately chimed in with directions. "If you follow this path up and around and then through the brush over there, you will find a dirt road," he said pointing in the opposite direction from which we had just come. "Follow that road to the left as it winds around, and soon enough you will find the sugar factory. I am also happy to tell you that it is still working, so at least you will find something you came for."

☭

Within fifteen minutes, we found ourselves before an expansive factory complex. This had to be it. Amidst small, unkempt houses stood a number of large, well-maintained, brick buildings with smoke stacks. Metal piping protruded from some of the buildings, and one white building with small windows and laundry lines appeared to serve as basic housing. Seeing the sheer size of the factory compared to other structures in the old section of Shepetovka, I could see why Nate remembered it. This was also where he learned his work ethic, where he played as a child, and where he bonded with his brothers, sisters, and friends.

I slowly walked along the factory fence and looked for the dry riverbed. Our approach was from the back of the complex but as we neared the entrance, I saw a dirt road running parallel to the main gate. Across the street was a broken-down shack, maybe a storage center, with spare wood pieces and metal tools lying around. It seemed abandoned and disorganized, but just behind it I could see a grassy slope that fell into a ravine and then proceeded higher to level ground. At the lowest point was a trickle of water, and alongside it, goats grazed.

We walked down the slope and then back up the other side, passing the goats and feeding them a bit of the bread we carried. Nate said he lived on a road near the stream and across from the factory. I thought that was where we were, but we couldn't find any roads. Searching the higher ground on the far side of the ravine, away from the factory, Yuri and I walked alongside what we thought was a forest. We made our way back to the entrance of the sugar factory and looked again: It wasn't a forest.

While lush and many trees deep, behind the leafy trees appeared to be an opening. We ran down the dirt road that extended along the front of the factory, and lo and behold, behind the trees was a small street running alongside the slope.

We strolled down the dirt road—more of a wide muddy path. It was lined with charming older houses, all made of wood and no larger than a few rooms each. Only a few had fallen into disrepair, with rotting porches or roofs that needed fixing. Some had a fresh coat of colorful, bright, paint, and in a faded, rustic way, reminded me of gingerbread houses. Most had weathered, white, picket fences, laundry strings hanging in the yard, and gardens full of flowers. Chickens and goats roamed free.

We approached two middle-aged women who were chatting over their fences, and introduced ourselves. Our script was rote by now.

One put down her basket of flowers to think, while the other peered at us in disbelief, hands on her hips. And while none of the names were familiar to them, they were very friendly. In fact, after talking for a while, one of the women ran inside and came out with a few packets of sugar made at the factory. She insisted that I take them home for my grandfather to see.

☭

Whether I'd actually found my grandfather's street, my trip to Shepetovka had a tremendous effect on me. As Yuri and I slowly strolled back to his house, he helped me talk through many of the things I was thinking, but had yet to articulate.

"*Nu*," he said thoughtfully, "are you disappointed we didn't find relatives?"

"No. I wasn't expecting any huge revelation. I mean, that would have been amazing, but I never considered it realistic. When we got on the train in Moscow, I had no idea what to expect, but this weekend has been an incredible journey." I struggled to find the right words. "I have to tell you that I loved gaining a better understanding of where my grandfather came from. The community I met—men in the synagogue, ladies on the street, your family—was inspiring. The people of Shepetovka welcomed me with open arms, and their warmth was so genuine. Thank you for inviting me, allowing me to be involved in the wedding, and being my tour guide today. It's something I'll never forget."

"It was nothing," he mumbled, looking down, a bit embarrassed. "So, you liked the wedding?" he laughed, changing the subject. "The drinking wasn't too much?"

"I loved it. Seeing your rituals come to life made me think that in some ways, even though Jewish weddings are different from Russian Orthodox ones, I got to experience how weddings are celebrated in Shepetovka. And the drinking? I did okay, right?"

"Yes, you did!"

Yuri paused as if thinking about what he wanted to say. "You know what got me thinking even more today? When we spoke with those men in the synagogue, I was heartbroken," he said, baring his feelings. "I don't know many Jews, and growing up here, I didn't then, either. I had heard of Jews, but never asked questions about where they went or anything. To think there used to be forty thousand Jews in this region, and today we went to the synagogue and there were four old men? To me, that's very sad."

"I know," I said softly. "They did say there were about five hundred remaining, but I have to think most of them are older. It makes me realize how dramatically things have changed since my grandfather grew up here."

We walked in silence, but I kept thinking of many things. Even though Yuri knew I was Jewish and he accepted me as a Jew, I hesitated to fully open up to him.

More than anything, this journey challenged me to think deeply about my heritage and the significance of passing down traditions from generation to generation. My Jewish identity always existed within me, but never in such a meaningful way. Seeing firsthand the impact of the Holocaust on my ancestors made me think differently about interactions with my grandparents, and strengthened my connection to them. The trip conjured up vivid memories of my grandparents saying things like, "David, I have a nice Jewish girl I want you to meet," or asking, "Who are you dating? Is she Jewish?" They always seemed to be poking or prodding, but never really insisting—yet by mentioning it, they let me know in their own way that it was important to marry someone Jewish.

"What about love?" I would ask them. "Isn't love important?"

"Yes, but finding both together is best," they would reply.

I never really understood why this was so important, until now.

For some reason, whether they didn't have the time, or thought it was too complicated to explain, they never mentioned that their parents grew up in villages that were eliminated. They didn't talk about the fact that my grandfather's family, who stayed in Ukraine, was never heard from after the war. Maybe they didn't want to scare me. Maybe they assumed I knew. Maybe it was my fault for not asking or being more curious. Either way, I wish we had discussed it.

Most likely, they saw that despite my Jewish upbringing, my connection to religion was tenuous, so they didn't want to be overbearing. I went to Hebrew school as a kid, but never enjoyed the experience. I became a bar mitzvah at thirteen, but recall it being more about the gifts than about assuming the responsibilities of a Jewish adult. I went to Israel as a teen, but focused more on meeting girls than on connecting to my heritage or the nation. I even learned about the Holocaust as a young adult, but after watching footage and reading the graphic accounts of genocide, I still considered it merely history. Embarrassingly, it made only a marginal impact.

Through it all, what I failed to realize was that my grandfather had lived the tragedy of the Holocaust. To him, it wasn't just history; it helped shape his life—and now it was part of my life, too.

Seeing, touching, and walking through Shepetovka made things real for me. Speaking with Jews who were struggling to keep their community alive was not only powerful, but motivating. What my Jewish education and childhood experiences couldn't instill in me, this journey had. Suddenly, my career and professional life paled in comparison to knowing my roots, traditions, and heritage. I saw that I was part of something greater than myself—a religious and cultural tradition that had survived despite the horrors of persecution. I decided then that I not only wanted to marry Jewish, but wanted to emulate my parents in building a family close to other relatives, so we could share in celebrating the Jewish holidays—together. I started to understand that I had a responsibility to ensure that my family's traditions, beliefs, and memories were passed on to my children. It was a heavy thought, but instead of weighing me down, it provided inspiration, pride, and purpose.

Days later, I returned to Moscow with a stronger awareness of who I was and who I wanted to be. The past few years of my life were gone, but this journey to Russia, and especially Shepetovka, had unintentionally helped me find a course for my future.

RISKING IT ALL

I returned to Moscow, to a job that now seemed tedious. Speaking a foreign language, meeting people from around the world, and living on my own in a foreign land had somehow lost its luster. I continued to enjoy Moscow's nightlife, but often my drunken thoughts and late-night conversations would lead me to serious territory. I questioned how much longer I should stay abroad, what was next for me, and who I wanted to become. Whether it was my newfound recognition of my roots and what it meant for my future, or the fact that I had lived in Russia for over two years now, my priorities were shifting.

It was during that summer of 1993 that I challenged myself to envision my life in ten years; where I wanted to live, what I wanted to be pursuing professionally, and the type of family life I'd want. To even think in decade-long increments was initially strange, even ludicrous. But as I sat down with more experienced businesspeople whom I'd met in Russia, they pushed me to establish longer-term goals, with specific steps on how to achieve them.

Still fresh in my mind, I wanted to integrate this goal-oriented thinking with the perspective I found in Shepetovka. To procrastinate would be to ignore a whole new part of myself. Oksana, whose advice and compassion had led me to Shepetovka, was now out of the picture. Our brief time together was special, but deep down I knew she would not be part of my long-term plan. I looked back on two years in Russia and four years in college—six years in which I couldn't articulate who I was or where I was headed—and felt that familiar sense of frustration dissipate. Taking steps towards a goal allowed a feeling of optimism to settle in its place. I was on the verge of something, and for once, I was calling the shots.

❧

Russia and its charismatic, populist leader, Boris Yeltsin, were also facing change-oriented challenges in the summer of 1993. Since assuming the presidency in July of 1991, Yeltsin had pursued both an international and domestic agenda. To his credit, he had many early international successes: the formation of the Commonwealth of Independent States, securing ownership of the former Soviet Union's permanent seat on the United Nations Security Council, and occupying former Soviet embassies abroad. At home, however, he faced ongoing challenges. His desire to continue pursuing policies that focused on economic reform was genuine. But even as he tried to consolidate power by surrounding himself with supporters who could pressure the legislature into accepting progressive policies, hardline foes consistently challenged him.

As early as 1992, Yeltsin found himself in a power struggle with the legislature. The opposition, led by Ruslan Khasbulatov, a nationalist who had the support of former communists, was determined to rework or possibly abandon economic reform. Khasbulatov quickly became Yeltsin's staunchest critic, highlighting the negative effects of Yeltsin's current policies. Increased violent crime, rampant corruption, skyrocketing inflation, and food shortages were pushing citizens to a breaking point. Khasbulatov represented their opinions and in an effort to weaken Yeltsin, pressed for increased legislative power. He argued that the 1978 constitution be upheld, and that parliament, not the president, was the most powerful arm of the Russian government.[9]

As the summer of 1993 came to a close, the constitutional conflict intensified into a bitter dispute. Yeltsin showed his frustration by taking the extraordinary step of claiming to dissolve the parliament and announcing new legislative elections.[10] Parliament responded by meeting in an emergency session. It voted to impeach Yeltsin, and elected Alexander Rutskoy, a Khasbulatov supporter, as acting president. With this, the constitutional crisis reached a boiling point. By October 4, civilian protestors supporting Khasbulatov barricaded the Russian parliament building, *Bely Dom* or White House, where the legislative body sat. Inside, Khasbulatov and his allies convened, not knowing if the tension outside would result in violence. Ironically, just two years earlier, Yeltsin had stood on top of a tank outside the same barricaded *Bely Dom*, defying the plotters of the 1991 coup, resulting in his well documented rise to power over Gorbachev.

That morning, October 4, I strolled lazily out of the tennis court into the main corridor of the real estate complex leading a group of Finnish executives to the exit. Despite my lethargy, I was confident the showing had gone well and that they would return, but in the back of my mind I wondered: *So what? Do I care?* My motivation had waned, but I continued working in good faith. I saw them to the door and after stopping in to the small grocery store and leaving unsatisfied, walked back to the office.

Over a year ago, the mayor of my hometown of Newton, Massachusetts had brought me a case of Fig Newtons while visiting Moscow, and I was craving a cookie. I opened one of the remaining treats, but alas, it was as expected, crumbly and stale. I ate it, anyway. Peeking into the usually busy waiting room, I was surprised to see no clients. Julie, Bill, and Clay hovered intently over the small TV.

"What's going on?" I asked.

"Something's happening near the *Bely Dom*," Julie said. "We're not sure yet, but it appears the military is preparing to surround it. Look—there's people milling about, but you can also see tanks approaching from outside the city."

"Really? Loyal to whom?"

"We think Yeltsin, but aren't sure. I think Khasbulatov is making a power play and won't leave the building," she continued. She enjoyed being the informed one of the group, and I could hear the self-satisfaction in her tone.

"You mean he and his supporters are in there?"

"That's what they're saying. It's unclear how many, but some," she said, eyes glued to the TV. "And, it appears those outside the parliament are trying to protect him in some way. It's as if they want to barricade the building so those loyal to Yeltsin can't get access to it."

Tanks were stationed across the river from the *Bely Dom*, a few armored cars idled near the building, and strangely, as Julie had mentioned, it seemed a crowd was growing at the front entrance. Nothing dramatic seemed to be happening, but with more and more military vehicles moving in from bases outside of Moscow, the afternoon promised to be quite interesting.

Clay looked at me and raised his eyebrows. He gently touched his reddish-brown mustache and smirked. I knew that look. He and I had become close over the past few months, visiting new bars, talking about life pursuits, and playing tennis. He was adventurous and lived every day like it was his last—squeezing as much opportunity and fun from it as he could. I nodded, but as we turned to leave, Julie tore into us.

"Oh, no!" she yelled, wagging her finger in our faces, "you are not going down there!" I had been at the center of the 1991 coup, after all. Clay was not necessarily hoping for an internal Russian conflict, but because he had been living in Texas in 1991, and had missed the coup, he vowed that if anything similar happened again, he would be there.

"We'll be fine," I explained. "Look at all the people gathering. We'll stay across the river so we can just get some pictures."

"Why would you go down there? It's stupid. You have no idea what's going to happen. Don't go." She was pleading, her face turning red with emotion. Maybe she really did care about our well being. "Charlie—tell them not to go," she said, grabbing his arm.

Clay and I looked at Charlie. He wasn't exactly our moral compass. And, as if on cue, he smiled, shrugged his shoulders, and said nothing.

☭

On the Metro, I checked my video camera to ensure it was working properly. Just as in the coup of 1991, I was drawn to the downtown activity, and felt once again that the wheels of history might be turning. When we emerged from the Metro station, we found ourselves

near the *Moskva* River, across from the *Bely Dom*, and were immediately engulfed in a bustling collection of people on the quay. We
were far enough from the *Bely Dom* to be safe, but close enough to
give us a great vantage point in case something did happen. Judging
from the crowd, we weren't the only ones who thought so.

"Look over there," Clay said breathlessly, stopping in his tracks. He
pointed to just beyond the crowds about fifty feet from the edge of
the river.

"Whoa—those are larger than in 1991," I exclaimed, looking at a
row of five tanks lined up, turrets down, facing the action across
the river.

"Yeah, I bet they could reach parliament if they wanted to," Clay
said.

"You think so? I don't know. Their aim would be horrible, I would
think."

"We might just see." Clay was smiling.

I recognized the atmosphere around us—so much like the coup
two years prior. A sense of shared concern hovered over the crowd,
onlookers occupied with quiet but intense discussions. It was obvious in peoples' lingering looks of concern, nervous cigarette smoking, and general watchfulness that they yearned for some hint of
what might come next. On days like today, Muskovites dropped
their aloof, unapproachable façade, and engaged anyone and everyone in nervous conversation.

"Do you know what's going on?"

"Who are those troops loyal to?"

"They won't really fire from those tanks, will they?"

The crowd was far larger than we expected, and with nothing really going on, people gathered on the concrete quay and the grassy
park area, watching the *Bely Dom* and the crowds clustered in
front of the building. Nobody really believed there would be any
type of military confrontation. With hordes of people across the
river and surrounding parliament, civilian casualties could be in the
thousands.

Clay and I found a spot overlooking the river and shot video footage of the crowds, the tanks and military personnel behind us. The

throngs of people on both sides of the river swelled. Emboldened by the peaceful coup of 1991, Russian civilians weren't skittish about interacting with the military, both on our side of the river and near the *Bely Dom*. Confused Russians, undecided on how close they wanted to get to the parliament building, cautiously crossed the bridge that spanned the river. Many went halfway and stopped, looking for a better view of what was happening. Others strolled to the opposite side, stood in front or to the side of the building, and waited for nothing in particular.

Time passed and very little happened. There was periodic activity near the entrance of the *Bely Dom*, but from where we were, without any radio or news, we had no idea what it meant. Military trucks could be seen approaching the access road to the entrance of parliament, but then backed away, without any clear intent. A few tanks pulled into position on the sides of the building, but remained inactive, waiting. Civilians on the grounds weren't intimidated or encouraged to leave, so they stayed.

Then suddenly, an unmarked black Volga pulled up behind Clay and I with its red siren wailing. A middle-age military official exited, met with a few other officials, and within minutes the military sprang to life. First, an older soldier barked orders to younger personnel. Then, soldiers scurried in and out of their tanks with purpose. Gray clouds of fumes spewed from their exhaust pipes, driving the crowds back from the area as onlookers gasped for clean air. Inside the tanks, soldiers rotated their turrets toward the *Bely Dom*, yet kept them aimed downward, facing the ground.

The crowd turned quiet and tense, waiting for something of consequence to occur. But as time passed, and it seemed nothing would come of this, a collective exhale was palpable.

"What's going on here?" I asked Clay. "Do you think those people near the *Bely Dom* don't realize there are tanks on this side of the river with guns aimed at them?" It was hard to believe.

"I have no idea. This looks like craziness," he muttered. He pointed at a tank. "Didn't you climb one of those in ninety-one?"

"I did, but these guys look more serious than the troops from the coup. They were young kids back then and not well organized—this looks different." The tanks once again began repositioning themselves. One of the more serious soldiers screamed something that we couldn't understand. In response, the gun turrets elevated their barrels, clearly preparing for something, with the *Bely Dom* now in their sights. We stood watching and waiting.

We turned around and I used my video zoom lens to follow what was happening across the river. I was in my own world, focusing on a single armored personnel carrier. It approached the *Bely Dom*, retreated, and began idling. *What's it waiting for? Why did it retreat and position itself on the side of the building?*

And then, without warning...BOOM!

The sheer volume of the blast stunned everyone within earshot. It was so loud and felt so close that I dropped my camera and hit the ground. I ended up sprawled face down on the pavement, wincing in pain with a strained groin caused by my sudden movement. The tanks behind us were shooting! Afraid to raise my head, I could only assume that damage was being inflicted on the *Bely Dom*. I remained frozen, as close to the ground as possible.

BOOM! BOOM!

The guns fired again and then again. I turned my head and was now facing Clay who was flat out next to me. BOOM! There went another. Beads of sweat were running down his face. The realization that bombs were being launched over our heads was unfathomable. As the minutes passed, we both moved to a more comfortable prone position. We waited. Ten minutes passed.

"Clay, you think we can get up?" I hollered over to him.

"No, and shut the hell up!" he replied.

Ten more minutes passed and I noticed others around us getting up or crawling to a safer location beside or behind the tanks. We cautiously edged to the side and slowly stood. There was nothing different about the row of tanks behind us. They stood as they had prior to the shelling, with one exception; small plumes of vapor rose from their barrels. I turned and then saw the impact on the *Bely Dom*. A cloud of black and gray smoke poured out of a portion of the building's crushed façade, with flames flickering intermittently in the plume. A bit higher than halfway up the building, windows on many levels were blown out, and dark smoke began crawling up the formerly pristine building. People on the grounds adjacent to the building fled as pieces of the building came crashing down to the ground. The bridge swarmed with crowds retreating to the far side of the river. Soon, another cannon explosion, and then another, each time as surprising and loud as before. Clay stood with his mouth open in disbelief.

Everyone was astonished that the tanks were actually firing. Not only were they shooting over us, but also over the river and the civilians who were in front of the parliament building. Their precision was amazing. They had now fired four to six rounds, each hitting the *Bely Dom* on the same level in a similar location. Black smoke continued to pour out of the windows, a shocking image that stopped most onlookers in their tracks. The *Bely Dom*, the symbol of a nascent democracy in Russia, was under attack by its own president.

☭

The bombing subsided, and as the minutes passed, it seemed as though the tanks were in a wait-and-see mode. Soldiers remained in their vehicles, and a hushed calm settled over the scene. It was eerily quiet, the kind that occurs after a violent New England rainstorm, when the fog rolls in and you can't tell what might come next. All eyes focused on the *Bely Dom* as it burned. The flames rose to engulf its upper floors. Speaking in hushed tones, everyone was asking the same question to nobody in particular, "Who was still inside?" "Were they all right?" and, "What will be the next move and by whom?"

A flurry of activity broke out across the river. An armored personnel carrier sped to the entrance, where a few people rushed out the door, jumped into the vehicle and drove away. Where was it going? Who was it loyal to? Rumors quickly emerged that the drivers were men loyal to Khasbulatov, rescuing a few of their own from the building, on their way to attack other buildings in Moscow. It was impossible to know for certain where they were headed, but within an hour, as if on cue, a plume of smoke rose to the north of the city, confirming an attack somewhere.

Then, some kind of armored humvee approached the building from the left, and climbed the lawn in front of the *Bely Dom*. It looked to be equipped with a protective shield that could allow troops access to the building while avoiding direct fire. But, instead of doing anything, it simply sat there. Gunfire began ringing out from across the river. Their source was uncertain. Against the bright blue sky and glare from the sun, a visual search was fruitless, but people's chatter said that snipers located in buildings around the *Bely Dom* were taking advantage of the great sight lines.

From across the river, it was tough to get a clear picture of what was actually happening on the ground. Were there soldiers or civilians hiding in the trees alongside parliament? Were there really snipers in the adjacent buildings, shooting at soldiers on the ground and in the White House? Were there civilian casualties? Clay and I came up with the bright idea of crossing the bridge to get closer to what we considered "the action." We were running on adrenaline, not common sense.

I followed Clay as he climbed up the grassy hill through the crowd, toward the bridge. It was far more crowded than we'd anticipated, so we had to push our way onto the bridge, and force ourselves against the current of people fleeing the burning *Bely Dom*. Once we reached the midpoint, we paused and took some pictures. We were witnessing an unbelievable historic event, one that was symbolically tragic for the Russian people, and unforgettable to foreigners. Just as in 1991, a sight like this seemed unimaginable in America; I was thankful for its rational system of checks and balances, which managed political conflict peacefully.

About twenty yards from the end of the bridge, the crowds began to thin. The sound of gunfire was closer now, no longer a faint popping sound, but a loud crackling, echoing between the buildings. It appeared the shelling was a prelude to more targeted combat. As we approached the end of the bridge, approximately fifty yards from the *Bely Dom* itself, we slowed down to assess. The tank fire left extensive damage. I fixated on the yellowish-orange glow glimmering through the dense smoke that billowed out a few windows, climbing up the *Bely Dom* façade, charring portions of the building. Heavy debris crashed to the ground, and a snowstorm of papers fluttered in the wind. Chunks of cement, window remnants, and office supplies lay at the foot of the building, where they had landed.

Closer to us, an overturned car lay on its side near the entrance of the bridge. Two people hid behind it, using it as cover. Given the river behind them, and the gunfire taking place overhead, it appeared safe. Clay looked at me and I knew he wanted me to follow him. Crouching low, we ran towards the car. While running I realized the crouching actually served no purpose. In fact, it probably slowed our progress, but for some reason, it seemed the safer way to go. We made it to the end of the bridge and scampered behind the car, next to the two young Russian men. Tucking ourselves as closely as we could to the underside of the vehicle, we took a breather. Our two newfound acquaintances periodically lifted their heads above the car, as if looking for something or someone on the other side.

We shared tidbits of information over the noise of the action. They confirmed that gunfire was being exchanged between those inside the *Bely Dom* and others stationed in surrounding buildings. It also became clear that a group of hardliners loyal to Khasbulatov remained inside. As we talked, bullets continued flying high above us, and an ambulance with a loud siren rumbled by, stopping just ten yards in front of us. With all roads closed in and out of the combat area, they were the only vehicles allowed closer than we were. Clay and I watched as four men carried a casualty out of the burning building and into the ambulance. The limp arms and legs hanging over the sides of the makeshift cloth stretcher told us this guy was probably not going to make it, and we exchanged nervous glances. We were enthralled by our proximity to the action, but there was such a thing as too close. This was different from the coup of 1991. It was deadly.

Sobered, we ducked down and reassessed. "Clay, I think we are too close. This is real bad shit and I think we need to get out of here—fast."

"I know. But give it a few minutes. Let's stay a while and see what happens. We're safe here for now."

I was incredulous. "You think so? Do you hear that gunfire?"

"Just chill. We'll be okay," Clay insisted, though he knew nothing more than I did. One of our Russian buddies chimed in, "Hey, my friend, this may not be the best time, but I am starting a business. You are a businessman, no?"

"I am," I responded half-heartedly. The combination of wailing ambulance sirens and the gunfire made it pointless to concentrate on a business pitch.

"Here is my card," he continued in English. "If you would need paper goods, copies, or printing supplies, my store will be open soon, and I would like to have you as client." He raised his eyebrows, smiling broadly.

I looked at him and then at Clay, dumbfounded. Was this really happening? His passion for his business and indifference to our circumstance made the exchange both implausible and fascinating. Sitting on the pavement, leaning up against the rusted underbelly of a car, surrounded by a hard line revolt that might roll back Russia's democratic reforms, this guy was still enamored with his idea of starting a business. It was almost inspiring, but so mistimed that I couldn't take him seriously. If there was one thing this journey to Russia had taught me, it was to expect the unexpected.

I smiled at him. "Okay, and good luck with this," I replied, waving his card.

I popped my head over the edge of the front panel of the overturned car and strained to get a better look at our surroundings. My body was contorted, one knee on the asphalt, one arm extended and gripping the front fender for leverage. Clay crawled behind me, trying to peer over my shoulder.

"Clay, look over there near the side of the *Bely Dom* in the trees. There are people over there looking at something." I pointed. "What do you think is going on?"

"I don't know, but it may be smart to get over there under the tree cover," he mused. "I know we are below the fire line here, but how do we know they won't just shoot down? I mean, look at us. If they do look down, we are sitting ducks!"

He had finally come around to my earlier point. "I'm with you," I said. The tree cover might help, but we had no way of knowing for certain. My knee started hurting so I lay down flat. Clay noticed something else.

"Look over there." He pointed at a cluster of civilians below the bridge. They seemed to be preparing themselves to move. "This is the second group I've seen doing this. They run from that spot under the bridge, to that ambulance, to those trees, and then further into the trees near the side of the *Bely Dom*. I don't know where they're going, but I've seen a few groups run the same route and nobody has been shot or injured. I think that's the way to go."

A new cluster of people appeared at the edge of the bridge near the slope down to the river. Quickly, they darted towards the ambulance as a group. They had to be running to someplace safe, right? "I guess we could run from here directly to the ambulance. You think that's safer than going back to the bridge?" I asked.

"Absolutely."

We both sat up on the pavement, our backs leaning against the car. Anxiety and dread were building in me. "But let's wait until the shooting lapses," I said. "It seems to be coming in waves and I'd prefer to run during a lull."

"No shit, Sherlock."

The trees we eyed ran alongside the *Bely Dom*, near the south face, and around the corner from the burning front façade. The artillery barrage seemed to have stopped. People were scurrying about in front of our location, trying to aid the wounded and evacuate those who wanted to escape the smoke-filled building. The ambulances awaited casualties, and other civilians like us were riveted to the scene.

Clay and I both noticed the pause in the action.

"Are you ready?" I asked him.

"Are you?" he answered, smiling nervously. He liked answering questions with questions. A trait I found highly irritating.

"Ready as ever—let's go."

We grabbed our stuff, said goodbye to our new friends, and ran behind the nearest ambulance. No shots. My heart beat fast inside my chest. Our backs now to the *Bely Dom*, we pressed up against the ambulance and were looking directly at our origination point on the other side of the river. Masses of people were still there, as were the tanks, which now faced us with their cannons still aimed at the White House. We strained to look over the rusted white hood of the ambulance and knew our next move would be the tough part. We would have to run into the trees, a distance of about twenty yards. Just then, I noticed a group of civilians running wildly from the trees in different directions, some towards us and others setting off in random directions. A fleeting thought crept into my mind. *Why do they look so scared?* I tugged at Clay to follow me. The chaotic dash in front of us created some semblance of cover. If we were ever going to go, this was the time.

Determined to get to the trees, I sprinted forward, towards the oncoming mass of people. I crossed the dead zone where there were neither ambulances nor onlookers, and made it to trees' cover. It was then I noticed that Clay hadn't followed me. From my new vantage point, I could see Clay peeking his head out from behind the rear of the ambulance. He waved, and jokingly smiled. What an idiot—funny to a fault. He took stock of his surroundings and burst from behind the vehicle, sprinting to a tree adjacent to me.

"What happened?" I asked. "Why didn't you come with me?"

"You can't just tap me and expect me to know you're running," he explained. "Before I knew it, you were gone!"

"Sorry about that. I was just ready to move and thought you were with me."

A new round of small arms fire erupted, and he yelled above it, "Let's move further into the trees and get away from the open space. Follow me from tree trunk to tree trunk."

He peered out from behind his tree, and made a dash further into the woods. It reminded me of years ago playing hide and seek with my brother. Hide, look to see if anyone notices you, assess surroundings, and find a better, more concealed hiding spot. Clay and I thought the same thing here. If we could get deeper into the woods, we'd be okay. What we didn't grasp was that we had just put ourselves in the most dangerous location of all.

While it was true that snipers were shooting at combatants in the *Bely Dom,* we were oblivious to the fact that there were also fighters coming up from the rear of the building, using the trees as cover, just as we were. Hidden to us from our previous vantage points, but now directly in front of us, these troops were dressed in full battle gear, guns ready, poised for action. I knew Yeltsin had called up troops to fortify the area, and figured they were loyal to him—probably just attempting to find a way into the building to end the revolt. Seeing them was reassuring. The snipers in the buildings had to know that their comrades were in the trees, so would logically avoid shooting into them. Great, I thought, our plan to take cover here was solid and we were safe. Curiously, however, as the troops approached, they looked more menacing than I expected.

We didn't misjudge something, did we? It was then I realized why the other civilians were running from the trees.

"Clay, I think we screwed up here—these are Yeltsin's troops, but... but they don't know who we are," I stammered, my mind racing through Russian words trying to figure out what I could yell to them to diffuse the potential situation.

"What? Holy crap! You're telling me! Let's get out of here!" Clay yelled, panicking at the sight of the soldiers' rifles pointed our way.

"Don't move quickly," I screamed, but it was too late. Clay turned to run and his sudden movement caught the eye of a soldier who lifted his rifle, and aimed, ready to fire at him. I couldn't believe what was about to happen.

"No! Stop! We're Americans," I screamed in English and Russian as quickly as possible. I jumped behind the nearest tree, hit the ground, and curled up in a ball.

It was too late. The soldier fired.

Clay had made it behind another tree trunk and was scared shitless. Bullets whizzed by—missing both of us, probably intentionally, as we hugged our protective trees.

"Go, get out of here!" A Russian soldier yelled with authority.

"Clay, I think he's telling us to go!" Blood pulsating through my body, my hands wet with sweat, I peered from behind the trunk, hands elevated. I imagined being barraged with bullets, but instead saw a line of soldiers, guns in ready position aimed at us, motioning with their heads to go. They *were* speaking to us.

"C'mon!" I yelled at Clay. We walked slowly from behind our shelters with our hands up.

Stopping briefly at the edge of the tree line, we looked and listened for snipers. Hearing none, we darted to a crowd of people watching the action from under an overpass near the river, seemingly safe from sniper fire. Out of breath, we found some open concrete and collapsed, thankful to be alive and unharmed.

"Dave, next time we're alone and I'm feeling a bit better than right now, can you remind me to kick your ass?" Clay said with a half-cocked smile, sounding like a true Texan.

"Yeah, I'm with you. That was stupid as hell."

☭

We sat motionless for a while, overwhelmed by our insanity and good fortune. I was exhausted from the wave of extreme emotions we'd experienced, my groin hurt from the strained muscle, and my clothes stuck to my sweat-drenched body. Darkness fell around us, and we could now see bullets' trajectories above and around us. The sparks of gunfire and the intermittent flares that followed each bullet illuminated the darkening sky. We were not in the line of fire.

We watched for two hours as a few obstinate rebels continued fighting Yeltsin's loyalists. Periodically, sporadic bursts of gunfire led to larger scale firefights. Ambulances came and went, and loud, rumbling tanks eventually surrounded the building. Final preparations were being made for a show of governmental force to take back the *Bely Dom*.

It was only a matter of time before this revolt would come to an end, but we were not going to be there to watch the conclusion. Physically and emotionally, we were drained, and sat mired in our thoughts. The *Bely Dom* continued to burn, and I questioned my actions that day and what the consequences could have been—I could have lost my life!

In the wake of my visit to Shepetovka, my actions were inexcusable, and I was overwhelmed with humiliation. I suddenly realized that if I wanted to act on my experience, on what I had learned and internalized in Shepetovka, now was the time.

Clay and I watched the intermittent gunfire, and with the backdrop of the glowing *Bely Dom* behind us, walked over the bridge to the other side of the river. Most of the onlookers had dispersed and those that remained took pictures and stood in disbelief, watching the burning building. We hopped back on the Metro and decided to get a drink at a popular Irish expat bar.

There, we met up with friends and told them about our exploits, including how scared and stupid we were. We knew we screwed up, and openly admitted it.

Our friends helped clarify what actually took place that day. We knew that when rebel legislators tried to take control of the *Bely Dom,* troops loyal to Yeltsin did what the military refused to do in 1991—assault their own capitol building. What we didn't know was that the shelling of the *Bely Dom* quickly led to the deadliest conflict in Moscow since the October Revolution of 1917. They informed us that over one hundred people were killed and many more were wounded. Yeltsin's assault was supported by the US, the Russian military, and most of the Russian elite, while the communists and radical nationalists led the opposition. We talked far into the night, discussing the fact that despite Gorbachev's initial Glasnost campaign and Yeltsin's perseverance toward a democratized Russia, the process of reforming the country would continue to be a long, complex, and challenging road. With the burning of the *Bely Dom*, the strife and frustration between the reformers and old-time hardliners had flared, too.

As we talked, another friend walked in, visibly shaken. She began to cry as she explained that one of her friends, an American woman, was shot in the back by a sniper close to the *Bely Dom*. The victim had been caring for two kids when one of them somehow got access to the roof and climbed up. She pursued the child, but on the roof-top from afar, she looked like an enemy combatant, and was shot. Nobody knew how she was doing, but we did know an emergency helicopter had been summoned from Finland and had taken her there for treatment.

Clay and I were heartbroken, and felt another powerful wave of shame. Was it fair that we had tempted fate and lived, while she was shot helping a child?

ON MY WAY

A few months later, after much deliberation, I loaded my bags into Vladimir's black Volga. I knew it was time to leave. I had spent two and a half years enjoying a life I had built on my own, and was ready to return home and take my next step. Vladimir finished his cigarette, threw it on the garage floor, and got behind the wheel.

Passing a recently built McDonald's on the highway from the city center to the airport, I looked out the back window of the car to say goodbye. In the distance was the city I had grown to love. I could still see the *Bely Dom* closest to me, the Kremlin walls, the dome of St. Basil's Cathedral, and I knew that Leninsky Prospekt and the disco were not far off. I felt for the people I'd met, but had to leave behind. They had already struggled so much, but were undoubtedly in for many years of challenging economic, political, and social times.

The Soviet Union, now broken apart, had become such a different place for me since I arrived. Originally a destination to immerse myself in a culture, learn the language, and bring people together, it had become both scary and enlightening. The politics had shifted dramatically, resulting in a future that was uncertain, but full of possibilities. I was confident that with time, business opportunities would be plentiful in Russia, but at what cost?

Closer to my heart, my perspective on life had changed. A new, deeper meaning attached me to my ancestors, my family, and my religion. This identity was now a priority, and living closer to home was foundational. The discovery of a direction for myself, informed by looking backwards to my roots, was the most important aspect of the journey, and it came as a surprise.

It also appeared that my dad's letter and its message, "Do not worry," was right on target. He couldn't predict my future, but he had the foresight to let me figure it out myself, knowing somehow and in some way, things would be all right. And they were. Over the course of the journey, a new inner confidence grew, fed by every new experience. I began to see the benefits of taking life in stride and not always trying to control the uncontrollable. And as the worry and fear of the past diminished, I became less intimidated by the future, too, and open to looking ahead with a more relaxed perspective.

I looked at my watch, wondering how much time I had to make the flight. Focused on packing and saying goodbye to friends, I had lost track of time and found I was an hour late in getting to the airport. I didn't think I would miss the flight, but it would be close. Vladimir was a great driver and went as fast as he could, but by the time we arrived at the airport, I only had forty-five minutes to get through the line at passport control.

The line was brisk, and within ten minutes I was face to face with the one person who controlled where I would sleep that night: the passport control officer. Dressed in his heavily starched military outfit and cap, he was no more than thirty with a bit of scruff on his chin, and appeared emotionless, almost robotic. His dead eyes looked at me.

"Papers?" he asked.

"Here they are." I passed them under the glass.

He opened the passport, reviewed the visa, and faster than he could read the documents to make sure they were legit, he handed them back.

"Not in order," he said curtly.

I remained calm. "What do you mean, not in order? What's wrong?"

"Not in order," he repeated.

"But my flight is leaving in thirty-five minutes. I have to get through."

"You can speak with my supervisor if you'd like," he suggested.

"Yes, let me do that."

"He doesn't arrive for an hour, so you can wait over there." He smirked as he said this, pointing to a security waiting area. He knew when my flight was leaving, yet his behavior was taking on the feeling of a deliberate performance.

I was livid, but maintained my composure. There was one thing I could do, but it was risky. For the three years I had spent in Russia, money always seemed to speak louder than words. If I offered a bribe here, especially to a uniformed officer, could I get in big trouble? I knew my papers were in order, so I figured he probably viewed me as one opportunity of many that day.

I took my passport from under the glass and held it below my belt, where he couldn't see what I was doing. I took a $20 bill out of my pocket, folded it, and placed it in my passport, and put the documents back under the glass.

"Can you check one more time?" I asked anxiously, looking away.

He said nothing, but grabbed the passport and visa.

He reached for it, opened the passport and took the money. I heard the loud cla-chunk of the stamp machine and knew I was okay. Unbelievable. He handed me the passport, and wished me a pleasant flight.

EPILOGUE

Russia was behind me, but would always be with me. The politics of the time I spent there was riveting, frustrating, enlightening, and sobering. Twenty years have passed, but I'm dubious that much progress has been made since 1993. Granted, I'm not as close to the action as I once was, but it appears that capitalism continues to grow even if it still only benefits the few. From an economic and political standpoint, those years in Russia made one thing clear to me: Capitalism, without the support of a government that promotes and enforces the rule of law, is not the perfect solution. It wasn't for Russia back then, and it wouldn't be now.

Beyond the dramatic economic and political changes I lived through, the opportunity to grow as a person made the greater lasting impression. No longer unfocused and nervous about my next steps in life, I left Russia feeling ready to jump into my life's next chapter, business school. My countless hours with Charlie, Jim, and other international businesspeople had been helpful in understanding their roles and responsibilities, but also shed light on how travel took a toll on their family and personal lives. This, combined with my newfound appreciation of my heritage, motivated me to make future choices that would allow me to build a strong family bond, while also enabling professional satisfaction.

Upon my return home, one of the first things I did was sit down at my mom's kitchen table with my grandfather. I showed him pictures of Shepetovka, gave him sugar from the working factory, and shared my impressions of his hometown, the people, and the unforgettable synagogue. He sat speechless, no doubt reminiscing over his past, but visibly pleased to know that Shepetovka was still on the map.

Today, I live in a suburb outside of Boston, Massachusetts. I'm a husband and father of two, and work in marketing at a firm that doesn't require much travel. I can devote my weekends to coaching or attending my kids' activities, playing board games by the fire, and taking my wife to dinner. These are the treasures of life, and I wouldn't have it any other way.

We are avidly involved in our community synagogue, and are raising our kids to love the traditions, music, and teachings of the Jewish people. One day, they, too, will learn about how their ancestors emigrated from Eastern Europe to America. I will certainly emphasize the effect the Holocaust had on our family, but I hope I can do it in a way that helps them understand it as a part of their family experience, not just as a part of history.

I also serve on my City Board of Aldermen, which is focused on contributing to our community in a positive way. The people of Shepetovka showed no boundaries in their acceptance of others unlike them, and came together as a community to maintain their old city while still investing in their future. These ideals of cherishing the past, adapting to embrace the new, and building a sense of shared community remain with me, and guide my sense of civic involvement.

Writing this memoir was a labor of love. To recall the trepidation with which I approached life and the fears I overcame while in Russia was a tremendously cathartic experience. Sporadically, I have kept in touch with both Charlie and Clay, who are doing well pursuing their respective businesses. Clay remains as adventurous and unpredictable as ever and we still call each other periodically just to confirm that our memories are, in fact, real. Over the years I have tried to reconnect with many of my Russian friends, but with our lives taking us in such different directions, we have shared no more than cursory exchanges.

For many, including myself, the time just after college can be scary. If you are approaching graduation or have recently finished school, I hope this memoir gives you a little pause and some reassurance—no decision you make now will lock you into sixty years of anything. Take your time. Explore your options. Possibly trace your roots to help create a foundation for your own story. Experience the world responsibly, but don't be afraid to take a few risks. Talk and learn from others. Then, dip your toe in the water. Eventually, you'll find your way.

ACKNOWLEDGEMENTS

Writing a memoir as a first time author takes a lot of time, patience, and effort. I truly loved every minute of it. But this project could not have been completed without the input and advice of so many.

My gratitude goes out to my friends and family who read the first, second, and even thirtieth version of my manuscript; Laurie Baker, Robert Barone, Mike Campanella, Yekaterina Dashkova, Margie Ross-Decter, C.J. Falcon, Barbara Gaffin, Phillip Gessert, Barbara Griswold, Leesteffy Jenkins, Anne Kalis, Lawrence Kalis, Sheryl Kalis, Darci Klein, Robert Kurson, Tara Mantel, Terry McBurney, Chris Noel, Cynthia Phoel, Ralph Ranalli, Cynthia Rehm, John Saxe, Michael Shelgren, Alan Spy, Keith Stern, Dean Whitney, Charles Venancio and Tom Yaroschuk. Thank you for your candid remarks, criticisms, and ideas. Your keen eye and focus are so appreciated.

To Sarah Cypher, the Threepenny Editor, who is worth so much more, thank you. Finding someone who does great work is a blessing, but someone who actually cares is even more valuable.

To my parents, Paul and Marilyn, your love and support taught me life lessons, allowed me to succeed and fail, and imparted the importance of love and family. I only hope to be as good a parent to my children as you were to me.

To my children, Ben and Talia, I love you both so much. Thank you for allowing me to write when I know you would have wanted me to play. I owe you many tickles and wrestles. While no letter similar to what your papa wrote to me is forthcoming, this memoir gives you insight into how both your mom and dad hope to support you in whatever endeavors you pursue.

Special thanks and never-ending gratitude to my wife, Anne. Your patience, understanding, love, and support have given me the freedom to write, the passion to persevere, and the confidence to complete this undertaking. Without your commitment to this journey, this would have never happened. I love you.

NOTES

1. "Leningradsky," *Moscow International Portal*, Department of Foreign Economic and International Relations of the City of Moscow, 2014, http://moscow.ru/.

2. Trudy Rubin, "In Pushing Gorbachev Plan, Bush Ignores the Desires of the Republics America Should Work to Ensure a Peaceful Transition to a New Form of Government," *The Philadelphia Inquirer*, August 16, 1991, http://articles.philly.com/1991-08-16/news/25807635_1_new-union-treaty-soviet-republics-soviet-union.

3. Voice of Russia, "Presidential Elections in Russia, 2005–2014," accessed on Dec. 5, 2013, www.voiceofrussia.com/elections_history/.

4. James L. Gibson, Marc Morjé Howard, *Russian Anti-Semitism and the Scapegoating of Jews*, (Cambridge University Press, 2007) 197-198, http://www18.george-town.edu/data/people/mmh/publication-7909.pdf

5. The Alma-Ata Declaration, Armenia-Azerbaijan-Belarus-Kazakhstan-Kyrgyzstan Moldova-Russian-Tajikistan-Turkmenistan-Ukraine-Uzbekistan, Dec. 21, 1991, http://lcweb2.loc.gov/frd/cs/belarus/by_appnc.html.

6. Arch Puddington, "Promise and Reversal: The Post-Soviet Landscape Twenty Years On," Freedom House, accessed January 14, 2014, http://www.freedomhouse.org/report/special-reports/promise-and-reversal-post-soviet-landscape-twenty-years.

7. *St. Petersburg Encyclopedia*, s.v. "Moskovsky Railway Station," by I. A. Bogdanov, accessed January 14, 2014, http://www.encspb.ru/.

8. Ibid.

9. John M. Carey, Matthew Soberg Shugart, and Scott Parrish, *Executive Decree Authority*, (Cambridge University Press, 1998) 67–68, http://books.google.com/books?id=2k9iI9iGVt4C&pg=PA76&dq=yeltsin+decree+1400+1993&ei=tZG3Sa3RGZaQyAST9rnXBA#v=onepage&q=yeltsin%20decree%201400%201993&f=false.

10. Carey, Shugart, and Parrish, *Executive Decree Authority*, 77.

ABOUT THE AUTHOR

David Kalis grew up in the Boston suburbs. He earned his B.A. in Soviet, East European Studies from Tufts University and an M.B.A. from The University of Chicago, Graduate School of Business. Following his graduation from Tufts, he spent two and a half years in Russia which formed the basis for this memoir. In 2007, after many years of talking about the idea of writing his story, he finally began the work. *Vodka Shot, Pickle Chaser* is the culmination of combing through his experiences, organizing his thoughts, and presenting his journey and the life lessons he learned along the way.

www.davidakalis.com